W9-BIQ-297

Understanding

the

Life of Birds

by

Patrick G. Coyle, Jr.

Summit Publications
Lakeside, CA   92040

Address orders to:
Summit Publications
11565 Sunset Knolls Rd.
Lakeside, CA 92040

Published in the United States
1987 by Summit Publications
ISBN 0-944423-02-7

Cataloging in Publication Data

Coyle, Patrick G., 1938 -
    Understanding the life of birds

    Bibliography: p. 279
    Includes index & glossary
    1. Birds - physiology. 2. Birds - anatomy.
3. Birds - breeding. 4. Aviculture. 5. Cage-birds.
I. Title
QL698.C695
ISBN 0-944423-02-7

Acknowledgements

I would like, first of all, to thank the following technical editors for their careful editing of this book. Although I assume complete responsibility for any errors in the book, I am very grateful to the following biologists for their analysis of the information presented:

Bill Toone, Curator of Birds, San Diego Wild Animal Park.

Wayne Schulenburg, Animal Care Manager, Ornithology Dept.,
San Diego Zoo.

Terry Mulroney, Animal Care Manager, Children's Zoo,
San Diego Zoo.

I also want to give a special thanks to Cyndi Kuehler, Avian Reproductive Specialist, San Diego Zoo, for reviewing the chapters on reproduction.

I also want to give thanks to:

Nicole Perretta, a young woman who added value to the book with her talented and accurate illustrations. To find an artist of such talent, who also has a good understanding of birds, was my good fortune.

Mike Kelly, for his patience and understanding throughout the writing, editing, and publication of this book. His knowledge of book publishing is extensive and he was most willing to share it.

Tony Costanza and John Dixon, for their valuable advice on photography. Their advice has made me a better photographer. However, any shortcomings in the photographs are purely my responsibility and not theirs.

Bob Longbotham, Joe Crosby, Dee Muschinske, and Martin Muschinske, for initially reading the rough draft chapters. Their encourgament to continue with the writing was most important to me.

Pam Anderson, for giving a "non bird person's" perspective to the editing of this book. She was very instrumental in improving the writing of this book.

Michael Coyle, for all of his legal assistance and advice in the preparation and production of this book.

Last but by no means least, I want to thank my wife, Phyllis. Without her this book would not have been completed. Her encouragement kept me going when the writing was hard or going slowly. She was involved in every aspect of this book, except the actual writing. She helped with design, editing, illustrations, and finally, production. That this book is finished is a tribute to her insights, good judgement, and patience, especially with me.

To

My Mother and Father

thanks for the genes
and the values

Foreword

For many years aviculturists have been divided into two separate factions. There are those associated with universities and the scientific approach, and those "backyard" aviculturists working from lore and tradition. In many areas they have very different views and opinions of each other's style. The one thing they have in common, unfortunately, is a lack of mutual respect.

These opinions did not form overnight, nor will they disappear overnight, or through the publication of any single book. However, this book represents an attempt to bring these two groups together. The truth is, both factions know a great deal and both are concerned with the same thing, the preservation of avian species.

There is a famous quote from a native American, Chief Settle, "What is man without the beasts? If all the beasts were gone, man would die from a great loneliness of the spirit. For, whatever happens to the beasts soon happens to man."

If a scientist wants to be critical, perhaps he would say that there is no death from "loneliness of the spirit." Maybe, maybe not. Even the scientist using technical jargon or complex reasoning would have to say that man ultimately can't survive without other life forms. One sees it spiritually, one sees it mechanically...neither are wrong, just misunderstood.

This book is written for aviculturists, but includes much information from the sciences along with understandable explanations of terminology which will enhance the aviculturists familiarity with the biology of birds. People fear what they don't know. With books like this perhaps the fear will begin to disappear, and be replaced with mutual respect and understanding. Through our enlightenment, the birds in our care will prosper.

Bill Toone, Curator of birds,
San Diego Wild Animal Park

Table of Contents

Unit 2. Feathers and Flight

Unit 5. Classification

Preface

There are many excellent ornithology books available for readers who have a biological or scientific background. There is also an abundance of "how-to" books describing the keeping and breeding of birds. Missing from the avicultural literature is a book describing the biology of birds for people who have no scientific background. This book is written to fill this need.

Understanding the Life of Birds is based on the author's years of experience teaching a course on the biology of birds to aviculturists with no scientific background. The purpose of this book is to stimulate interest in the subject, as well as being educational. It provides the bird owner and aviculturist with an understanding of the anatomy, physiology, reproduction, development, natural history, genetics and taxonomy of the avian species. The style of this book is similar to what one would expect from a series of lectures on aviculture - straight forward descriptions of avian biology, with many comparisons to the biology of other familiar species.

Writing a biology book without facts would be like trying to justify your last year's income tax to the IRS without using numbers. It would certainly be less complicated, but it wouldn't be effective. The same is true of bird biology. It would be easier to understand without any technical material, but it wouldn't increase our knowledge of birds.

This book attempts to present the biology of birds without getting too detailed. The goal is to present the information accurately, without the technical material becoming predominant. The attempt here is not to make an avian biologist out of the reader, but rather to inform him about the biology of birds. This will help the reader to care for and breed birds in a more informed manner.

The book concludes with a brief discussion of habitat destruction and its effects on birds and other wildlife around the world. It is hoped that by the end of the book the reader will have gained not only an appreciation for birds but also for the many similarites between their biological systems and those of other animals. In so doing the reader will become more aware of the interdependence of all living things. Finally, there is a plea for captive breeding of endangered species and a global approach to wildlife conservation.

Introduction

Before looking at a book on the biology of birds (ornithology), we need to take a look at the meaning of this word. The word ornithology is derived from the Greek word "orneo" which, means bird and the Greek word "logus," which means study of or discourse. Thus, ornithology means the "study of birds."

Aviculture derives from the Latin word "avi," which means a bird, and the Latin word "cult," which means to cultivate, plow or till. So, aviculture is the "cultivating of birds." Almost all words beginning with "orni" or "avi" have something to do with birds.

Ornithology is the scientific study of birds. The word science derives from the Latin word "scien" which means knowledge. A scientist, therefore, is someone who works with knowledge. In this sense, we are all scientists. Not surprisingly, the dictionary defines a scientist as one who "specializes in science." Science is defined as "systematized knowledge derived from observation, study, etc." **The point is, you don't have to be a scientist to be scientific.** In the keeping, breeding, and studying of birds, being scientific is very important.

What are the fundamentals of being scientific? The scientific method is a systematic approach to problem solving and inquiry into the unknown. Using the scientific method is very important because it eliminates "beliefs," "gut feelings," and intuition in the approach to a problem or situation. The first step in the scientific method is observation. Science deals with things that can be observed and results that are reproducible.

Observation usually leads to data, which should be written down. Written data can then be made available to others. Using this data, we can now form a hypothesis, "hypo" means before and "thesis" means arranging. A hypothesis is actually an educated guess.

Next, more specific data must be collected to support the hypothesis. If the data supports the hypothesis, then it is accepted. If the data does not support the hypothesis, then another hypothesis is proposed. This new hypothesis will likely be a better educated guess because we have gained insight from the data which eliminated the first hypothesis. Each hypothesis brings us closer to a final conclusion.

For conclusions to be accepted by the scientific community, or by people in general, the data supporting the hypothesis must be reproducible. The need for aviculturists to be scientific is great because they are doing most of the research on breeding birds. Unfortunately, few records are being kept and the data base is usually much too small to be reliable.

Let's use as an example, a breeder who is trying a new feed to see if it would improve breeding success. The typical approach would be to put all of the breeding birds on the new feed and keep records of the offspring produced. If the number of offspring is increased, the breeder assumes that the new feed was the reason. It may have been. However, there are many other factors which could affect the number of offspring. Some of these factors are, age of the birds, environmental conditions, such as heat, rainfall, presence of predators, or vermin, etc.

For this experiment to be meaningful, one must establish a control group of similar birds for comparison. As an example, half of the breeding birds can be put on new feed and the other half kept on old feed. There should be no other variables. Do not change nest box size, time of nest box placement, vitamins in the water, etc., during this experiment. Otherwise, you will not know which variable has an effect, good or bad, on breeding.

The data from experimental birds and control birds can be compared and one can meaningfully assess the effect of the new feed. Few breeders like to use the control method. If they are using a new feed, it is probably because they suspect it will help their breeding. Therefore, they are reluctant to allow half of their birds to remain on the old diet. However, without the use of control groups, the results will always be suspect.

For example, one could legitimately argue that the birds could have produced as well on the original seed. One could also argue that the birds could have produced even more offspring if kept on the original diet. Without a control group, there is no way to prove either viewpoint.

For reasons we still do not understand, some years are more productive for breeding than others. If you switch to a new feed on one of these good years, you may assume that it is the feed which caused the good breeding. In fact, the feed may have been irrelevant to the increase that year, or could possibly have reduced the increase from what it could have been.

Be scientific by keeping good records, eliminating variables, using control groups, and collecting lots of written data. And finally, share your data with others so that we can all become more productive managers in the breeding of our birds.

Figure 1.1 Young cockatoo (*Cacatua galerita galerita*).

1   **Breeding Behavior**

Reproduction

The reproductive system is the most mysterious of systems. It is the system whose workings we understand the least. This system imparts little in the way of benefits to the adult birds, yet they will sacrifice their health and sometimes their lives to insure reproductive success. What forces are buried deep in the heredity material of the bird to cause this strong need to procreate the species?

Reproduction is a complex system, which like all physiological systems of the body, depends on the efficient workings of the other systems. But, very few of the other systems depend, in any significant way, on the reproductive system.

The reproductive system is an unusual system. It is the one system that is not involved in maintaining the health of the bird. Failures in the reproductive system rarely result in health problems for the individual. At worst, the individual would not be able to produce offspring.

The function of the reproductive system is the procreation of the species. This system insures the survival of the species rather than the survival of the individual bird.

The reproductive system is the system of greatest interest to the aviculturist, since the primary goal of most aviculturists is breeding. Unlike humans, reproductive behavior in birds is not a conscious decision. Humans often make decisions as to when and how many offspring they will have. Birds do not have these options. The breeding behavior of birds is controlled primarily by hormones. Song, territorial and courtship behaviors, nest building and nesting are all initiated and controlled by hormones.

It becomes obvious then that the secretion of these hormones is paramount in successful breeding. The first significant indicator that breeding is imminent is the tremendous enlargement in the gonads (ovaries and testes). During the breeding season the testes of the male may enlarge to as much as 200 to 300 times their normal non-breeding size. Like the testes, the ovary significantly increases in size during the breeding season. The enlarged testes and ovaries then begin to secrete the male and female sex hormones which control the breeding behaviors. Figure 1.2 shows the testes in the process of being enlarged.

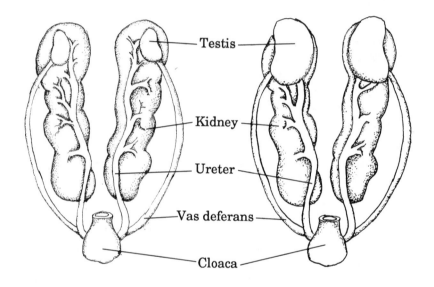

Figure 1.2 Male testes showing enlargement during breeding season.

Let's take a look at the cause of this significant increase in gonad size. Here again hormones are involved. Follicle stimulating hormone (FSH) and luteinizing hormone (LH) secreted by the pituitary gland, located in the brain, are the prime stimuli to this gonad enlargement.

FSH and LH stimulates the enlargement of the gonads, which then secrete increased amounts of the sex hormones. This increase in sex hormones stimulates breeding. Therefore, the control of breeding is ultimately under the control of the two pituitary hormones, FSH and LH.

Therefore, any factors which will increase the secretion of FSH and LH will have a significant impact on breeding. What are some of these factors?

Table 1.1 lists some of the factors which stimulate the pituitary to release FSH and LH. Not all of these factors are important in all species. It is a combination of some or all of these factors which stimulate the hormonal secretions. No one event is responsible for initiating this sex hormonal release.

Table 1.1.   Stimuli for Breeding Behavior.

Temperature
Length of day
Rainfall
Behavior of mate
Availability of food
Psychological factors

An important thing to remember is that the bird does not have to breed in order for its own survival. The bird has to eat, drink, and be able to stay warm, dry and away from predators. But, the bird does not have to breed to survive or to be healthy. Therefore, a bird will breed only when all environmental and psychological requirements are met. This is a very important fact in terms of avicultural success. The aviculturist must attempt to meet, as much as possible, all these environmental and psychological conditions.

The seasonal nature of most avian reproduction has definite adaptive value. With a significant enlargement in gonads the bird's weight increases. This weight increase maintained throughout the year would be a burden on the bird. Birds in captivity, with their flying requirements significantly reduced and a ready source of food, often have more clutches and a longer breeding season than in the wild.

The seasonal nature also allows breeding to occur when the conditions, such as the availability of food and warm weather are most favorable for the successful raising of young. Since breeding is such an energy requiring process, a bird doesn't start breeding unless there is near certainty that success will be achieved.

The decision to breed is not a conscious one, but rather a behavior that has been programed into the genetic material of the birds over many generations. Those birds that attempt to breed when conditions are unfavorable are usually unsuccessful and therefore do not pass on their genes to their offspring. Those who do breed in favorable conditions are usually successful and thus pass on these beneficial genes to their offspring. This is a good example of natural selection.

Male sex organs

The primary sex organs in the male bird are the paired testes. The testes are bean-shaped organs located in the abdominal cavity slightly above and forward from the kidney (Figure 1.2). Testes size varies, depending on the season.

Each testis contains many seminiferous tubules which produce sperm cells. Between the seminiferous tubules are the interstitial cells which are responsible for the production of the male sex hormone, testosterone. The sperm cell and testosterone production increases, due to the increase in the testes size during the breeding season.

Originating in the testes, and ending in the cloaca, are the paired vas deferens. The vas deferens serves as a passageway for the sperm cells to pass to the cloaca so they may be transmitted to the female. The vas deferens also increases in size during the breeding season. It also serves for sperm storage.

Most species of male birds lack the organ of penetration, the penis. An example of this is the less primitive species, such as the psittacines and song birds. Sperm deposition is accomplished by aligning the vent opening of the male with the vent opening of the female and depositing the sperm cells in the female cloaca.

Mating is generally accomplished by the male balancing himself on the back of the female, curving his vent region under that of the female until the openings are aligned. This is a precarious position, although some birds actually mate while flying.

A consideration for the aviculturist is to have strong, firm perches upon which the female can balance herself with the male on her back. Thin perches make it much more difficult for the female to get an adequate grip. Having perches of varying sizes may make the difference between a successful mating or mating failure. Some birds mate on the ground or in the nest box. One legged males have been successful breeders.

More primitive birds such as ratites, Galliformes, storks, flamingos, duck, geese and some others do have a grooved penis. This penis does become erect and increases the efficiency of guiding the sperm cells into the cloaca of the female bird.

Female sex organs

The female reproductive system has some similarities to the male reproductive system but there are obviously some specific differences. The main
organ in the female is the ovary. Unlike the paired testes, there is only one
ovary located on the left side near the kidney. The right ovary and oviduct
become very small (atrophied) and non-functional in most species of birds.

The ovary, like the testes, has two basic functions, the production of the
gametes (ova) and sex hormones. The ovary, which greatly increases in size
during the breeding season, contains thousands of primary follicles, each of
which can give rise to yolk and germ cells. So, a female bird is capable of
producing thousands of eggs during her lifetime.

Originating at the ovary and ending at the cloaca is a long modified tube
called the oviduct or fallopian tube (Figure 1.3). This figure shows that the
different segments of the oviduct have different names. These segments also
have different functions which will be discussed later in the chapter on egg
formation.

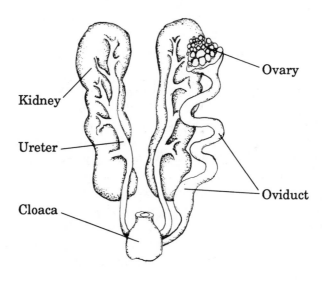

Figure 1.3   The female reproductive system.

Specific cells in the ovary and some of the cells lining the follicles produce and secrete the female sex hormones estrogen and progesterone. These hormones are very important in bringing the female into breeding condition.

Territory

As the sex hormone levels begin to change so do the behavioral patterns of the birds. One change that takes place is an increase in the activity of establishing and defending territory. Many a person has been chased down the street by a blackbird in very aggressive defense of it's territory. Birds at this time have also been known to attack their own reflections in windows, interpreting their own image as that of an intruder.

What is a territory? Territory is any space which will be defended by the bird, usually against males of the same species. Territory may be different from the home range of the bird. The home ranges is the overall area visited by the bird as opposed to the specific area to be defended, the territory.

For reasons still not understood, birds who have established territory have a psychological advantage over intruders, some of whom may even be physically superior. Therefore the territory is usually successfully defended.

A male is as likely to fight over territory as he is to fight for a mate. What is it about territory that makes it so important? Once the territory is established it reduces the interference from other males in the courtship of a mate, copulation, nest building and the raising of young. The established territory also gives the pair the almost exclusive access to the available food which is so essential in the successful raising of young. There will be less squabbling over nest sights and nesting material as well.

The establishment of territory spaces out the various members of a given species in their home range. This spacing greatly increases the potential numbers of offspring possible. Fighting is an energy draining process and must be reduced if the species is to successfully procreate itself.

The territory, being somewhat small, becomes a much more secure place for the occupying birds. The pair soon learns the territory well. They can then better exploit the food sources, nesting materials and escape routes that are necessary during an attack by a life threatening predator.

Territory also plays a psychological role in the breeding of birds. Males with desirable territories attract and keep a larger number of females than males with a less desirable territory. In a typical aviary setting with more than one pair of the same species, often only one pair will establish a breeding territory and breed. Larger aviaries reduce this problem.

Some birds require a small territory or are non-territorial and are there-fore successful in a colony breeding situation. Zebra finches and cockatiels are a good example of this. Putting two pairs of Cuban melodious finches (*Tiaris canora*) in the same flight will result in the males fighting to the death of one them, before territorial limits are established.

There are still many arguments among aviculturists as to the efficacy of colony breeding. While colony breeding makes the best use of aviary space, there seems to be more and more evidence that most birds breed best when not in a true colony situation. By placing birds in separate aviaries, ones which are close together, the aviculturist will significantly reduce the physical interference which occurs when more than one pair is kept in the same flight. Being close together, the pairs will still be influenced by each other's breeding behaviors.

One of the main advantages of a colony is to allow the birds to pick their own mates. The best of both worlds may be achieved by breeding the birds in a colony the first year. This colony situation allows them to establish their own pair bonding. Once the pair bonds are formed, the pairs can be moved to individual flights the next year.

Another concern is the establishment of a feeding territory. This is rare, but if it occurs in a community aviary, the territorial pair must be removed. If they are not removed, the other members of the community may starve to death or may not have enough food to sustain their own breeding attempt.

Once a breeding territory is established, courtship can begin. Courtship takes many forms, from the prolific songs of the song birds to the colorful strutting of many ground birds. To be sure, not all birds establish territory and some that do, choose their mate before the territory is established. Since some species mate for life and some for a few minutes, few definite state-ments can be made about the breeding behavior of birds as a group. There is tremendous diversity in the successful procreation of the various species.

Courtship

Successful courtship begins with courting a bird of the right species, sex and maturity. Innate genetic patterns almost always ensure the courtship of the proper species. Birds raised by foster parents will, if in the same aviary, often try to court the foster species. Likewise, the courting of the opposite sex is genetic, although not infallible. However, those who do mistakenly court the wrong sex will, of course, be unsuccessful in breeding and will therefore effectively remove themselves from the gene pool.

Figure 1.4   Male Gouldian finch courting a female.

Courting a bird that is mature is important. As you would surmise, the age at which maturity is reached varies tremendously from one species to another. Zebra finches can mature in as little time as 3 months. Most psittacines are not fully mature for breeding until they are 2 years old. Large birds such as macaws and cockatoos do not mature until 3 to 5 years of age.

Although young birds can be bred by the aviculturist, there are some inherent dangers. Younger female birds tend to become egg bound. We know little about the causes of egg binding, but in young birds it may be because the oviduct has not fully matured. The first egg of the first clutch is often the most difficult egg to move through the oviduct.

Another problem inherent in breeding young birds is that they often don't copulate effectively, thus resulting in many infertile eggs. And finally, young birds are often not adequate parents. They may not incubate properly or they don't feed the young when they hatch.

One would assume that "the birds will know when they are ready to breed." There is probably a lot of truth to this statement, but problems can arise when a young, immature female is placed with an older experienced male. The male may influence the immature female to begin breeding before she is physically ready or capable of breeding. Although many birds will try to breed at a young age, it is unwise to permit this. Separating pairs or removing nest boxes will prevent young birds from breeding too early which can be potentially harmful.

Pair bond

The result of courtship is ideally the formation of a pair bond. A pair bond is a nonaggressive, mutually beneficial relationship between a sexually mature male and female bird. This pair bond may be strong and last as long as both mates are alive. In other species, the pair bond may last only during the breeding season or may not be formed at all.

The need for the pair bond in breeding is obvious, but many an aviculturist has been fooled into thinking that mutual preening and social behavior is a pair bond. This is especially a problem in some of the social parrots in which the sexes look alike. Two males or two females may be quite cozy and act like a pair forming a pair bond but are simply "making do," or exhibiting the "any port in a storm" philosophy. Fertile eggs will tell you that you have a true pair who have formed, at least for this breeding season, a pair bond. In aviculture a pair means one female and one male bird, not just two birds.

Song

If one were to play a word association game with the word "bird," most people would say flight or feathers. The next most common associative word would probably be song. Bird songs are as diverse as bird sizes and shapes. There are actually thousands of different bird songs. By aesthetic criteria, we probably would not call most of these sounds a song. However, to the bird making these sounds, the sounds are very much a song.

For man a song has to be melodious. This is not true for birds. A bird song is a series of notes expressed in a sequence in a distinct pattern, not to be confused with bird calls. Although both are vocalizations meant to impart information, the song tends to be more rhythmic and is under the control of the sex hormones. Calls are much more involved with survival. Table 1.2 compares, in a superficial way, some of the functions of bird songs compared to the functions of bird calls.

Table 1.2. Comparison of Bird Songs and Calls

Functions of Bird Songs	Functions of Bird Calls
attract mate	food has been located
maintain pair bond	distress
maintain territory	alarm
stimulate breeding behavior	aggression/intimidation
	locate others in flock

Vocalization in mammals is possible because of a structure called the larynx. Air movement, caused primarily by the diaphragm, moves over the vocal cords in the larynx producing sounds which are manipulated and resonated by the mouth, tongue and teeth. The vocalization structure in birds is called the syrinx.

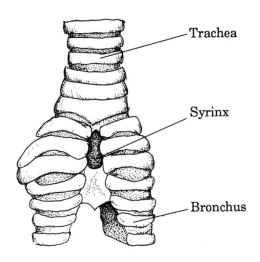

Trachea

Syrinx

Bronchus

Figure 1.5   Avian syrinx.

The larynx is not capable of producing the tremendous sound variation found in birds. To accomplish this, birds have a structure, unique to birds, called the syrinx. In most birds the syrinx is found where the two bronchi of the lungs join to form the trachea (Figures 1.5 and 1.6). Almost all parts of the syrinx and upper respiratory tract play some role in the production of the various sounds produced by birds. No other animal group has a syrinx and none make the complexity of sounds found in the avian world.

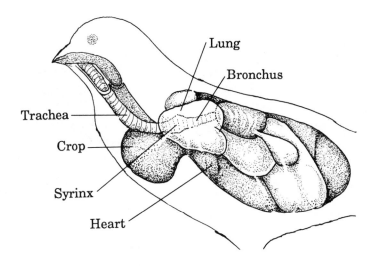

Figure 1.6   Avian syrinx and its location in the bird.

Nesting

Many animals build nests but none build nests with the variety and sophistication of birds. Bird nests are used primarily for breeding. The idea of a bird's nest being analogous to one's home is, for most species of birds, not valid. Although birds sometimes use the nest to escape predators and unfavorable weather conditions, the nest is used primarily to keep the eggs and the developing young protected from unfavorable conditions.

If the nest is to serve these functions, then location is supreme. The nest must be, as much as possible, out of the sun, wind and rain. It must also be in a position where predators will not observe it or will have a difficult time reaching the nest.

These are important considerations for the aviculturist. Although the aviculturist knows that predators cannot get into the aviary, the breeding birds may not. Again, since breeding is such an energy draining process for the parents, birds will only attempt breeding if there is a high chance for success. Nests available to predators have a poor chance of being successful and over generations those birds who are genetically programmed to avoid this will pass on these beneficial genes on to the young.

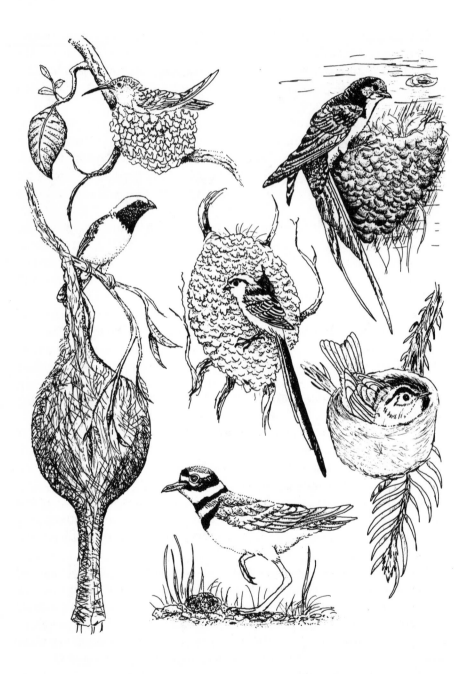

Figure 1.7 A variety of avian nests.

Choosing the nest site and building the nest are all important components of the breeding behavior of most birds. The implication for the aviculturist is to provide as many different nest sites as possible. This reduces the possibility that breeding will be stopped because the birds don't like the nest box or the site chosen by the aviculturist.

Nest building seems to be important to the breeding of cockatoos. They will often remove most of the nesting material deposited by the aviculturist and then proceed to make their own by chewing up any available wood. Having pine boards available for this purpose is advisable, especially for those aviculturists who provide some form of metal nest site such as metal trash cans.

Lovebirds like to use palm fronds, but will use other materials. Gouldian finches have a reputation as very poor nest builders, but if given adequate nesting material they will build nice domed nests. Sisal twine cut into two to three inch pieces works well. Long grasses, such as Bermuda grass, will also be used if made available to the birds.

The point here is, if we are to successfully breed many of these difficult birds we will need to know more about their natural history. When we attempt to breed a certain species of bird it would be helpful to go to a local library (preferably a college or university library) and try to find some field studies on that particular species. With this information one would have a better chance of satisfying the needs of breeding birds in terms of nesting sites and materials.

Copulation

The ultimate goal of courtship is successful breeding and successful breeding depends on consummating the relationship. Copulation is the method by which sperm cells are deposited close to the ova, thereby allowing fertilization of the ovum by a sperm cell. If fertilization is successful, the resulting zygote will begin to divide into many cells forming the embryo.

The urge to mate and specifically to copulate is hormonal. As the testosterone level increases during the breeding season, the urge to copulate becomes quite strong. Different species of birds have been observed attempting to copulate with various objects including large buttons on a night gown, avian dummies and even the human fist. There are even reports of birds attempting to mate with miniature gliders being flown by hobbyists.

In some situations this mating urge becomes so strong as to turn violent. More than one aviculturist has had a female cockatoo maimed or killed by a normally loving mate turned aggressive during the breeding season. This phenomonon appears to be more an artifact of captive breeding than of cockatoo behavior in the wild. One solution to this problem is to clip the wings of the male so that it is easier for the female to escape. Another precaution is to have an opening at both ends of the nesting box, again so that the female can more readily escape the aggressive male.

Sperm cells are ejaculated in a fluid called semen. In mammals, semen represents the combination of sperm cells, seminal fluids and prostate fluids. The primary role of these fluids is to nourish and protect the sperm cells. Birds lack both seminal glands and a prostate, so avian semen does not contain any seminal or prostate fluids. The seminal plasma of birds is therefore quite different from mammals, the significance of which is still unknown.

Figure 1.8   Lovebirds copulating.

Sperm cells (spermatozoa) are produced by the testes. Avian sperm cells tend to be small compared to those of mammals. The number of sperm cells ejaculated per ejaculation is tremendous. In chickens the semen volume is between 0.5 to 1 ml and contains an average of seven billion sperm cells. Research with turkeys has shown lower semen volumes but a higher concentration of sperm cells. While little work has been done on sperm counts of most species of birds, it is reasonable to assume that the sperm counts are also as high.

Why such a high sperm count when only one sperm cell nucleus is required to enter the ovum for successful fertilization? Research with chickens has shown that an ejaculate must contain 70 million sperm cells for optimum fertility. This still seems like a tremendous overproduction. Some probable reasons for large sperm counts are as follows.

There are some sperm cells which are not motile. The movement of those that are motile is random, thus many are not going up the oviduct but in other directions and therefore will not encounter the ovum. Furthermore, it takes the collective enzymes from many sperm cells to breakdown the membrane of the ova allowing one sperm nuclei to enter and join with the female nucleus. In humans, at least 1,000 sperm cells are required at the ovum to release enough enzyme so that one sperm cell nucleus can enter the ovum.

One peculiarity in avian sperm production is that the testes are in the body cavity. In mammals, the testes are outside of the body cavity and if they remain inside the body cavity, the higher temperature causes infertility. Having the testes outside the body is a problem for birds because it would disrupt the sleek flying surface necessary for efficient aerodynamics.

How do birds produce fertile sperm cells in a body cavity that is warmer than that of mammals? We don't know, but there are some hypotheses. One is that the sperm cells are produced at night when the body temperature is typically lower. Also the sperm cells are stored in the lower part of the vas deferens near the cloaca, which can be as much as four degrees C cooler than the body cavity temperature.

Once insemination (copulation) is completed, usually requiring a very short time, the sperm cells are in the cloaca of the female. They may be stored there for a time, which varies from one species to another. After storage, the sperm cells begin their ascent up the oviduct destined to make contact with the ova. In chickens, this movement through the oviduct occurs in as short a time as 26 minutes.

Ordinarily, only one insemination is necessary to fertilize the eggs, but the greater the number of matings, the greater the chance that all the eggs will get fertilized. In chickens, the highest percent of fertile eggs occurs two or three days after normal insemination, with good fertility lasting up to five or six days but dropping off rapidly after that. Fertilization has occurred as long as 35 days after mating in some birds.

Female canaries placed with a male for only a few matings have produced four or more fertile eggs. Female turkeys show an even greater ability to store sperm cells, laying 12 to 15 fertile eggs after a single insemination. Some turkeys have laid fertile eggs two months after insemination. While the number of matings does increase the chances of fertility, increased matings have no effect on the number of eggs laid.

The number of eggs laid will be determined by the number of follicles released (ovulated) from the ovary. How many follicles are released is genetically determined, but this may be influenced by environmental and psychological conditions. The genetic component means that for any given species a clutch size is usually predictable. Birds which lay a predetermined number of eggs are called determinate layers.

Most birds in aviculture are determinate layers. They lay a specific number of eggs per clutch and then cease laying for a time regardless of whether the eggs are removed or not. There are exceptions to this, such as when Zebra finches lay two or three times the normal clutch size. In spite of their attempt to populate the world with offspring, they are still considered to be determinate layers.

Indeterminate layers are those birds that attempt to lay a certain clutch size and will continue to lay until that clutch size is attained. This can be beneficial to anyone desiring to get many eggs. If, as is the case in chickens, the eggs are pulled as they are laid, the hen will continue to lay for a long period of time. Indeterminate layers can be very beneficial to humans who have a stake in the bird's reproductive capacities.

Unfortunately for the aviculturist, the psittacines and song bird species are determinate layers. Pulling their eggs rarely increases the clutch size. Pulling the eggs will, however, often increases the number of clutches by stimulating the birds to go back to nest sooner than they would have otherwise. For example, when umbrella cockatoo eggs are pulled they often lay again within six weeks. Gouldian finches often lay again within a few weeks after the eggs are pulled. However, the birds don't read this book and many will simply quit breeding for the year when a clutch is pulled.

Figure 1.9   A typical indeterminate layer and a determinate layer.

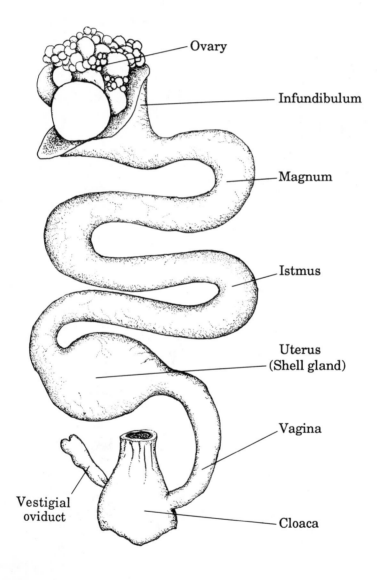

Figure 2.1   Female reproductive system.

2   The Egg

Egg formation

In chickens, release of the ovum (ovulation), into the first part of the oviduct (infundibulum), occurs within 15 to 75 minutes after the previous egg is laid. Ovulation has not been studied in many other species, but in those birds in which it has been studied, the time between the laying of the previous egg and ovulation varies. For example, in the pigeon, ovulation occurs four or five hours after laying. Once in the infundibulum, the chicken ovum begins a 24 hour (more or less in other species) journey down the oviduct (Figure 2.1) ending when the fully formed egg is laid.

Ovulation stimulates smooth muscle contractions in the oviduct. This causes the oviduct to engulf the ovum which is mostly yolk (vegetative pole), but contains the chromosomes from the hen (animal pole) on the surface. The oviduct can be stimulated by, and will engulf, any similarly shaped object. In one experiment, a cork ball was placed in the infundibulum, resulting in the production of an egg with a "yolk" of cork. If there is a simultaneous release of two yolks at this time, the egg will be a double yolked egg. The egg remains in the infundibulum for no longer than 20 minutes, which is enough time for fertilization to occur.

From the infundibulum, the now (hopefully) fertilized egg will pass into a glandular area called the magnum. This is where the layers of albumen (egg-white) are deposited around the yolk and embryo. The depositing of the albumen takes about four hours in the chicken. Albumen is made of protein and is synthesized from both essential and nonessential amino acids.

The egg now passes into a narrow area of the oviduct called the isthmus, where the shell membranes, made of keratin, are deposited around the egg. Initially, the membranes cover the albumen very tightly, but quickly loosen up. The egg remains here for an of average of one and one-quarter hours.

Next is the area where the egg spends most of its time. The egg will spend the next 18 to 20 hours in the uterus also called the shell gland. Here in the first five hours, the egg gains some water and minerals in a process called plumping. The remaining 13 to 15 hours are used to form the egg shell. Any pigmentation (coloration) of the egg shell occurs here also. The hard shell is then covered with a thin protective layer of protein called the cuticle.

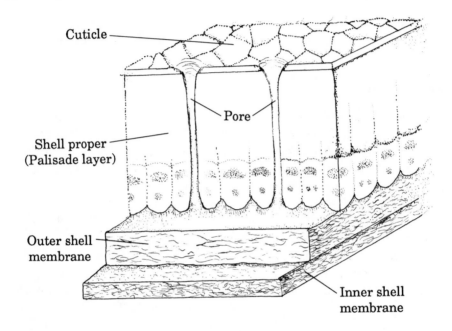

Cuticle

Pore

Shell proper
(Palisade layer)

Outer shell
membrane

Inner shell
membrane

Figure 2.2   Egg shell structure.

The primary part of the egg shell is called the palisade layer (Figure 2.2) and is composed primarily of calcite crystals. Calcite is made up of the compound called calcium carbonate. The carbonate is made by the bird, but minerals such as calcium, magnesium and phosphorus cannot be synthesized by any animal and therefore must be ingested from the diet.

These calcite crystals are deposited on a framework of protein much the way stucco is deposited around chicken wire. This structural relaionship between the calcite crystals and the protein results in a very strong covering for the egg. In addition to adding strength to the egg shell, calcium also provides a source of calcium for the developing chick. The components of the typical chicken egg shell are shown in Table 2.1.

The average total weight of a chicken egg shell is 5 grams. Of this weight, 2 grams or about 40% is actually calcium. The deposit rate for calcium is approximately 125 mg/hour. This converts to a rate of 25 mg. deposited in 12 minutes. With a normal plasma calcium level of about 25 mg., the bird must replenish the plasma calcium level every 12 minutes during the formation of the egg shell. This requires that a tremendous amount of calcium be available in a very short period of time.

Table 2.1   Components of the chicken egg shell.

Calcium carbonate	94%
Magnesium phosphate	1%
Calcium phosphate	1%
Protein	3-4%

Where does this calcium come from? What sources replenish this plasma calcium? Since it is almost impossible for the bird to consume and absorb that much calcium every 12 minutes, the calcium must already be somewhere in the body. Almost all of it has been previously stored in the bones.

A female chicken on a low calcium diet will form normal egg shells, at least for a while. Since the chicken normally has about 20 grams of stored calcium and the egg shell contains 2 grams of calcium, the hen must be liberating 10% of her stored calcium for each egg. Obviously this cannot continue.

That a bird can lay a clutch of normal eggs under these conditions can be attributed to the depositing of calcium in bones, called medullary bones, before egg laying begins. Medullary bone, found only in female birds during the breeding season, adds to the weight of the bird making flight a little more energy requiring. One stimulus for the formation of medullary bones is the sex hormones. In medullary bone, the red marrow is slowly replaced by deposits of calcium (Figure 2.3). Once the egg laying is completed, the medullary bones return to normal.

Medullary bone is very significant for the aviculturist. It is important to provide good calcium sources (see chapter on nutrition) a couple of weeks **before** the egg laying begins, so that the hen may build up the calcium in the medullary bones. Putting calcium sources in the aviary after nesting behavior is noticed may be too late for normal egg formation.

Medullary bone is not the only source for calcium during egg shell formation. The other bones of the body contribute significant amounts of calcium. There are also marked changes in the absorption of dietary calcium at this time. When the shell gland is inactive approximately 40% of the

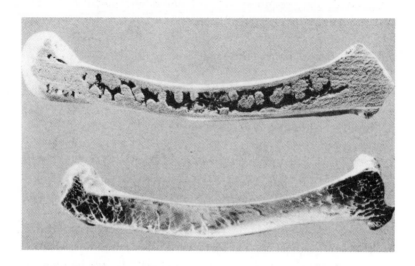

Figure 2.3   Medullary bone (top) compared to normal bone.

ingested calcium is absorbed from the gut. During egg shell formation the absorption rate of calcium from the digestive tract into the blood steam increases to 72%.

Permeating the egg shell are thousands of pores which pass from the shell surface to the internal shell membranes (Figure 2.4). These pores are essential for the intake of oxygen and the ability of the developing chick to get rid of the waste product carbon dioxide. There is a negative side to these pores. They represent passageways for the entry of microorganisms which could destroy the chick.

A crack in the egg shell is serious because of the possibility of microorganisms entering the egg and because of increased water loss. Cracked eggs can be saved. A small piece of sterile chicken egg shell can be used as a patch. Then use some thin (watery) albumen (egg white) as a glue (paraffin and Elmers glue have also been used). Place the small piece onto the shell so that it completely covers the crack. Incubation of the egg can then continue.

The gain or loss of water is another problem posed by having pores in the egg shell. Because water forms a gas and it can diffuse into or out of the egg. Too much water going in or coming out of the egg would be disastrous for the chick. For this reason the amount of water in the air (humidity) around the egg is very important to the successful hatching (see incubation).

Figure 2.4   Air bubbles passing through egg shell pores.

The egg is a marvel of nature. It is almost a world unto itself. The egg contains everything necessary for the full development of the chick except for oxygen. Even the shape is interesting (Figure 2.5). Obviously, the somewhat round shape of the egg facilitates its movement through the oviduct and out of the vent during egg laying. The shape of the egg is also structurally very sound. Examples of strong curved structures such as tunnels and arches come to mind.

There is another factor in egg shape. Why do we not find eggs that are round like a golf ball? One reason is that they would roll out or around the nest too easily. The oval shape of the egg means that the egg will not roll in a straight line.

Some eggs are so shaped that they will roll in a complete circle, thus ending up after the roll, in the almost the same place they were when the roll began. Birds, such as murres, who nest in such precarious places as cliff ledges have elongated, pointed eggs which are thus less apt to roll the ledge.

That large birds lay large eggs and small birds lay small eggs is obvious. However, the larger a bird is, the proportionally smaller is the egg compared to its weight. For example, the ostrich egg is only 1.7% of its body weight as compared to the wren whose egg is 13% of its body weight.

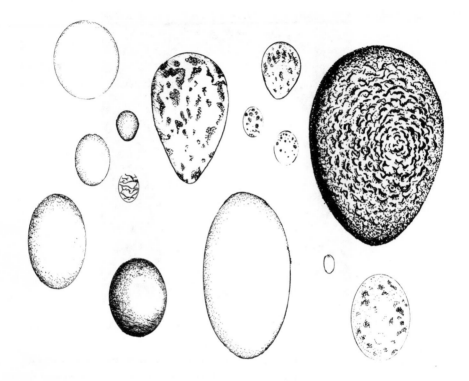

Figure 2.5   A variety of egg shapes and sizes.

The egg shell thickness also changes with egg size. The larger the egg, the thicker the egg shell. This relationship is stated as a proportion. The thickness of an egg shell is proportional to 0.456 power of the weight of the egg.

The primary compounds making up the egg can be seen in Table 2.2. As in almost all biological structures, water is the dominant substance.

Table 2.2   Composition of a chicken egg

Compound	Percent
Water	65.6%
Protein	12.1%
Lipids	10.5%
Glucides	0.9%
Minerals	10.9%

Constituents of the egg

We can get a better idea of the composition of the egg by looking to see where these various compounds are actually located in the egg. Table 2.3 shows the location in the egg where the various organic and inorganic components are found.

Table 2.3   Components of the egg by area.

Component	Yolk	Albumen	Shell
Protein	16.6%	10.6%	3.3%
Carbohydrates	1.0%	0.9%	-
Fats	32.6%	Trace	0.03
Minerals	1.1%	0.6%	95.1%
Water	50.0%	90.0%	0

The yolk, with its high concentration of fats, is where the fat soluble vitamins A,D,E & K are found. Albumen, with its high concentration of water, is the storage area for the water soluble vitamins, B complex and C.

The development of the egg can be better followed if we again review the structures of the egg (Figure 2.6). First is the egg shell which serves to protect the developing chick from physical damage, infection, chemicals and water. Looking inward, we next see the inner and outer shell membranes. Between the two membranes on the blunt end of the egg, is a small air chamber which will get larger as incubation proceeds.

Next is the albumen. Albumen is composed of three proteins. Mucins and globulin make up approximately 5% and albumen makes up the remainder. Albumen is formed as a jelly-like mass, but when the egg is fully formed there are different forms of albumen. The albumen which directly surrounds the yolk is watery, thus allowing free rotation of the yolk. This watery albumen is surrounded by the thick jelly-like albumen, which is again surrounded by more thin watery albumen.

Passing thru the thick albumen are two twisted cords called the chalaza. The chalaza attaches to the yolk on either side and passes along the long axis of the egg. The chalaza holds the yolk in the center of the egg. The lighter animal pole (embryo) should always be up and the heavier vegetative pole (yolk) should be down. When the egg is turned the twisted chalaza are responsible for maintaining this relationship regardless of egg position.

Next is the very familiar yolk. The size of the yolk depends on the type of bird. Precocial birds are those birds such as chickens, ducks, quail, etc. whose young are born fully feathered, eyes open, mobile and eating. Altricial birds are those birds such as finches and parrots which are born with few feathers, eyes closed and are unable to feed themselves.

Precocial birds have a yolk that is from 35 to 50% of the egg volume, as compared to the altricial birds whose yolk represents about 20% of the egg. Why such a difference? When precocial birds hatch they must begin to feed on their own. This is awkward at first. The reason most precocial birds survive this hit and miss attempt at feeding is that they still have 15 to 30% of the yolk. This yolk was pulled into the abdomen just prior to hatching and will sustain them until they can ingest adequate amounts of food.

The altricial birds don't have to feed themselves and so having the yolk in reserve at hatching is not as important. Most altricial birds have used up much of the yolk by the time they hatch.

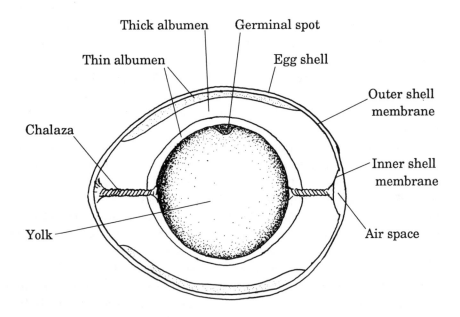

Figure 2.6   Avian egg structure.

Last, but certainly not least, is the animal pole or embryo. Once sperm and ova join together, the resulting cell is called a zygote. This single celled zygote is now capable of dividing and producing all of the cells of the mature bird. Since all cells ultimately come from the zygote they will all have the same genetic material as the zygote.

This genetic material was contributed equally by each parent. Each parent contributes genetic information strands called chromosomes to the young. The chromosome number varies in birds depending on the species. We will use as an example a species of bird which has 80 chromosomes in each cell. The male bird would contribute 40 chromosomes in the sperm cell and the female would contribute 40 chromosomes in the ova. Therefore, the resulting zygote would have 80 chromosomes. See chapter on genetics for a more elaborate discussion of how the sperm cell and ova end up with only 40 chromosomes in each.

Egg laying

Once egg formation is completed, the egg moves into the vagina. From the vagina, the egg moves into the cloaca from where it will be laid. Most passerine birds, such as finches, lay one egg per day until the clutch is complete. Larger birds have a longer time between laying. Parrots often lay an egg every other day until the clutch is complete. Large birds, such as cockatoos, have a 3 to 5 day span between each egg laid.

Although birds don't have conscious control over ovulation and the formation of the egg, they do have conscious control over the actual laying of the egg. Otherwise birds flying overhead or sitting on a perch would be dropping eggs everywhere. Birds whose nest have been disturbed will often cease laying. Since the next ovulation will not occur until the egg is laid, this disruption may affect the clutch size.

Often the number of hours between each egg being laid in a clutch increases as more eggs in each clutch are laid. This probably relates to the fact that as more eggs are laid, there are less egg materials (albumen, yolk, etc) available to form the egg, thus it takes longer to form the egg. The last egg laid in a clutch is often the smallest and later clutches tend to have smaller eggs.

There are some breeders who purchase first clutch birds because they claim that they are bigger. Since the genetic composition of the first clutch would be the same as the second and the care and feeding for both clutches are usually the same, this hypothesis is very weak We need more research in this area. However, many breeders have observed that when birds such as cockatiels are overbred, some young produced later that year are smaller.

The time of day when the eggs are laid varies from species to species. Many birds lay their eggs in the morning. Many parrot type birds tend to lay their eggs in the afternoon. Unless the laying schedule is exactly on a 24 hour cycle, the time of day will vary. For example, if a bird lays its egg every 28 hours then the time of laying would be four hours later each time.

Exactly what determines clutch size is not well understood. If we understood the causes of large clutches, we would have a better chance of increasing clutch size. The main determining factor in clutch size for any given species is heredity. In most cases there is a strong correlation between species survival rates and life span relative to the clutch size. In other words, birds who don't live very long will need to be replaced at a faster rate than those that live a long time, if the species population is to be maintained.

Other factors which affect clutch size are age, size of nest, time of year, and environmental conditions. What effect food availability has on clutch size has not been studied sufficiently in birds, but in many mammals there is a direct correlation between food availability and litter size. A correlation between amounts and types of food affecting clutch size have significant implications for aviculturists.

In 1973 a German scientist named H. Lohrl performed experiments with a small passerine bird called the Great Tit. He used two different sized nest boxes, one which had a diameter of 3 1/2 inches and one which was approximately 8 inches in diameter. There were no differences between hatchability, size of young, or mortality in the different sized boxes. However, there was a difference in the clutch size. Over a two year period, the birds using the larger boxes produced more offspring than those using the smaller boxes. So, for this particular species of bird, the size of the nest box had a definite effect on clutch size.

Other important unanswered questions are, how does the bird know when she has laid a certain number of eggs? Does she count? Does she go by the feel of eggs against her brood pouch? It is obviously unproductive to produce more eggs than the birds can incubate, not to mention feed.

One factor which DOES NOT have an effect on clutch size is the number of matings. It does not matter if the male copulates with the female one time or eighty times, the clutch size will be the same in either situation. For example some birds will copulate many times over a period and lay only one egg. The turkey on the other hand will often copulate only once and lay more than a dozen eggs.

Incubation

Incubation is somewhat similar to pregnancy in mammals. However, in birds, both parents may be "pregnant" since in many species both parents incubate the eggs. Having this "pregnancy " outside of the body is a definite advantage for a flying animal. Can you imagine a bird trying to fly with six developing eggs carried in her uterus? Table 2.4 shows the typical incubation times and normal clutch sizes for some commonly kept avicultural birds.

Table 2.4   Incubation Time and Clutch Size.

Type of bird	Incubation Time (days)	Typical Clutch Size	Fledging Time (days)
Finches	12-14	4-6	21-22
Canary	12-14	4-6	21-22
Budgerigar	17-18	5-7	30-35
Cockatiel	17-18	4-6	30-35
Amazon Parrots	25-26	4-6	55-56
Conures (Aratinga)	23-24	3-6	50-56
Pionus	25-26	4	60-70
Macaws	27-28	2-3	80-100
Mini-Macaws	25-26	3-4	56-60
Cockatoos	22-28	2	65-85
Grass Parakeets (Neophemas)	17-18	4-6	28-32
Rosellas	20-21	4-6	30-32
Polytelis	19-20	4-6	35-40
Eclectus	28-30	2	72-80
Lories & Lorikeets	23-28	2-3	70-90
Kakarikis	18-19	5-8	42-45
Hanging Parrots	19-20	3-4	30-31
Parrotlets	18-21	3-8	28-34
Asiatic Parakeets (large)	27-28	2-3	50-55
Asiatic Parakeets (small)	23-24	4-5	47-50
Lovebirds	22-23	3-7	42-48
African Gray Parrot	28-30	3-4	80-90

Once laid, the egg contains everything necessary for chick development, except oxygen. The other necessities for normal chick development are proper humidity and heat. In most cases it is the role of the parent birds to impart the heat to the egg and to affect the humidity around the egg. The ability to effectively do this is critical to the survival of the chick in the egg. The other primary role of the parents is to provide protection for the eggs against preditors as well as protection against enviromental stresses.

An interesting exception to this are the megapodes of Australia and the East Indies who lay their eggs in a mound of decaying vegetation or other mounds and sand (Figure 2.7). The incubation temperature is provided by either the sun or the heat given off by the decaying vegetation. Parents control the temperature by adding more or less material to the nest and by opening or closing the opening to the nest. Superficially this would seem like a good way for the parents to get out of the work of incubation. However, observations have confirmed that these birds spend up to 10 hours a day manipulating the mound to maintain the proper incubation temperature.

In birds of avicultural interest, the incubation is done by the parents or by artificial incubators. Many birds begin incubation after the first or second egg is laid. This provides greater protection for the eggs, but has some definite disadvantages. One is that the young will hatch out at different times, some may be 3 or 4 days apart. Sometimes, the last hatchling cannot effectively compete for food and does not survive.

For the precocial birds, hatching at different times could be disastrous. For this reason most precocial birds don't begin incubating until the last egg has been laid, thus ensuring that all the eggs will hatch within one day of each other. Altricial birds, such as the finches, typically wait until the clutch is complete or almost complete before incubation begins.

The obvious question here is, how does the bird know when the clutch is complete? Is it the feel of the eggs in the nest or the feel or better yet lack of feeling of the eggs in the oviduct? If it were the feel of the eggs in the oviduct, then no species would begin to incubate until the last egg was laid, but, as we know, some birds begin incubation with the first egg. The behaviors of incubation are hormonally controlled. But, we still do not know what brings about these hormonal changes.

Incubation patterns vary tremendously. In some species only the hen sits (grass parakeets), in others only the male sits (emus) and in many species the parents alternate (cockatiel). Where both parents do sit, the role of the male may be minor, as in many finches, or they may share the incubation equally. In some species both parents sit at the same time.

Figure 2.7   Megapode mound for egg incubation.

In situations where the female does almost all the sitting, such as the grass parakeets from Australia, the male's role is to feed the female who rarely leaves the nest. Generally, birds that don't feed the female, will share the incubation so that the female can leave the nest to feed herself. Because the female is a much more drab color in most species, she is much less conspicuous on the nest than the more colorful male.

There are other patterns of incubation. As mentioned earlier, the megapodes lay their eggs in mounds and then care for them. It takes as much energy to construct and maintain the mound as it would to directly incubate eggs.

Some birds have an incubation pattern that requires no energy at all. They lay their eggs in the nest of other birds. This is called brood parasitism. Not only do the brood parasites get out of incubation, but they also avoid building the nest and feeding the young.

Since many birds will throw any eggs which look different and foreign objects from the nest, it is important for the brood parasite's eggs to look similar to the host eggs. For this reason most brood parasites lay their eggs in nests of specific species of birds (Figure 2.8).

An example of this is a group of African finches called wydahs. The pintail wydah (*Vidua macroura*) parasitizes the nests of the red eared (common) waxbill (*Estrildae troglodytes*). The wydah lays her eggs in the waxbill nest and they usually hatch first. The wydah chicks resemble the waxbill chicks, exhibiting a gape and begging posture similar to the host chicks (Figure 2.9). Parasitic chicks generally grow faster than the host chicks, ensuring their share of the food supply and the survival of their species.

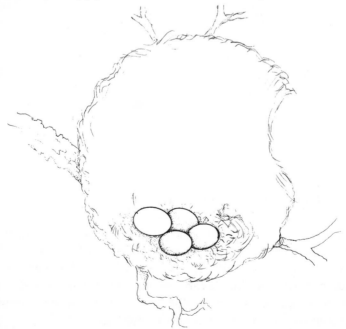

Figure 2.8   Parasitic eggs in nest.

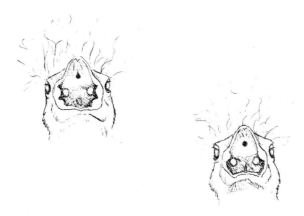

Figure 2.9   Similar gape marks of wydah and waxbill.

The incubation behavior in general is so strong that many birds will incubate eggs from other birds even though the size may vary as much as 100%. Some have been shown to incubate objects such as dice, light bulbs, golf balls and fake eggs.

Birds such as society finches (*Lonchura striata*) will often begin incubating eggs placed in the nest by an aviculturists even though they are themselves not breeding. Even male birds are known to do this. Society finches have also been known to feed young placed in their nest even when they are not themselves breeding at the time. For this reason, society finches make excellent foster parents, especially for the Australian finches. This breeding behavior may indicate that incubation in society finches is a strong innate behavior, not as intimately connected to cyclic hormonal control. Or it may indicate that, in the society finch, the sex hormones are easily stimulated, resulting in this breeding behavior.

Just because a bird sits on an egg does not mean that the egg is being efficiently incubated. Remember that feathers are excellent insulators, therefore they don't transmit much heat to the outside world or to the egg. Therefore, birds develop an area called a brood patch.

The brood patch is basically an area with few feathers and an increase in blood vessels necessary to transport blood and thus heat to the area. Because of this increased blood supply, the area looks like it is inflamed. Generally, those birds doing the incubating develop the brood patch. If both parents incubate, both will develop a brood patch, although there are many exceptions to this.

This transfer of energy during incubation is the prime stimulus for the growth of the chick. Growth is very much affected by the egg temperature. As temperatures rise, so does the rate of growth. However, a point is reached where the increase in temperature is detrimental (called denaturation) to the enzymes which control the metabolism of growth. It would seem ideal then to keep the temperature as high as possible but without reaching the point of denaturation.

How birds can do this with continual changes in ambient (surrounding) temperatures is remarkable. Especially when one considers the penguins and skuas which lay and incubate their eggs in the polar regions where air temperatures are consistently below freezing.

Research indicates that the incubating bird can detect small changes in the temperature of the egg and act accordingly. The detection of these temperature changes probably comes from receptors in the brood patch. Birds, whose brood patches were anesthetized, incubated eggs whose temperatures rose to well above normal. The birds, apparently unable to detect the increased temperature in the egg, made no attempt to lower the egg temperature.

Some ingenious research was done using temperature controlled water circulating through a copper egg, which doves were induced to incubate. When the eggs got cold, the incubating bird would respond by shivering, fluffing the feathers, and shortening the neck. When the eggs got warmer than usual, the bird responded by panting and smoothing out the feathers and elongating the neck.

Incubating birds are not the only source of heat determining the temperature of the egg. The developing chick will produce metabolic heat which increases daily as chick size increases. It is estimated that by the end of the incubation period the chick is providing 75% of the heat required to maintain normal development. The average temperature of the egg tends to increase, as much as 2 degrees Centigrade, from the beginning of incubation until hatching.

There are significant variations in incubation temperatures between the different species of birds. There is also variation in terms of the egg's position. Eggs in the center of the clutch tended to be warmer than those around the edge.

Breeders who artificially incubate their parrot eggs typically use a temperature between 98.5 to 99.5 degrees Fahrenheit depending on the species. Information on incubation tempertures is very sketchy because of the poor methods and inaccurate thermometers used by many breeders.

The energy expenditure of the incubating birds is very high. In the species studied, from 15 to 25% of all the energy produced by the parent bird per day was used to incubate the eggs. Research with the zebra finch showed that birds kept in constant temperatures below 58 degrees Fahrenheit were unable to impart enough heat to the eggs for normal development and hatching. Any temperature below this would require at least 40% of the birds energy expenditure, an amount that would cause the parents body temperature to drop below normal. This would be detrimental to the health of the parent birds.

The avicultural implications are that birds should not be encouraged to breed at these low temperatures. Even those who might be successful at these low temperatures would pay a high price in terms of their own health and welfare.

The low temperatures would greatly slow down the growth of the chick, since the growth rate is primarily determined by the temperature of the egg. Lower incubation temperatures have been shown to cause defects in cockatiels. Work with some quail have shown that a decrease in incubating temperature of only 4 degrees Fahrenheit would increase the incubation period by as much as 6 days. Constant egg temperatures below this will result in poor hatchability. Finch and parrot eggs are much less tolerant of temperature changes than those mentioned above for the quail.

However, in parent incubated eggs, the temperature may safely drop below these levels if the drop lasts only a short time. Many birds leave the nest for periods of time during which the egg may drop to ambient temperature, but will still be viable when the sitting bird returns to the nest. The implication here is to not give up on an egg just because it may be cold. Even eggs which are near hatching have become cold and still hatched normal chicks when reheated. Eggs hatched in an incubator are not as tolerant of these temperature drops and thus do not survive them as well.

While chicks may survive temporary drops in temperature during the incubation period, they rarely survive increases in temperature above normal. This is especially true in the first week or so of incubation. The developing embryo is very sensitive to temperature increases at this time. High temperatures will affect the rate of chick development or denature the enzymes of the chick, resulting in death.

One final concern when incubating eggs is contamination by microorganisms such as bacteria. Care should be taken to ensure that the nest, incubator and anything contacting the eggs, especially hands, are clean.

Figure 3.1 Hoatzin feeding young.

3   Chick Development

Egg turning

Egg turning serves several purposes. First, turning the egg will move the embryo to a different position relative to the albumen and to the egg shell. Since the bird derives nutrition from the albumen and calcium from the shell, this movement will result in a better use of food resources. The egg turning also decreases the chance of the a developing chick sticking to the shell membranes.

Also, by turning the eggs, the lower side, which is the cooler side, is brought into contact with the brood pouch and thereby warmed up. The turning of the eggs would also result in a more even distribution of temperature through all of the eggs in the clutch.

Turning begins with incubation and continues until the chick pips into the air space. Egg turning is much more important in the first half of the incubation period than in the second half. There is a significant variation in the rate at which eggs are turned. Some birds turn their eggs only once an hour and some as often as every 8 minutes with many rates in between.

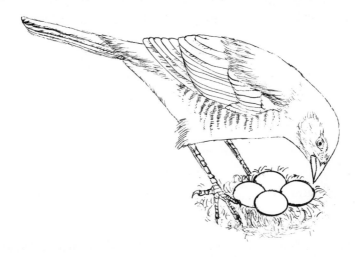

Figure 3.2   Egg turning.

Egg turning is critical to successful hatching in most species. If artificially incubated chicken eggs are turned only once a day, the hatching rate drops to 15% of normal. Many aviculturists turn their incubator eggs every hour. A habit they may have developed because the automatic turning devices typically turn the eggs once every hour. Yet there are aviculturists who have been successful by turning the eggs as little as 5 times per day.

During egg turning, it is important to turn eggs in a different direction each time. This will prevent the coiled chalaza from unwinding and therefore being unable to move the embryo to the upper surface of the yolk. It is also advisable to turn the eggs an odd number of times per day. Therefore, during the night, the embryo is not always on the same side. Nightime is typically the longest period that the eggs sit without being turned.

Egg humidity

Another important factor in the hatchability of eggs is humidity. Humidity is significant because it will determine the amount of water that is evaporated from the egg. If the humidity around the egg is low, too much water will be lost from the egg. This moves the chick away from the egg shell and some of its nutrient sources. If the humidity is too great, the egg will not lose water at the normal rate. This will decrease the size of the air space and the chick may drown during pipping.

Although there is not as much scientific data on humidity as we would like, many breeders are having success incubating their parrot eggs at a relative humidity of approximately 50%. At an incubation temperature of

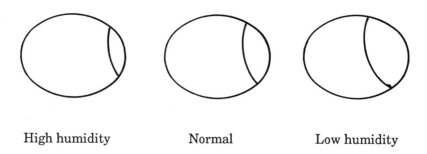

High humidity   Normal   Low humidity

Figure 3.3   Effect of humidity on air space of cockatoo egg at 20 days.

100 Fahrenheit, the relative humidity of 50% corresponds to a wet bulb reading of about 85%. A wet bulb reading is simply a thermometer whose bulb is surrounded by water, usually drawn to it by a cotton wick.

Because evaporating water has a cooling effect, the wet bulb will have a lower temperature reading than a dry bulb (thermometer). How much lower will depend on the amount of water in the air (humidity). More water in the air means less evaporation which then causes a higher wet bulb reading. On the other hand, if the amount of water in the air is low, there will be more evaporation and thus more cooling, which will lower the wet bulb reading.

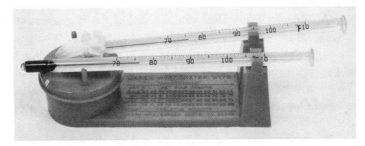

Figure 3.4   Typical wet bulb thermometer.

Therefore, the wet bulb reading will be determined by the amount of moisture in the air as well as the temperature. If the temperature in the incubator changes, both dry bulb and wet bulb readings will change, but not to the same degree. By using tables, the dry bulb reading and the wet bulb readings can be used to calculate the relative humidity. The relative humidity is the amount of water the atmosphere is holding, relative to the maximum amount of water it can hold at a specific temperature. Relative humidities above 100% are called rain.

At an incubation temperature of 100 degrees Fahrenheit, the ideal relative humidity of 85-86% will yield the highest hatchability in parrots. The ideal hatching humidity is generally higher than the incubation humidity. Once the chick pips into the air space, most aviculturists increase the humidity or move the hatching chick to an incubator with a higher humidity. The higher humidity prevents the chick and the shell membranes from drying out during the hatching period.

As egg development continues the egg weight drops. This drop is due to many factors such as the evaporation of moisture just discussed. No other organic matter or minerals are gained or lost during the incubation period. Therefore, the weight changes must relate to the loss of carbon dioxide and other gaseous waste products, as well as the water loss. The only two substances which normally enter the egg at this time are water and oxygen. Most of the metabolic processes which take place in the egg involve the conversion of carbon, hydrogen, oxygen, and nitrogen, etc. to compounds which make up most of the organic materials. These organic materials form the many cells of the growing chick.

Studies of South American parrots by English aviculturists, John and Pat Stoodley, indicate that a 16% weight loss over the incubation period results in the best hatching and healthiest chicks. According to Table 3.1 the loss in grams of a 20 gram egg over an incubation period of 21 days should be about 3.2 grams. This calculates to a loss of 0.152 grams per day, assuming the egg loses 1/21 of its weight each day.

The egg will not lose the same amount of weight everyday, but the 0.152 grams per day figure gives one a guideline as to how well the egg is developing. There are no absolutes here. Eggs have hatched with normal chicks when weight losses have been more and less than 16%. Earlier books recommended an ideal weight loss of 13%, for birds such as chickens, quail and ducks. The Stoodleys' study was done primarily with South American parrots. Much more hard data must be accumulated to determine if these values are correct for other species of avicultural interest.

Table 3.1   Daily weight loss at 16%

Data:

> Egg weight = 20 grams
> Incubation period = 21 days
> Weight loss in 21 days = 16%

Calculations:

Expected weight loss in 21 days:

> 20 grams x 0.16 = 3.2 grams

Expected daily weight loss:

> 3.2 grams / 21 days = 0.152 grams/day

Embryo development

Development of the embryo within the egg proceeds at a very deliberate pace and sequence determined by the hereditary pattern. Each time a cell divides (mitosis) it is capable of producing two new "daughter" cells. So the zygote undergoes mitosis, producing two new cells. These two new cells each produce two new cells, so we are now at the four cell stage. These 4 cells produce 8 cells which produce 16 cells which produce 32 cells, etc. These cell divisions continue through the development of the chick. Later on growth is tremendous. For example, the chick would go from say 16,000 cells to 32,000 in a short period of time. This initial collection of cells is called the embryo.

Initially the cells produced from the zygote are unspecialized. Then the cells begin to specialize. How cells, all of which have exactly the same chromosomes, and hence the same genetic potential, can specialize into different cells is still pretty much a mystery.

Yet, this specialization does occur and it is at least predictable, if not understandable. Initially, the cells form three specialized tissues called endoderm, mesoderm, and ectoderm. These tissues will then go on to form the other tissues of the developing chick. (Table 3.2).

Table 3.2   Specialized Tissue Formation.

Endoderm forms:
>   Digestive tract and its glands
>   Urethra
>   Respiratory system
>   Pituitary gland

Mesoderm forms:
>   Skeletal, smooth and cardiac muscle
>   Cartilage and bone
>   Blood and blood vessels
>   Kidneys and gonads
>   Dermis of the skin

Ectoderm forms:
>   Epidermis of skin
>   Feathers and nails
>   Lens of the eye
>   Most sense organs
>   Nervous tissue

Tissues and organs form in the order in which they are needed. The circulatory system with its transport function is needed early for the continued development of this mass of cells. The heart, blood vessels and blood develop early. By the third or fourth day, blood vessels can be seen when the egg is candled. Presence of these blood vessels is one of the earliest positive indicators of fertilization (Figure 3.5). The brain and lungs will develop last since neither will be used until the chick hatches.

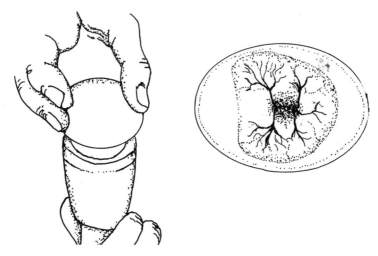

Figure 3.5 Candling of an egg.

The growth of birds and the growth of mammals proceeds at a very different pace. Most mammals progress slowly through the growth phases from birth to adult size. Birds, on the other hand, achieve up to 80% of their adult size before they even leave the nest.

Humans use about 15% of their life span to grow from birth to adult size, as compared to birds who spend less than 1% of their life span to achieve adult size. These figures ignore the gestation period, which is just as dramatic. A human takes approximately 270 days to develop from fertilization to birth, as compared to a bird such as the cockatiel, which takes only 18 days or so. Even large birds, such as the ostrich, which will equal a human in weight, only requires a gestation period of 60 days before hatching.

The short incubation period and the rapid growth rate are undoubtedly necessary due to the vulnerability of birds in the nest. Adult birds, as well as the chicks, are most vulnerable to predators when they still in the nest. If the nest is approached by a predator, there is, in most nests, only one way out. And, this exit is often occupied by the entering predator. So for the survival of the individual and of the species the reproductive process needs to be as short as possible.

Another factor in the rapid growth rate is the fact that in many species the fledged birds will be on their own within a few weeks after they fledge. There is no time to "leisurely pass" through the juvenile period. The juvenile must have all of its physiological systems, including the nervous system, fully developed if they are to survive. Within a few weeks after leaving the nest, the juveniles are completely on their own.

Although most birds are "on their own" shortly after fledging, there are many exceptions. These exceptions occur in those species which require the learning of a behavior, such as hunting for prey. Birds of prey are good examples of birds which stay with the parents longer since learning to find, stalk, and successfully attack prey is much more difficult than the finding of fruits and seeds.

Hatching

Until this time, the chick has played a passive role in its own development. In hatching this is no longer so. The chick plays the major role in hatching. Prior to hatching there are two changes which take place. First, some chicks develop distinct hatching muscles at the base of the neck. These muscles are so prominent in some chicks that they look like some kind of abnormality. The other change is the development, on the upper mandible near the tip, of a small pointed structure called an "egg tooth."

Using the "egg tooth" (Figure 3.6), the chick pushes against the shell, first scoring the inner surface and with continued work will actually puncture through the shell. The chick will continue the pipping around the blunt end of the shell until the egg shell is weakened. Then with forceful pushes, using its legs and neck with the well developed neck muscles, it will push the two ends of the shell apart. In some species this process takes days and is a very energy draining process.

After hatching, the neck muscles get smaller (atrophy) and return to the more normal shape. Also at this time the "egg tooth" will separate from the beak and fall off. These changes take from one to four weeks, depending on the species of bird.

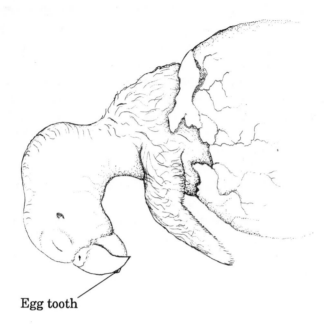

Egg tooth

Figure 3.6   Egg tooth and well developed neck muscle.

As hatching becomes imminent, the air space undergoes significant enlargement in size. In cockatoos it occupies almost 25% of the egg volume. Approximately 3 days before the actual hatching, the cockatoo chick will pip through the egg membranes into the air space. The air space is usually at the blunt end of the shell, but sometimes (abnormally) appears at the pointed end. Expansion of the lungs and air sacs occurs and the chick is now breathing on its own for the first time. One indication of this is that the chick can be heard to peep at this time.

Once into the air space, the chick then pips a hole in the shell allowing air to enter the air space. The chick now has adequate oxygen necessary for the rigorous work ahead. Shell pipping usually takes from 1 to 3 days for a cockatoo. There is evidence that in many species, the peeping sounds made by early hatching chicks are a stimulus to initiating pipping in the other chicks. Again, this would have real adaptive value in precocial birds where hatching of all the chicks at the same time is important. This pre-hatching peeping may also serve to identify and bond the chicks to the parents.

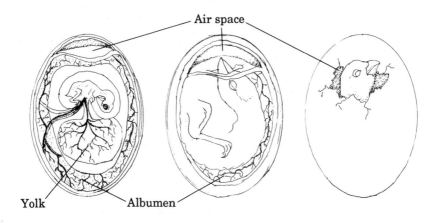

Figure 3.7   Chick pipping into air space and through shell.

Now that the chick is breathing air, the network of blood vessels in the inner membranes are no longer needed for gas exchange and are drained of their rich blood supply. Also, at this time, the yolk sac is drawn into the abdominal cavity. In precocial birds this represents approximately 40% of the original yolk. This significant reserve is necessary because the precocial chicks are not fed by the parents, but are instead "taught" how to feed. This trial and error learning is possible because the chick has a few days reserve of nutrition available to it in the yolk.

In altricial birds, the yolk which is drawn into the body cavity represents at the most 10% of the original yolk. Remember, the altricial yolk was smaller than the precocial yolk initially. This internal yolk means that the altricial bird can survive for at least a day without the need to be fed. However, in situations where a chick takes a long time to pip, the yolk may be almost completely consumed at hatching. Therefore, immediate feeding may be necessary.

Parent birds rarely assist the chick in the pipping process and it is questionable as to whether the inexperienced aviculturist should either. However, there are cases where aviculturists have successfully helped chicks hatch who would have otherwise died. The danger is that the over anxious person may assist the chick before the yolk has been adequately drawn into the abdominal cavity. This will result in the hemorrhaging of the membrane blood vessels and thus death to the chick. To help or not, is a difficult decision. Most chicks don't need this well-meaning assistance.

Once hatched, the survival of the chick depends, in most cases, on the parents. Table 3.3 gives some indication as to the role actually played by the parents. In the precocial birds, the role of the parents is primarily educational. Whereas, in the altricial birds, the young are dependent on the parents for warmth, protection and nourishment.

Table 3.3   Maturity of the young when they hatch (adapted from Nice, 1962).

I. Precocial
   Eyes open, down-covered, leave nest first day or two.
      1. Completely independent of parents (megapodes).
      2. Follow parents, but find own food (ducks, shorebirds).
      3. Follow parents and are shown food (quail, chickens).
      4. Follow parents and are fed by them (grebes, rails).
II. Semi-precocial
   Eyes open, down-covered, stay at nest although able to
      walk, fed by parents (gulls, terns).
III. Altricial
   Eyes closed, little or no down, unable to leave nest, fed
      by parents (finches and parrots).
IV. Semi-altricial
   Down covered, unable to leave nest, fed by parents.
      1. Eyes open (herons, hawks).
      2. Eyes closed (owls).

Feeding the young

The first role of parents, after hatching, is to brood the young so that the young will dry. In the absence of this brooding, the heat loss due to the evaporation would be more than the young chick could handle. Once the young are dry, the hardest reproductive task of all begins.

Feeding of the young is an energy draining task for the parents. It begins shortly after hatching and continues until a few weeks or months after the young are fledged. This may take as long as two to six months, as is true in the larger birds such as cockatoos.

In most species both, parents take part in feeding the young, although in some birds, the role of the male is to feed the female who then in turn feeds the young. Feeding by one parent alone is a difficult task, but it can be done as shown by hummingbirds where the female performs every reproductive function herself, except copulation.

Figure 3.8   Feeding regurgitated food to young.

Regardless of whether the various species feed primarily on fruit, seed, or insects, the chick diet must be higher than usual in protein. Many species who don't normally feed on insects, begin to consume insects and other small animals at this time because of their high protein content. A study of house sparrows showed a non-breeding diet of 3.4% animal matter and 96.6% vegetable matter. Analysis of the diet of chicks indicated a diet of 68.1%

animal matter and 31.2% vegetable matter, indicating a radical change in the diet of the parents during the breeding season. This increased need for protein during the breeding season has significant implications for the aviculturist.

While there are many different methods of feeding, the finches and parrots both swallow and then later regurgitate the food for their young to eat. There are important advantages to this method of feeding. First, the swallowing of the food allows the parent to carry much more food than would be possible if carried in the beak.

Secondly, the food being in the crop gets partly digested by the enzymes of the adult, an aid to the chick. Digestive juices tend to get regurgitated with the food, also aiding in digestion by the chick. The regurgitated food also contains bacteria. Bacteria are normal and beneficial in the digestive system of the adult (see chapter on digestion). Regurgitated food may be a way of establishing these beneficial bacteria in the chick.

Young birds can open their mouth very wide. This is called gaping, which serves many purposes. It obviously greatly increases the size of the opening through which the food is passed. Gaping, along with "hunger begging," is also a stimulus to the parent bird to feed the young. It is also a stimulus for initiating gaping in nest mates. Gaping is a strong reflex in chicks and many will continue gaping even though their crops are filled up, especially if other chicks in the nest are gaping and making begging sounds.

When gaping, the wide-open mouth becomes the dominant feature of the bird. Many altricial chicks have mouth linings which are quite colorful. The bright colors typically seen in these species are yellows, reds and oranges. Some finches have small reflective structures at the corners of the mouth, presumably to guide the parents in the dark nests.

The parents tend to pump food down into the chick's stomach, in a coordinated effort with the chick. This feeding requires the beak of the parent to be inserted into the gaping beak of the chick. The most dramatic example of this occurs in hummingbird feeding. Here the female inserts almost the full length of her beak into the mouth of the young. How she does this without impaling the chick is remarkable. In other species the beaks are placed together in a "scissor position."

The feeding instinct is a very strong. So strong that some times youngsters from the first clutch will assist in feeding the young of subsequent clutches. This is a real advantage in fostering. Watching a Bourke's parakeet feed a much larger fledged cockatiel is quite a sight.

One unknown regarding this feeding instinct is, how does the parent bird decide which young to feed or better yet, does the parent make any decision at all. Obviously the clutch size must play some role in this decision. A large clutch means more mouths to feed and thus many more trips to the food source and more food to be spread around. Little is known about how these decisions are made.

When a chick is fed, it will stop gaping long enough to swallow. The parent will then feed another gaping bird and thereby spread out the feeding. But in a large clutch of say 9 birds, there will always be begging and often by a chick that was fed "two chicks ago" and another that has, at this point, received no food. We don't know how the parent decides who will get fed?

Empirical observations indicates that small clutches tend to produce fledglings that grow faster and are larger when fledged, than are the fledgling of a large clutch from the same parents. This does not mean that the adult birds from a small clutch will necessarily be larger than adult birds from a large clutch. A bird, small as a fledgling, may still develop into a normal sized adult bird.

Feeding the young is a full time job. Small passerine birds have been observed to make between 30 to 60 feeding visits per hour to the nest. Initially, nestlings will eat their own weight in food per day. By the time they fledge, nestlings are eating only one-fourth of their body weight in food. Although the relative amount has decreased to one-fourth, the absolute amount of food required has increased because the weight of the chick has increased. Because of this increase in the amount of food consumed, the feeding trips increase as the chicks develop.

Nest sanitation is a must. "Don't foul one's own nest" is a cliche we hear often. For birds, it has real meaning. Fecal materials represent waste and non-digestible products which must be gotten rid of. The nest must be kept clean and dry or microorganisms such as bacteria will grow. Most birds keep their nest clean and dry. This is done in many different ways.

Some chicks, such as hummingbirds, can forcefully expel their fecal material from the cloacal opening. Hummingbird chicks will back-up until their vent opening is above the nest rim and then expel the fecal material into the air. Peeking into a hummingbird nest is not without its hazards.

In a variation on this expulsion, birds in enclosed nests tend to expel their fecal material against the nest walls, often on the upper sides of the walls. This then keeps the fecal material away from the nestling who are usually huddled in the center of the nest.

In many species, such as swallows, warblers and sparrows, the waste materials are excreted in small fecal sacs (Figure 3.9). These membranous fecal sacs can then be eaten or carried from the nest by the parents. While the eating of the fecal sac may sound distasteful, there may be benefits to the parent bird. Welty suggests that the fecal material in young hatchlings may have food value resulting from the inefficient digestion of the hatchlings.

Figure 3.9   Fecal sac removal.

Along with feeding, the other primary role of the parent is brooding. In the altricial birds, thermoregulation (temperature regulation) is very poor. This along with the lack of feathers necessitates brooding by the parents. Brooding, like feeding, is a strong instinct and birds will sometimes brood chicks other than their own.

The daytime brooding is strong in the first week after hatching and decreases significantly there after. Studies indicate an average decrease in daytime brooding time of 6 to 8 percent each day. Night time brooding continues through much of the incubation period.

Table 3.4 shows some of the external and behavioral changes that take place in a small altricial bird such as a finch during the 13 to 14 days between hatching and fledging.

Table 3.4   Changes in finch development after hatching.

Day	External development & behavioral changes
1	Elevates head and gapes at any movement in the nest. Begins to expel droppings.
2	Eyes start to open. Some feathers show through skin.
3	Eyes open. Pushes upward with wings & legs. Some control over where droppings are deposited.
4	Growth is progressing rapidly. More efficient use of legs. Makes louder sounds. Primaries erupt thru skin.
5	Birds face nest opening or feeding parent. Leg development allows birds to stand. Preening attempted.
6	Young move around the nest. Begin to exhibit fear of disturbances. Responds to parents alarm sounds.
7	Young active in nest. Exercising, stretching and preening are common behaviors. Decrease in rapid growth rate. Young begin to remove feather sheaths.
8	Very aware of events around them. Thermoregulation is much better.
9	Most feathers fully formed.
10	Very active in preening. Begins to peek out of nest. Becomes more inquisitive.
11	Thermoregulating well. No longer requires brooding.
12	Much wing stretching.
13	Fledges due to parental calls or following fledged nestmates.

Fledging

Once the bird has grown enough to be able to fly, it generally leaves the nest. This is called fledging and the fledged bird is called a fledgling. Table 2.4 (page 29) shows the average number of days in which various birds spend in the nest after hatching.

One of the most significant changes in the fledgling occurs just prior to leaving the nest. The young bird will experience a weight loss. This "slimming down" is a natural event caused by changes in their eating pattern, most likely brought about by the need to decrease weight for flight. Once the fledglings leave the nest, most don't return.

Fledging is stimulated by a number of factors. Weather is a factor, as is hunger. Other fledglings leaving the nest are often a stimulus. Also, parents anxious to nest again, will often drive the young from the nest. This sometimes results in feather picking or injury to the young, if they are not yet ready to leave.

When young leave the nest prematurely, there is usually a problem. Heat stress, insects in the nest, parents not feeding, parental pressure or dead birds in the nest are a few reasons for early fledging.

Once the young leave the nest, they are fed by the parents for weeks or months, depending on the species of birds. At this time, the parents demonstrate to the young the ways to find, obtain, and consume food. Once the young learn these important "lessons" they leave the parents, most never to return to the parents or their parent's territory.

4   Skeletal System

Introduction

The avian skeletal system is a versatile structure. It must be sturdy enough to support the bird's weight on the perch and on the ground. This skeletal system must also be sturdy enough to withstand the constant pulling which results from muscle contraction. On the other hand, it must be light-weight enough for flight. The avian skeletal system is a marvelous compromise between the need for strength and the need for a light-weight structure.

Functions of the skeletal system

The avian skeletal system, like those of other vertebrates, is an internal skeleton (endoskeleton) which serves many purposes. One purpose is to provide a network upon which many organs, in one way or another, attach. Along with the muscles, the skeletal system plays a dominant role in the support that is necessary for movement, be it walking, running or more commonly in birds, flying.

The skeletal system also serves as protection. Skull bones protecting the brain and vertebrae (backbone) protecting the spinal cord are good examples. The ribs are important in protecting the delicate internal organs. Calcium storage is another function of the skeletal system. And finally, the bone marrow of the skeletal system serves as the primary site for the production of the three types of blood cells.

Bone Modifications

In most vertebrates, the skeletal system must support the animal's weight when the organism is standing, regardless of whether it is a two legged or a four legged animal. When perched or standing on the ground, all of the weight is supported by the legs. However, in flight the support changes from the legs to the wings. Obviously, the bird's skeletal system must be modified to accommodate the varying demands placed upon it.

Primary modifications of the avian skeleton are the fusing of some bones and the elimination of others. By fusing bones together, greater strength is achieved. The trade-off of course is a loss of flexibility. One example of this fusing can be seen in the area of what would be the hand in humans (Figure 4.1). Other examples are the hip (pelvic) bones, and many of the vertebrae, which when fused provide rigidity for walking, perching and flying.

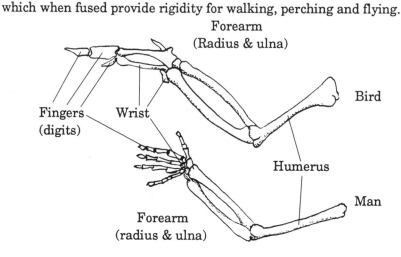

Figure 4.1   Comparison showing the fusing of "hand" bones of birds.

One of the most characteristic features of the backbone in most bird species is this rigidity. An exception to this would be the penguins who have a very flexible backbone. This probably relates to the need for the flexing of their body while swimming. Because most birds have a rigid backbone, their necks tend to be proportionally long and quite flexible.

Another significant modification of the avian skeleton occurs in the pectoral area, the area where the wings (arms) attach to the body. The backbone, ribs and sternum form a strong structure which provides strength for attachment of flight muscles. These bones also provide protection for the heart, lungs and internal organs.

Pneumatized bone

Another compromise to flight is the pneumatization (filled with air) of many bones (Figure 4.2). Most of the large bones have air sacs which penetrate down deeply into the bones. Diving birds such as the grebes, loons and penguins lack the hollow bone, an adaptation, no doubt, to the difficulty of diving with bones full of air. The long bones of large birds, such as swans, have been used as primitive flutes. Charles Darwin, the famous naturalist, was reported to use a pipe made from the wing bone of an albatross.

These air passages within bone can be a real problem for aviculturists attempting to eradicate internal parasites living within the respiratory system. The air sac mite *Sternostoma tracheocolm* is an internal parasite found in many birds. However, this mite has a serious effect on the health of some species such as canaries and Gouldian finches. Many air born treatments simply drive the mite deeper into the air sacs, where it patiently waits for the noxious gas to pass. Therefore, systemic (in the blood) treatments seem to be more effective at controlling air sac mites than are air born treatments.

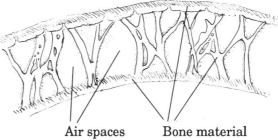

Air spaces   Bone material

Figure 4.2   Pneumatized bone.

Skeletal system

For purposes of comparison and illumination, let's compare the specific bones of birds with those of humans. The bird skeleton, like that of man, is divided into two major systems. They are the axial skeleton and the appendicular skeleton. (Table 4.1).

Table 4.1   Bones of the axial and appendicular skeleton.

Axial skeleton	**Appendicular skeleton**
skull	scapula (shoulder blade)
vertebrae	clavicle (collar bone)
ribs	wing bones ("arm")
sternum (breast bone)	pelvic girdle (hip bones)
	leg & foot bones

Skull

First, we will compare the skulls. The first obvious difference is the absence of a heavy jaw and teeth. In its place, the bird has a light weight beak. This beak must serve not only the eating and chewing functions, but in the absence of hands, the beak must serve as a manipulating instrument as well.

The next obvious difference is the size and position of the eyes. The eyes are proportionally larger and, in many species, positioned more toward the center. Moving at high speed, such as in flight, requires good vision.

Pneumatization (air in bone) of the skull occurs in most birds. A definite advantage in flight, but a real disadvantage when accidentally flying into something. With thin bones surrounding the brain, it does not take much of a collision to cause brain damage or to cause life threatening cerebral bleeding.

Like man, the lower mandible of birds is freely movable. Many birds take this one step further, having the ability to raise or lower the upper mandible (Figure 4.3). This allows a wider gape which is significant when the young are being fed and for those birds that collect insects "on the wing."

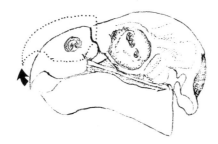

Figure 4.3 Upper mandible flexibility.

Tongue

Although the tongue is not bone (it is a fibromuscular organ), it is the modifications in bone and muscle which allow birds to extend their tongue to extraordinary lengths. This extension allows birds such as hummingbirds and woodpeckers to probe deep into recesses searching for what otherwise would be unobtainable food sources.

Vertebral column

The vertebral column of birds, like man, is divided into five areas: cervical (neck), thoracic (chest), lumbar (back), sacral (hip) and caudal (tail). While man has a total of 26 of these vertebrae, birds have many more, some having more than 60. As discussed above, many are fused for rigidity, except for those in the cervical (neck) region. Where mammals have only seven cervical vertebrae, birds may have as many as 25.

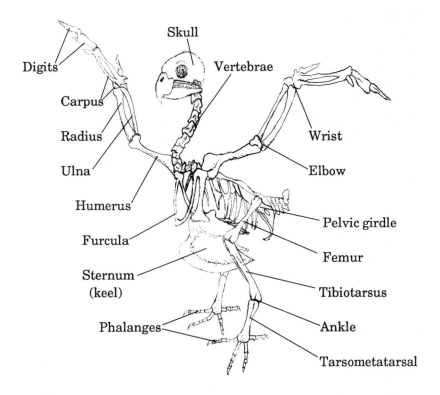

Figure 4.4   Avian skeleton.

Sternum

The sternum (breastbone), which connects the ribs in front, is one of the most noticeable differences in the avian skeleton. The avian sternum is much more developed than in mammals. It has a large flattened plate, called a keel, used for the attachment of flight muscles. The edge of this keel is quite noticeable when feeling the chest of the bird. Aviculturists often check the keel when inspecting a bird. If the keel is sharp and the muscle mass concave (curved in), the bird is not healthy. The bird could be sick or simply in poor health. Neither of these are acceptable to the aviculturist.

Pectoral girdle

In man, two bones, the scapula (shoulder blade) and clavicle (collar bone), form the pectoral girdle, which is the primary attachment point and support for the humerus. In birds, there are three bones forming this girdle. They are the scapula, the coracoid and the furcula. The furcula corresponds to our clavicle and is referred to as the wish bone. The main bone of the wing, the humerus, attaches to this pectoral girdle, thereby attaching the wing to the body of the bird.

Humerus

The bird's humerus is shorter and stronger than the humerus of man, owing to the tremendous force exerted on it in flight. Major flight muscles attach to the humerus, making this bone the most important bone in terms of the strength needed for flight. A break or weakness in the humerus will prevent the bird from flying.

Radius and ulna

The radius and ulna are slightly modified and fused. Man can lay his hand palm down on a table and then turn it over so that the back of his hand now lies on the table. This flexibility is due to man's ability to rotate his forearm using the radius bone. Because of the fusing of the radius and ulna in birds, they are unable to "turn over their wings." Having a more stable, stronger wing for developing the lift necessary for flight, more than compensates for the loss of flexibility.

Carpel bones

It is in the wrist and finger bones that the bones of birds and man are vastly different. Table 4.2 shows these differences. Man has eight carpel (wrist) bones, bird's have two; man has five metacarpal bones, birds have three; man has five fingers, birds have three. The wrist and finger bones are modified for the attachment of the feathers.

Table 4.2   Comparison of the wrist and finger bones of man and birds.

Bones	Man	Birds
carpel (wrist)	8	2
metacarpel (palm area)	5	3
fingers	5	3

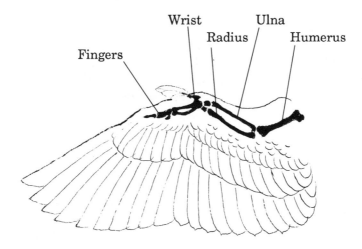

Figure 4.5   Wing showing relative position of bones.

Pelvic girdle

The avian pelvic girdle, like that of man, consists of two pelvic bones. Each pelvic bone is formed by the fusing of three bones, the ilium, ischium, and the pubis. Where these bones meet is a cavity called the acetabulum, which is the attachment point for the large leg bone called the femur. The avian pelvis is much longer proportionally than the pelvis of man and is open in the forward portion to facilitate egg laying.

The avian pelvis, like that of man, is dimorphic (shows a sexual difference). Because of egg laying, the pelvis of the female is wider apart than that of the male, especially during breeding season. Also, the female pelvis tends to be more pointed.

These differences are sometimes used to determine the sex of birds whose sex cannot be determined externally. This is not particularly reliable, however, because it is not pronounced in females who have not yet laid their first egg. Also, when the bird is handled, muscle contraction tends to pull the pelvic bones together leading one to assume that the bird is a male. To be more reliable, the pelvis should be palpated while the birds is perching. This can be accomplished by forcing the bird to perch while still holding the bird in hand.

Femur

Since birds use their legs for basically the same purposes as man, one would not expect the avian leg bones to be greatly modified from those of man, and, in fact, they are not. The femur has somewhat the same shape as the human femur, although it is shorter. When man stands the femur is an obvious bone. This is not true in birds. Because the femur is close to the body, it tends to be covered by the wings and is usually not visible.

Fibula

The bone that is most visible, and therefore, inaccurately called the femur by many, is the fibula. It is this observation that causes some to say "look at that bird, his knee goes the wrong way." This mistaken observer is actually looking at the bird's "ankle" rather than its knee. One has to look at the bird a little closer to see the birds knee because it's often obscured by the wing. The tibia is the main bone of the "drumstick" that is so popular when fowl is the main course.

Tarsals

Now we see significant differences. The tarsals (ankle), metatarsals (arch), and phalanges (fingers) are highly modified. Some of the tarsal bones are fused to the end of the tibia (now called tibiotarsus) for strength, which again results in a loss of flexibility.

The remaining tarsal bones are fused with the metatarsal bones, forming a bone called the tarso-metatarsus. This is a significant difference. Man walks on his tarsal, metatarsal and bottoms of his phalanges. The bird's tarsal and metatarsal bones are not even touching the ground. Birds walk on their phalanges (Figure 4.6). In other words, birds stand on their toes.

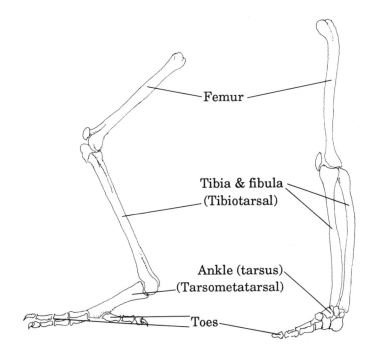

Femur

Tibia & fibula
(Tibiotarsal)

Ankle (tarsus)
(Tarsometatarsal)

Toes

Figure 4.6   Avian leg and foot bones compared to human.

Although the bone material is the same in all vertebrates, the modifications of this bone is quite different in birds. All of these modifications to the skeletal system make birds the marvelous running, jumping, and flying machines that they are.

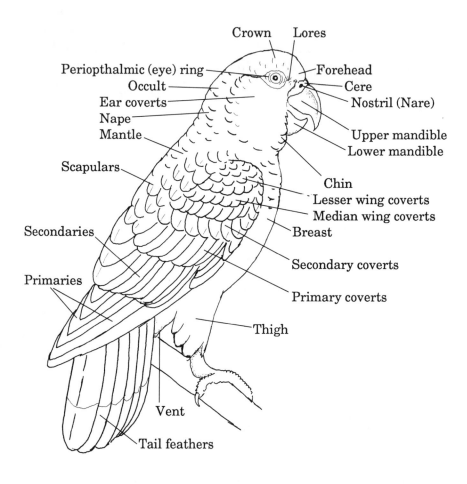

Figure 5.1 Avian topography.

5   Muscular System

Introduction

Skeletal muscles are used primarily to move bones. In so doing, some form of movement such as walking, running, or flying is accomplished. A description of the biochemistry of skeletal muscle contraction is beyond the scope of this book, but a look at some of the characteristics of skeletal muscle is in order.

Muscle contraction stimulus

As we know, the stimulus for muscle contraction is the nerve impulse. The impulse is the stimulus, but the actual trigger for muscle contraction is the release of calcium ions. The release of calcium ions results when the nerve impulse reaches the muscle. Therefore, calcium is a critical component of the contractile process.

Since the heart is a muscle, physiologically very similar to skeletal muscles, calcium is important in the efficient contraction of the heart muscle, as well. Because the concentration of calcium in seeds is very low, there is a significant possibility for the development of calcium deficiencies in aviary maintained birds (see Nutrition).

Skeletal muscle cells

In birds, as in mammals, the number of skeletal muscle cells is genetically determined. Once the bird reaches adulthood, there is no increase in the number of muscle cells. This is again true for the heart muscle cells as well. How then do we get stronger and how do our muscles get bigger, if there is no increase in the number of muscle cells?

Both of these changes are brought about by an increase in the size of the individual muscle cells (hypertrophy). So, as the muscles are built-up, we see not an increase in the number of cells, but an increase in the size of the cells. When the activity level is reduced over a period of time, the size of the cells decrease (atrophy), with a resulting decrease in size of the overall muscle.

Birds kept in cages or small flights rarely have the opportunity to exercise their flight muscles. The muscles tend to atrophy. More importantly, the cardiac muscle begins to atrophy, resulting in a heart which is much less efficient. Although very little research has been done with birds in this regard, there is accumulating evidence that a lack of exercise in humans results in many health problems, not the least of which is decreased life span.

Birds need to exercise in order to maintain maximum long term health. Birds kept in cages for breeding should be put into a flight during the non-breeding season. Pet birds should be taken from the cage daily and allowed to exercise their muscles. They can do this even though their wings are partially clipped. Ideally, birds should be kept in flights which are long enough to allow them some sustained flying space.

One may argue that some birds breed very well in small cages. However, small cage living does not maximize the bird's health any more than your health would be maximized by living in a closet sized room with windows, a TV and gourmet meals served three times a day. Even prisoners are allowed periodically to visit the exercise yard. My premise is that birds that are allowed to exercise will be healthier, live longer, and be much more productive in the long run.

Antagonistic muscles

Muscles only shorten when they are stimulated. Therefore, they can only pull. Since muscles pull and do not push, the muscle that pulls the wing down cannot be the same muscle that pulls the wing up. There must be a muscle on the other side that pulls the wing in the other direction. This is called an antagonistic muscle.

An example of this in man would be the relationship between the biceps and triceps muscles. The biceps on the front of the upper arm pulls the forearm upward toward the shoulder. The triceps on the back side of the upper arm pulls the forearm downward away from the shoulder (Figure 5.2).

Avian muscles, like those of mammals, only pull and so we would expect to see antagonistic muscles in birds, and we do. Therefore, we would expect to see muscles on the chest (ventral) side to pull the wings down and muscles on the back (dorsal) side to pull the wings up. However, for streamlining purposes, there are very few muscles on the back (dorsal) side of the bird.

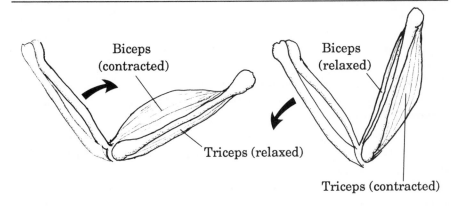

Figure 5.2   Antagonistic arm muscles of man.

Because of the rigid backbone in most birds, they don't need dorsal muscles for structural support of the back. They do, however, need antagonistic muscles to pull the wing up, so that it can again be forcefully pulled down to obtain lift. Having all antagonistic muscles on the chest (ventral) surface creates a problem. Birds overcome this by extending the uplifting muscle (supracoracoideus) tendon up over the scapula and then down to attach on top of the humerus. This form of attachment acts like a rope and pulley (Figure 5.3).

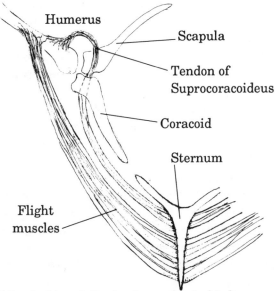

Figure 5.3   Antagonistic chest muscles in birds.

Muscle mass

The amount and distribution of skeletal muscle in birds varies depending primarily on the life style of the bird. Excellent flyers, such as the swallows and hummingbirds, devote 25 to 35% of their muscle mass to flight muscles and only approximately 2% to leg muscles. This results in superb flyers, but birds who are quite awkward when on the ground. When was the last time you saw a hummingbird walking around?

Predatory birds such as owls and hawks tend to have as much muscle mass in their legs as in their flight muscles, providing them with strong legs for grasping prey. And, as one would expect, ground dwelling birds have more muscle mass in their leg muscles than in flight muscles.

Skeletal muscle cells

Not only do avian skeletal muscles differ in size and distribution, they also differ in color. Some are red in color and some are white to pale in color and some are a mixture of the two. The "dark" and "light" meat of a roasted turkey is a good example of this. To understand this color difference, let's take a closer look at skeletal muscle cells.

The red or "dark" cells are red because of the presence of a compound, closely related to hemoglobin, called myoglobin. Myoglobin is a compound that holds a reserve of oxygen. Since it takes a lot of oxygen for sustained activities (long flights), the red muscle cells are found in those muscle used for endurance activities. Red muscle cells tend to be smaller in size than the white muscle cells.

The white muscle or "light" cells lack color because of the absence of myoglobin. More important than the lack of color, however, is the lack of oxygen reserve. These cells are used for short-term, high energy activities. Activities which do not require much oxygen, but in the absence of oxygen cannot be sustained for any length of time.

Therefore, birds which are strong distance flyers, such as swallows or plovers, have flight muscles which possess predominantly red muscle cells (not to be confused with red blood cells). Birds such as quail, pheasants and other gallinaceous birds have a very strong flight for a short distance, because of a predominance of white muscle cells in the flight muscles. As many hunters know, if compelled to repeat these flights in a short time, they very quickly become fatigued.

Figure 5.4 Quail (poor distance flyer) vs. plover (strong distance flyer).

These white muscle cells tend to undergo hypertrophy (muscle cell enlargement) much more than the reds, and therefore, the white cells are much larger, as is the overall muscle. An example would be to compare a bicyclist who rides four hours a day with a weightlifter who spends much less time "pumping iron" with his legs. They would show very different leg development.

The bicyclist's aerobic activity is stimulating the development of red muscle cells and therefore does not show much hypertrophy. On the other hand, the weightlifter's high energy, short-term actively stimulates the development of white muscle cells and therefore much larger legs. Although both would be described as having strong legs, neither would be good at the other's activity.

The same thing is true in birds. Each species has developed a certain percentage of red and white muscle cells and this limits, or allows, specific types of muscular activity. Although very little research has been done on the muscle physiology of birds, changes similar to those in man probably occur. In man, the studies have shown that the percentage of cell types can be changed by changing the type of activity, assuming again, the limitations of one's genetic potential. In other words, the ratio of red and white muscle cells is not permanent and can be changed with changes in activities.

Muscle contraction

Muscles not only provide movement, they are also important in posture. The type of muscle contraction, such as in flight, is characterized by a shortening of the muscle and is called an isotonic contraction. Muscle contraction in which the muscle is prevented from shortening is called an isometric contraction. It is the isometric contraction that is important in posture and, for most animals, in standing or sitting. Isometric contractions are also used to stabilize the wing during gliding.

Perching

Standing on a perch for long periods of time, such as in sleeping, could require the expenditure of large amounts of energy. However, birds have developed several unique methods to hold on to the perch which require a minimum of energy expenditure. One method is the use of a toe-locking mechanism. For normal perching, the muscles of the lower leg would contract, pulling on the tendon attached to the toes, which pulls the toes into a closed or perching position. This activity, however, requires energy.

When birds are perching for any period of time they will "squat," while keeping the lower leg muscles relaxed. This causes the lower leg bone (tarsometatarsus) to stretch the tendon, which will pull the toes into a perching position, all without any muscle contraction (Figure 5.5).

This ingenuous mechanism does however have its drawbacks. To fly from the perch, the bird must first stand up to release the stretched tendon, thereby opening up the toe grasp. A startled bird, trying to fly before releasing, could find itself flying around the perch in a circle because of the unreleased toe grasp. Or at best, releasing his grip while hanging upside down.

Other skeletal muscle functions

Along with movement and posture, skeletal muscle can also be used for defensive and offensive purposes. Skeletal muscles move the beak for biting, and wings are sometimes used as weapons. Also, birds with spurs can put quite a dent in your leg. Ostriches can break a human leg with their kick.

Skeletal muscles are beneficial to the bird's body in other ways. During muscle contraction, compounds such as glucose and fats are broken down to release energy for the contractile process. This is a very inefficient process.

A good portion of the energy in glucose and fats is used not to power the muscle, but rather is lost as heat.

Some of this heat is retained by the bird and used to maintain body temperature. In fact, shivering is a mechanism of involuntary skeletal muscle contraction. These muscle contractions are not initiated for movement, but rather for the purpose of producing the heat needed to maintain body temperature in cold environments.

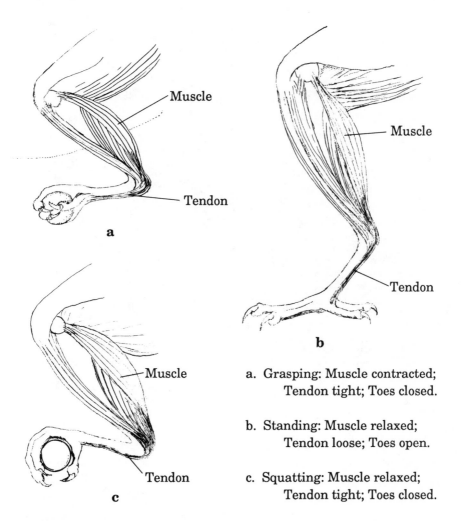

a. Grasping: Muscle contracted; Tendon tight; Toes closed.

b. Standing: Muscle relaxed; Tendon loose; Toes open.

c. Squatting: Muscle relaxed; Tendon tight; Toes closed.

Figure 5.5   Toe locking mechanism.

Figure 6.1 Feathers are especially important to aquatic birds.

6   Feathers

Introduction

Feathers are unique to birds, and all birds have feathers. They are the structures which distinguish birds from other animals. We all know of their significance to flight, but feathers have many other functions as well. They are excellent insulators, insulating the body against changes in temperature. Feathers protect against physical damage and damage from the sun. They are also a barrier to keep water from the skin. Oily feathers increase the buoyancy of water birds. Feather colors are important in camouflage, as well as in courtship displays.

How are feathers uniquely structured to perform all these functions? First, and foremost, feathers have a high concentration of keratin. Keratin is the same protein found in the fingernails and hair of mammals, as well as the nails, beaks and leg scales of birds. Keratin is also the dominant fiber in wool.

Keratin is well suited for its role as the main structural component of the feather. It is strong, light weight and insoluble in water. The mature feather is not living and therefore will not grow. One advantage of this is that no energy must be expended to support the mature feather. The disadvantage is that although quite durable, the feathers do begin to deteriorate over time and must be replaced periodically in a process called molting.

Feather structure

Feather structure is a marvel of ingenuity. The main structure of the feather is the shaft, which runs from one tip of the feather to the other tip. There are two main parts to the shaft (Figure 6.2). The first part is called the quill (calamus), which is found mostly inside of the skin follicle from which it developed. The quill actually penetrates the skin. At the lower end of the quill is an opening through which the developing feather received its blood supplied nourishment.

The remaining portion of the shaft is called the rachis. The long rachis is grooved and flattened on its sides and constitutes most of the shaft. As a concession to flight, the rachis is hollow to save weight. At the point where the quill ends and rachis begins (obvious by the beginning of the vanes), a secondary feather called the afterfeather can be found .

The afterfeather is usually down-like and small, although in some birds, such as the emu, it is quite large. The afterfeather serves many functions, one of which is insulation. Being close to the skin, the afterfeather may serve to increase insulation.

The primary function of the strong and flexible rachis is to support the branching parallel structures forming the vane. Vanes may be symmetrical, or in some feathers, the inner vane tends to be much longer than the outer vane, whose barbs are often stiffer.

The main structures of the vane emerge, like branches, from the shaft on either side and run parallel with one another. The vane of the feather is divided into two parts, the first being the barb which projects, branch-like, from the shaft. Barbs tend to be stiffer near the tip of the feather and tend to be longer toward the center of the vane and shorter on either end of the vane.

The second part is the barbule, which projects from the barb in the same branch-like way that the barb projects from the shaft. Barbules are too small to be seen with the naked eye and have even smaller projections called barbicels. These barbicels are nature's "Velcro." They hook together giving stability and strength to the feather.

There is a real advantage to this, for like "Velcro", if the barbicels are pulled apart they can be hooked together again. This is usually done while the bird is preening. If the feather were one solid structure, any damage would be permanent. With feathers structured as they are, most damage is the pulling apart of the barbicels, which can easily be hooked again. The flexibility of the barbicels could also be a weakness, but the barbicels remain hooked even under the most rigorous flight. Some feathers such as down feathers lack barbicels and thus have a soft "downy" feel.

Feather types

There are five or six different types of feathers depending on the species of bird (Figure 6.5). The most common type is the contour feather. Say the word "feather" to almost anyone, the image in their mind would most likely be the contour feather. As the name suggests, the contour feathers are those which make up most of the body plumage, thereby keeping the bird warm

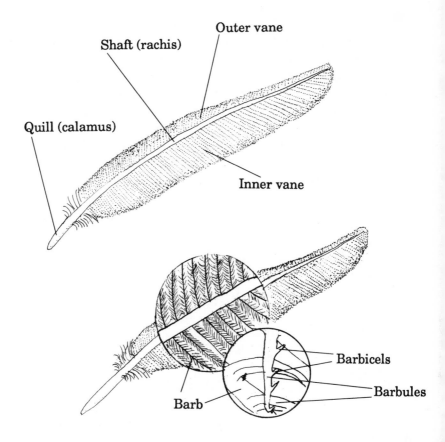

Figure 6.2   Feather structure.

and protected. The primary and secondary flight feathers are also contour feathers. Vanes of the plumage feathers tend to be symmetrical, whereas the vanes of the flight feathers are asymmetrical.

The primary flight feathers are the outermost flight feathers and are attached to the bones in the "hand" region (refer back to Figure 4.5). As their name suggests, they are the largest of the flight feathers. Most birds have 10 primaries, but some, like the finches, have only 9 and others have 11 or 12. Also attached to the "hand" are three or four small feathers called the alula. These feathers, which actually attach to the "thumb," increase lift, especially when the birds are flying upward at a great angle.

The secondary flight feathers attach to the forearm. There is quite a variation in the number of secondaries per species. Hummingbirds have only 7, finches have 9 while some of the large soaring birds have as many as 20.

Covering the base of the flight feathers on both the inner and outer surfaces are contour feathers called coverts. The greater coverts cover the primary flight feathers and are more typical of flight feathers having asymmetrical vanes. The lesser coverts cover the secondary flight feathers and are more like a body feather than a flight feather. By covering the quills of the flight feathers, the coverts make the wings more solid, as well as smooth, and therefore, aerodynamically more efficient.

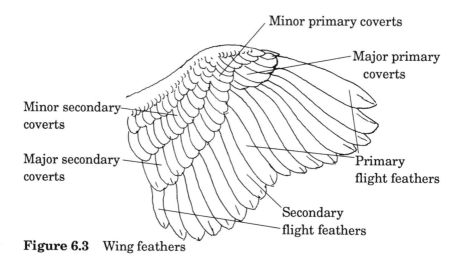

Figure 6.3 Wing feathers

In cases where the bird's wings must be clipped to reduce flight, the coverts are significant. These coverts can be used as a guideline for clipping the wings. Generally, if the wing clipper follows the coverts, staying to the outside of them, no blood vessels or nerves will be encountered. Therefore, the bird will feel no pain, nor will there be any bleeding. This is analogous to cutting your finger nails.

Care should be taken so that blood feathers, also called pin feathers, are not cut. Blood feathers are the new feathers coming in. Each of these new feathers has a cavity containing a rich supply of blood, necessary for their growth. Because they are filled with blood, a cut of the blood feather will result in a serious blood loss. The best way to stop the bleeding of a blood feather is to grasp the feather at the skin line and pull it out. Then, put pressure over the bleeding site until the bleeding stops.

Tail feathers are also contour feathers. Usually, the tail feathers have barbs which continue to the end of the shaft, resulting in a stronger feather. There are a multitude of modifications of tail feathers, an example of this being the long, highly modified tail feathers of the African finches called the wydahs (Figure 6.4). Most bird species have between 6 and 12 tail feathers, but there are some species which have as many as 32.

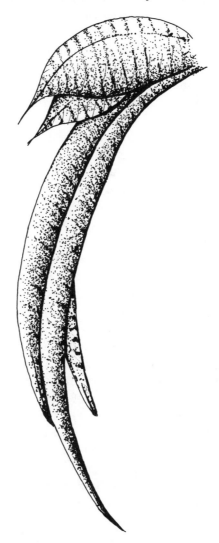

Figure 6.4   Wydah tail feathers.

There are far too many other modified contour feathers to mention here. Many of them are modified as plumes used for display, especially during the breeding season. These modified feathers can be raised during display. The beautiful display of the male peacock is a prime example.

The total number of contour feathers varies from one species to another. This range can be appreciated by realizing that hummingbirds have around 900 contour feathers as compared to a Whistling Swan which has over 25,000. When the size difference is considered the hummingbird actually has more feathers for its body weight than does the swan.

In small birds, feathers comprise 7.1% of total body weight, as compared to only 6% in larger birds. Realize also that the total number of feathers changes with the seasons, reflecting the importance of feathers in the regulation of body temperature. The relationship between size and body temperature will be covered in the chapter on circulation.

We now move from the dominant contour feathers to two other types of feathers. The semiplumes and adult down feathers will be considered together because of their similarity. These feathers lack the interlocking barbs and are therefore soft. Both are primarily used as insulation to aid in temperature control (thermoregulation). The primary difference between the two is that the semiplumes have a distinct rachis (shaft), whereas the down feather does not. As you may guess, birds that spend time on or in the water, or in colder climates, have a greater number of these feathers.

The fourth type of feather is the filoplume. Filoplumes are thin, almost hair-like feathers. These feathers are richly supplied with tactile nerve endings and are very sensitive. They are quite common, and are believed to play a role in controlling feather movement during flight.

Next are feathers called bristles, which as the name suggests, are quite stiff. This stiffness occurs because of the absence of any barbs along the outer portion of the shaft, leaving the feather almost vaneless. They are found almost exclusively around the head and neck. Bristles tend to surround the openings of the nostrils, eyes and ears, where they filter out foreign matter from the air. The bristles, like the filoplumes, are also tactile. They are considered by some ornithologists to be analogous to whiskers in mammals. Bristles aid birds, such as the nightjars, in capturing insects.

The last type is the powder-down feather. These feathers produce a fine powder, much like a talc. The powder is actually made of skin cells which are covered with keratin. This powder is believed to aid in the maintenance of the feathers. Birds without preen glands have a much higher concentration of powder-down feathers. As the bird is preening or fluffing much of this fine

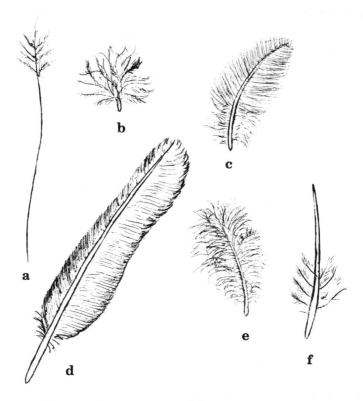

Figure 6.5   Feather types: **a**. Filoplume; **b**. Down; **c**. Body contour;
d. Flight contour; **e**. Semiplume; **f**. Bristle.

powder is shed into the air. Anyone who has kept a cockatoo in the house can
attest to the fine white power which quickly accumulates on everything.

Preening

Obviously, with feathers being as critical to survival as they are, birds
spend a lot of time taking care of them. The most obvious activity is preening.
In preening the bird can re-hook the barbules, spread oil from the preen
gland over the feathers to waterproof, preserve, and also clean them.

Most birds have an oil or preen gland (uropygium) located on the lower
back, just in front of the tail. The ostrich-like birds, some parrots, and
pigeons lack an oil gland. There are many discussions as to how important
this oil is as an agent for waterproofing the feathers. We do know that this

oil is important in keeping the feathers in good condition. One piece of evidence to support this is the observance of how much faster feathers deteriorate once they are molted and lying on the ground.

Figure 6.6   Preening bird.

Bathing

Bathing is an important part of the feather maintenance. Birds who live where there is very little water tend to take dust baths. All avicultural birds should have bathing facilities available to them at all times. Glass pie plates or a similar shaped dish, such as baked enamel dishes, work very well. They are inexpensive and can always be put in the dishwasher for periodic cleaning. Household bleach works quite well for cleaning and disinfecting water dishes.

Molting

In spite of the birds best efforts at feather maintenance, the feathers eventually wear out. The only solution to this dilemma is to replace them. Since it would be very hard for the bird to sense exactly which of the thousands of feathers need replacing, the bird replaces most of them in a process called a molt.

Most bird have either one or two molts per year. There are also partial molts which usually occur just before the breeding season and involve those plumage feathers used in breeding displays. Molting may also serve to rid the bird of feather parasites.

Almost all birds have at least one molt per year during which all of the feathers are renewed. Molting occurs in a distinct and predictable pattern. The feather loss pattern is different in various species, but is consistent within the species. As an example, in a primary molt in the finches, the primaries are lost first at the wrist joint and then are lost in an outward sequence. The secondaries molt from the two outer feathers and then move toward the center. In the tail, feathers molt from the center outward.

Because of the flight and protective functions of feathers, they are lost in a pattern which is least disruptive to these functions (Figure 6.7). When a bird molts, bare patches of skin are not visible. In the molting process the incoming feather literally pushes out the older feather it is replacing. A bird with bare skin is not molting and is most likely feather plucking itself or being plucked by other birds. Disease may also cause feather loss.

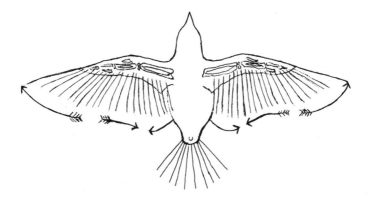

Figure 6.7   Pattern in which flight feathers are molted.

Molting is an energy draining process. The production of each new feather requires the production of many cells, as well as the production of large amounts of the protein keratin. For example, penguins during their 19 day molt experience a weight loss of 50%. Most birds don't lose this amount of weight, but all experience a significant increase in their metabolic rate. The average increase is between 20% to 25%.

Therefore, molting is a very stressful time for birds. The birds are not as well protected by the contour feathers of the body and their flight is not as strong. Both of these conditions result in a period of time that is psychologically, as well as physiologically, hard on the bird. The birds should have adequate amounts of food and a good source of calcium at this time.

Experiments have shown that a shortage of food for only one day during the molt resulted in defective feathers. Other studies have shown that when the diet contained 3% proteins there was a repression of molting, at 5% protein levels molting proceeded at an intermediate level, and at 9% protein levels the molting was normal. Before and during the molt, nutrient supplementation would probably be helpful.

Disturbances should be kept to a minimum at this time. This is not the time to clean your aviaries, move the birds to a new flight, trim nails, or to perform other potentially disruptive activities. Nor should birds be shipped during their molt. The length of time necessary to complete the molt varies tremendously, depending on the species of bird, the time of year, and the bird's diet. Finches typically complete their molt in a few months, whereas eagles may require as long as two years to finish a complete molt. Some birds molt continually through out the year.

Feather growth

Like finger nails, feathers grow from the base, not from the tip. As the feather grows, the tip moves away from the blood supply and therefore is no longer living. Therefore, any impact that you wish to have on the feather, such as enhancing color, has to be accomplished before or while the feather is forming. Anything that you do after the feather is formed, such as color feeding, will have no impact on the fully formed feather.

The stimulation and control of molting is hormonal. The primary endocrine gland in molting appears to be the thyroid gland. Hormones from the pituitary and gonads also affect feather growth. The interrelationship of these hormones during the molt is complex, and will require much more research before the process is fully understood.

Although hormones are the primary stimulus for feather growth and development, there are other stimuli. One prime stimulus is the loss of a feather. When a feather is pulled out, it will be replaced before the next molt. If the replacement feather is pulled out, it also will be replaced.

In chickens, a feather from the same follicle can be pulled out three times in a row and will be replaced. When pulled a fourth time, however, the feather is not replaced until the next molt. Little research has been done on other species, but it is reasonable to assume that most birds would respond in a similar way. It is important to realize that broken feathers are not replaced until the next molt, unless the broken feather is pulled out.

Many aviculturists use this rapid replacement of a pulled feather to more quickly determine the sex of a young dimorphic bird. Dimorphic birds are those species in which the males are visually different than the females. When a contour feather is pulled, it is replaced. The replacement feather usually bears the color of the adult and thereby indicates the sex of the dimorphic birds sooner than waiting for the normal adult molt.

When the feather first erupts from the feather follicle, it is covered with a protective sheath of keratin (Figure 6.8). The core of this new feather is filled with blood and so these feathers are called blood feathers (Figure 6.9). This rich blood supply is necessary to sustain the rapid growth of the feather. Because the outer covering of keratin wraps the feather so tightly, the maturing blood feather is called a pin feather. After these feathers grow, the young bird will strip off this outer protective sheath, allowing the now mature feather to unfold.

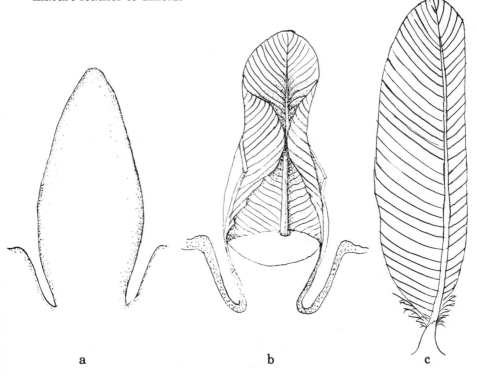

a   b   c

Figure 6.8   a. Newly erupted feather surrounded by keratin sheath.
b. Sheath stripped away and feather opening.
c. Fully emerged feather.

Figure 6.9
Blood feathers.

Color

To understand color in the avian feather, we must first understand a little bit about color and light. Light is a form of energy which travels in a straight line in small packets called photons. Light, as it comes from the sun or house lights, is called white light. White light is made up of different wavelengths of energy, each with the capacity to produce the perception of various colors.

The color spectrum is represented by the familiar colors of the rainbow. It is important to realize that color is, for each of us, a unique experience, since we cannot describe color in any way other than to point to that color.

So, we don't really know what color other people or animals actually perceive. We have learned to say "red" when we see the wave length of light represented by the color red and therefore we all agree that "red is red." But in reality, we don't know what the others see when they look at red.

What is it that makes something appear red? The perception of most colors has to do with pigments. Pigments are substances which absorb varying wavelengths of light. For example, a red pigment is one which absorbs all wavelengths of the light, except for red. The red wavelength, not being absorbed, will then leave the pigment and enter our eye, thus we see red. Green pigments would absorb all the wavelengths of light except green, blue pigments would absorb, etc. Some pigments absorb all wavelengths but two or three, thereby resulting in the different hues we see.

A pigment that absorbs all the wavelengths of light emits no wavelengths and therefore appears black. A pigment that does not absorb any wavelength of light therefore emits all wavelengths (white light), and the object appears white. Since black absorbs all wavelengths, and these wavelengths represent energy, a black object will be much hotter than a white object, when both are placed in sunlight.

Feather color

Much of the coloration of bird feathers is produced by the presence of pigments in the feathers. There are many feather pigments, one of the most common are the melanins. Melanin is the same pigment found in the skin, hair and eyes of humans. It is synthesized by the bird from the non-essential amino acid tyrosine. The B vitamin riboflavin is important in the formation of melanin and therefore must be in adequate supply when the feather is forming. Otherwise, inferior color will develop. Melanin, in varying concentrations, is responsible for producing the following colors: black, brown, red-brown (rufous), and dull yellow.

The second group of pigments producing feather color are the carotenoids (lipochromes). Carotenoids cannot be synthesized by the birds and therefore must be obtained in the diet. This means, then, that the diet will have a strong influence on any colors produced by these pigments

Most birds who use carotenoids for coloration change them biochemically before they are deposited in the feather. This biochemical change is genetically controlled. In other words, not all birds can bichemically change and deposit the carotenoids. For example, a black and white bird, such as the sea gull, will not become a red bird, regardless of the amount of carotenoids in the diet. Carotenoids cannot be chemically changed by the sea gull into the pigment form used in feather coloration.

However, birds, such as canaries, who can chemically change the carotenoids, can have their feather color enhanced by the addition of carotenoids to the diet. This addition must occur before the feather is formed. The addition of carotenoids later won't increase the color in feathers already formed.

There are two primary types of carotenoids, the carotenes and the xanthophils. The carotenes are made of the atoms carbon and hydrogen. They produce the colors red to orange. The carotenes are usually changed (metabolized) before they are deposited in the living feather. For example, beta-carotene is converted to canthaxanthin, resulting in the red color of some canaries, the red head of Gouldian finches, and red of many parrots.

The xanthophils are chemically different in that they are made of carbon and hydrogen as well, but also have oxygen atoms in their structure. This group of pigments typically produces the colors of yellow, orange, and red. For example, the xanthophil called zoonerythrin produces red, whereas zooxanthin produces the yellow found in egg yolk, bird's legs, and canaries.

A third and distinct group of pigments are the porphyrins. These porphyrins found in feathers are related to the red color producing porphyrin group of the hemoglobin molecule. These pigments are synthesized by the bird. However, only one family of birds, the touracos, have the ability to produce them. The two pigments producing these unique and unusual colors are the green producing turocoverdin and the red producing pigment turacin.

Structural colors

There is another way, besides using pigments, to produces color in avian feathers. This way involves structural colors which affect color primarily by scattering light. When light is scattered, different wavelengths travel in different directions. By scattering light, different wavelengths of light reach the eye and thereby produce the perception of color. The blue color of the sky is produced by scattering, as are the colors of large bodies of water. This scattering can be affected by moisture, smog, and the particles in the air, hence the many color changes in sunsets.

The structural colors in birds are categorized into two groups. First, and most common, are non-iridescents. Feather structure, rather than pigments within, are most important here. Air cells in the feathers tend to scatter light. An example is gray hair in humans. Hair turns gray as pigments are lost and increased air cells affect the perception of hair color. In birds, most blues are produced by scattering, as are the white colors. If all wavelengths are scattered the same direction, white light produces the perception of white.

The second group of structural colors are those produced by iridescence. Iridescent colors are determined by feather structure, but are dependent on position. In male hummingbirds, when viewed in one direction, the color is an iridescent red, but when viewed from another angle it appears black.

Actually, many of the colors of birds are produced by the combination of pigments and structural colors. The bright green typical of many parrots is produced by a combination of carotene and scattering. By scraping the surface of these green feathers, the color won't be lost, but it will change.

Table 6.1   Summary Of Color In Birds.

A. Pigments:
   1. Melanin:
      Can be synthesized by the bird.
      Similar to melanin found in human hair, eyes, and skin.
      Produces colors: Brown, red brown (rufous), and dull yellow.
   2. Carotenoids (lipochromes):
      Cannot be synthesized by the birds.
      Two types of carotenoids:
         a. Carotenes:
            Produces red-orange colors.
         b. Xanthophils:
            1. Zoonerythrin: produces red.
            2. Zooxanthin: produces yellow (i.e. egg yolk).
   3. Porphrins:
      Related to the pigment in hemoglobin.
      Turacin produces the unique red color in touracos.
B. Structural Colors:
   1. Non-iridescent:
      Air cells in feathers scatter light.
      Most blue and white are produced this way.
   2. Iridescent:
      Affected by position of the bird.
      Hummingbirds often exhibit these colors.
C. Combinations Of Pigment and Structural Colors:
      Found in many birds.
      The bright green of some birds combines carotene and scattering.

Functions of color

Coloration in birds serves many purposes. Colored feathers are an important component of the courtship displays exhibited by many birds during the breeding season. Coloration can be protective by making the bird look bigger or more vicious than it really is. It may also be protective by allowing the bird to more readily blend in with its environment. Or it may have the opposite effect of allowing the bird to stand out so that it may be more easily located by its peers in dense jungles.

Figure 7.1   Avian wing - the symbol of flight.

7   Flight

Introduction

Flight, a gift taken for granted by birds, but much envied by man. There are mammals that fly (bats) and insects that fly, but no other animal is as proficient and beautiful a flyer as the bird. How convenient it would be to move so easily from one place to another. Oh, if man could only fly.

Birds have the greatest amount of freedom of any vertebrate. No need for all our mobile machines. Avian flight is truly conservation of resources at its best. No depletion of oil reserves here. One can only speculate how different this world would be, if man could fly.

The ability to fly has many advantages for birds. With minimum energy output, birds can cover long distances in a short period of time. This allows birds to exploit food sources otherwise unavailable. Because of flight, birds occupy more ecological niches (sites) than any other animal, except insects.

Flight also decreases the bird's vulnerability to predation. Birds can fly away from most predators. Also, it can roost in places that are inaccessible to most predators. However, many are still exposed to birds of prey.

For protection against predators, most other animals must have a coloration that allows them to blend in with their environment. Because birds are less susceptible to predation, they can develop a vast array of colors. These bright colors allow the birds to maintain contact with each other, without endangering themselves.

Characteristics of air

It is easier to understand flight if we think of air as a fluid, rather than the gas that it is. We are all aware of the pressure exerted when we enter a body of water. Air exerts a similar pressure. We are not as aware of this air pressure because it is so much less than the pressure of water. In both cases, the pressure is exerted by the molecules of air or water.

In a body of water, most of the pressure is exerted by the water molecules . In air, the pressure is exerted by a combination of molecules, including the gases of nitrogen, oxygen, carbon dioxide, and some others.

During swimming, we push against these water molecules and propel ourselves forward. Propulsion can be increased by increasing the surface area of the "propeller." This can be done by putting our fingers together and using our hand like a paddle. By adding swim fins to one's feet, we increase the surface area and thereby increase propulsion.

The same principles for propulsion in water hold true for propulsion in air. A primary difference is that the air pressure is so much lower than the water pressure. Therefore, the force exerted by the propellor must be much greater to cause the same amount of propulsion in air.

Water weighs about 8 pounds per gallon. Since a gallon of water occupies less than one cubic foot of volume, a cubic foot of water would weigh at least 8 pounds. By comparison, a cubic foot of air weighs less than 1/10 of a pound.

When we add more water, we increase the number of molecules, thereby increasing the water pressure. The farther down you go into the water, the greater the pressure. This pressure increases because there are more water molecules piled on top of each other, and you. Although not as heavy, the same thing is true for air.

Therefore, the higher one goes in the atmosphere, the less the pressure. The lower the altitude, the lower the pressure will be. So, the greatest air pressure will be at sea level. Even with all the "blankets" of air piled on top of us, the air pressure is only 14.7 pounds per square inch (psi). This means that at every point on our body where the air touches us, it will exert a pressure of 14.7 psi. It is this air pressure that is used to develop lift for flight.

Lift

How do birds fly? Let's take a look at the phenomenon of lift. The Italian scientist, Bernouli, proposed that high velocity results in lower pressure. This is a somewhat simplistic view of Bernouli's theory, but it is a workable one for us. Look at the drawing of an airfoil in Figure 7.2.

Notice that air striking the air foil at point A will divide, half going over the upper surface and half going over the lower surface. Regardless of the direction the air takes over the wing, it will reach point B at the same time. Because of the shape of the airfoil, the distance traveled over the upper surface is greater than the lower surface. Therefore, if the air traveling over the upper surface is to reach "B" at the same time, it must travel faster than air traveling over the lower surface. According to Bernouli's principle, the air

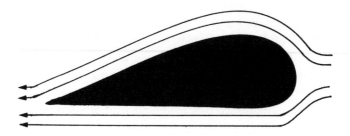

Figure 7.2   Air foil.

traveling faster will spread-out the molecules, thus producing a lower pressure on the upper surface of the airfoil. The lower pressure on the upper surface means there is more pressure on the lower surface and the airfoil will rise. This is lift.

Tilting the wing upward will decrease the distance traveled by air on the lower surface and increase the distance traveled on the upper surface. This will have the effect of decreasing the pressure on the upper surface even more, thereby increasing lift.

However, if the airfoil is tilted too much, the air on the upper surface cannot follow the upper surface of the airfoil and lift is lost. Lift can easily be demonstrated by placing ones hand out of the open window of a moving car. By tilting the hand slightly one can feel the lift. Turn your hand perpendicular to the ground and you will feel, not only the loss of lift, but a tremendous amount of drag.

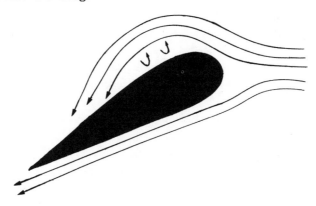

Figure 7.3 Effect of wing tilting.

The wings of birds are very efficient air foils. They are fairly smooth and proportionally long. Longer wings will result in greater lift. So birds that fly long distances or are gliders have long wings. The longer wing does not allow as much maneuverability, nor is it as strong as a short wing. However, because of the gain in lift, the decreased strength and maneuverability is a worthwhile compromise for the long distance flyer. Birds that fly short distances and do a lot of maneuvering, such as hummingbirds, have short wings.

Although there is a lot of variation in wing shapes, there are four basic avian wing shapes (Figure 7.4). Oceanic birds, such as the albatrosses, who do a lot of gliding, have a wing shape that is long and narrow. Soaring birds, such as eagles, need a wing with a large surface, but they also need a wing which allows some maneuverability during the capture of prey. Birds that need a rapid take-off, such as pheasants and some finch type birds, need a wing that is quite wide compared to its length. Finally, high speed flyers, such as swallows and many birds of prey, have a wing type that is short, but narrow, allowing a great amount of maneuverability.

Figure 7.4 Basic wing types: **a.** gliding (e.g. albatross); **b.** rapid take-off (e.g. pheasant); **c.** high speed flyer (e.g. swallow); **d.** Soaring (e.g. eagle).

Another important characteristic of the avian wing is the ability to fold the wing against the body surface. The flexible wing and the ability to repair the wing by molting new feathers, make the avian wing far superior to the airplane wing, to which it is often compared. Imagine birds trying to get into their nest if their wings were fixed in position, not to mention the problem of inadvertently taking off in the middle of the night due to a heavy breeze.

Yet, lift is not enough. Lift won't get the glider up, nor will it keep it there. There must be a force to move the wing forward, thereby creating lift. Airplanes accomplish this with the use of a propeller or jet propulsion. Birds must use the wing, not only as an instrument for developing lift, but also as the instrument to achieve forward progress (propulsion). The way birds accomplish this is quite complex and differs from one group to the next.

The hand region containing the large primaries is responsible for most of the propeller action of the wing. Most of the lift is provided by the remainder of the wing. The secondary flight feathers attach to the forearm area and provide most of the lift. During non-gliding flight the "hand" does most of the moving.

During the down stroke the wing provides lift, but during the up stroke the wing is turned so as to decrease resistance. The forearm and upper arm move very little during this time. Primaries provide some lift as well. Experiments have shown that cutting the secondaries won't prevent the bird from flying (some control may be lost). However, cutting the primaries, even just the tips, will significantly reduce flight and sometimes prevent it altogether.

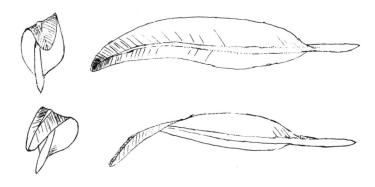

Figure 7.5   Feathers as a propeller.

Additionally, the hummingbird has the ability to forcefully pull the wing up in such a way as to develop lift on the up stroke. This lift on the up stroke cancels out the lift of the downstroke, allowing the hummingbird to hover in one place. The movement resembles a figure 8 drawing (Figure 7.6) and is very important to the hummingbird when feeding.

Figure 7.6   Figure eight movement by hummingbird.

It is important to remember that the feathers, as well as the wings, change shape in flight. During each wing beat, the primary feathers go through different shape changes (Figure 7.5). These shape changes are determined by the air pressure, shape of the feather, and the strength of the vane and barbs.

The barbs of the primary feathers are thicker at their base than at their tips. This results in a streamline shape much like an airplane propeller. The primaries are the feathers which strike the air edgewise and therefore need this streamlining.

Tail feathers

Wings are not the only structures used for flight. Tail feathers play an important role as well. Lift created by the tail supports the tail region on an even plane with the front of the bird. Tail lift is necessary because the wings are in front of the bird's center of gravity. Therefore, the bird would be "tail heavy" if it were not for the lift developed by the tail.

By acting as a rudder, the tail can affect turning and twisting. The tail is also used as a brake during landings (Figure 7.7). Pheasants have a long tail used for maneuvering around their wooded environment. The marine dwelling loons have a stubby tail and must take off and land in almost a straight line. Tail feathers are also important in the hovering behavior of birds of prey.

Figure 7.7   Using the tail as a rudder.

Figure 8.1 Hummingbirds have a well developed cerebellum.

8   Nervous System

Brain

Control. This one word sums up the most basic function of the nervous system. The key to this control is the brain. One could argue that all the remaining organs and structures of the body exist solely to nourish, protect, and move the brain to wherever the brain decides it wants to go. Given the speed with which some birds move, the avian brain needs to produce quick responses.

The nervous system of birds, like those of mammals, is divided into two basic parts. First, is the central nervous system, which consists of a brain and spinal cord. The second part is the peripheral nervous system which is composed of nerves and ganglia.

We shall begin our inquiry with a look at the avian brain. The avian brain is proportionally smaller than the brain of mammals and is not as well protected. As a compromise to flight, the bones surrounding the brain are thinner and therefore much lighter. The significant areas of the brain discussed here are the cerebrum, thalamus, hypothalamus, and cerebellum. There are many other areas of the brain, but a discussion of them is beyond the scope of this book.

Cerebrum

The cerebrum is that part of the brain associated with intellectual activities such as insight, hindsight, intuition, perception, and the ability to solve problems. Compared to mammals, most birds do not have a particularly well developed cerebrum (Figure 8.2).

Some birds do have a proportionally large cerebrum, notably the owls, crows and parrots. These birds do exhibit some degree of intelligence, although not to the degree to which they are given credit by some pet owners. Many parrots have been trained to recognize words, and to respond to verbal and visual commands, but it is doubtful that they respond to a conceptual phrase such as "this way." The ability to problem solve is not an attribute of even our most intelligent birds.

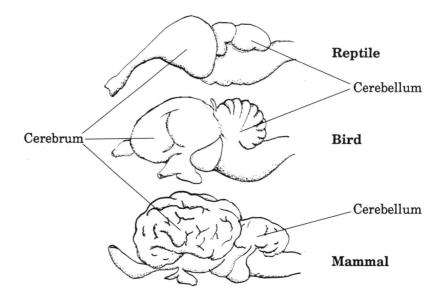

Figure 8.2   Comparison of the cerebral cortex of three animals.

Avian behavior

Birds do many things well, but most of their behaviors are innate. In other words, most bird behaviors are not a function of observation, followed by analysis, and then reaction. Birds use very little analysis. They simply observe and then react. These reactions have been programed into their genetic material somewhere in the species' past.

For example, birds do not observe nest building by birds of their own species and then go out and build a similar nest. Instead, the nest building is innate, the blueprint residing somewhere in their genetic material. Therefore, even if they have never seen a nest built by a bird of their species, a weaver is capable of building a sophisticated nest quite similar to those built by their species for centuries (Figure 8.3).

Behavior is a complex subject which involves knowledge from other disciplines such as, neurphysiology, endocrinology, physiology, anatomy, ecology, etc. Because it is open to interpretation, animal behavior does not always lend itself to the same level of scientific investigation as do many other subjects. In recent years, the study of behavior (Ethology) has become more scientific and hence much more valuable..

The study of animal behavior requires many hours of observation and interpretation. Because the words used to describe behavior often imply some human motive or purpose, conveying this information is also difficult. Applying human attributes to other species of animals is called anthropomorphism and must be guarded against.

For example, we may see a bird attack another bird and assume that the attacking bird is "mean." In reality, the attacking bird may be simply reacting in a reflex way to protect its territory, nest site, or mate. Or, one might ask, do birds feed their young because they "love them" or because the feeding behavior has been programed into their hereditary material? The distinction is quite significant and must be understood, if we are to have any impact on the breeding behavior of our birds.

There will be no attempt in this chapter to explain a lot of specific bird behaviors. However, throughout this book, behaviors will be mentioned and, when possible, explained. The goal of this unit will be to introduce the basic concepts of animal behavior.

The most basic behavior of higher animals, such as birds, is called a reflex. A reflex is a behavior whereby the incoming nerve signal does not go to the brain, but goes directly to an effector organ, such as a skeletal muscle. The advantage of this type of behavior is speed. There is no lost time sending the message to the brain and then waiting for some interpretation before sending the signal to the effector organ. An example of a simple reflex is the eye blink.

Most behaviors are much more complex than a simple reflex. However, many of these behaviors, such as the reflex, don't involve

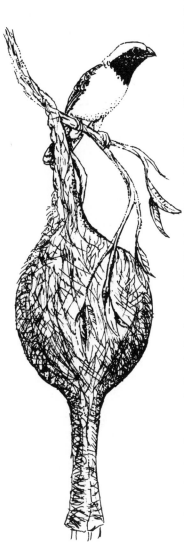

Figure 8.3   Weaver nest.

conscious thought. This type of behavior is called instinctive or innate behavior. Most avian behavioral patterns involve instinct.

These instinctive patterns can sometimes be a problem. Getting a wild caught bird to try new foods is, as many a frustrated aviculturist will attest, a difficult task. Birds have some innate feeding preferences and are also influenced by the feeding preferences of their parents.

Instinctive patterns can be beneficial to the bird. The need for some instinctive eating patterns is obvious when one considers a bird, such as the toucan. If a toucan were intellectually capable of deciding to be a seed eater, it would be in trouble. Its beak is modified for feeding on fruits and other soft foods, rather than for cracking seed, and hence would be ineffective as a seed eater. This "decision" to eat seed could be life threatening to the bird.

Figure 8.4   Toucan is a typical fruit eater.

In higher animals, such as birds and mammals, many of these instinctive behaviors are affected by learning. For example, the song of many birds has both an inherited and a learned component to it. The more we learn about bird behaviors, the less sure we are that they are simply instinctive.

An example of this involves the ability of fledglings to fly. Often, when young birds leave the nest, they don't fly well. However, in a few days, they fly quite well. The early assumption was that the fledglings fly better in a few days because of practice. To test this hypothesis, experiments were performed where some nest mates were temporarily prevented from flying. When these fledglings were released with their clutch mates, who had been flying for three days, there was no difference in their flying abilities. These results suggest is that the early inability to fly well has nothing to do with practice. Rather, it is the physical maturity of the fledgling which determines the young bird's flying abilities.

The age at which learning takes place is also significant. A bird may readily learn a behavior at a certain age, but is incapable of learning or modifying that behavior at another age. Working with a behavior at the wrong age might lead one to conclude, incorrectly, that the bird is incapable of that behavior. For example, in humans it is known that children under ten years of age can learn a language much faster than adults.

How is learning defined? Learning is the changes in behavior due to experiences, rather than changes in behavior due to maturity. There are various types of learning.

Habituation is a process whereby an organism becomes progressively less responsive to a repitition of a given stimulus. In the extreme case, the bird hardly responds to the stimulus. A bird who finally stops fluttering about when people walk by the cage is an example of this behavior. Aviary birds who get used to the aviculturist's daily routine are another example.

Conditioning is another type of learning. This type of learning is brought about by the reinforcement of a response to a stimulus the bird has previously not encountered. For example, chicks being hand fed will often get excited when hearing the bell of the microwave oven used to warm the food. They have become conditioned to the fact that when the microwave bell rings, they will get fed.

Most animal training is brought about by the "positive feedback" of conditioned learning. A good example of this is giving birds a favorite food when they demonstrate the desired behavior. Giving the bird more attention is another positive feedback.

Negative feedback techniques, such as depriving the bird of food or physically harming the bird, are a very poor way to achieve behavioral goals. Some of them may work, but at the price of negatively affecting the personality of the "trained" bird.

Hitting or shaking a bird as part of negative feedback training rarely works. This is because physical punishment is not a part of the birds' normal behaviors. In some animals, such as the dog, being physical is a part of their normal behavior toward one another. Although this type of training may work, it is questionable whether hitting or shaking any animal is a good training technique.

Trial and error learning is a third type of learning. We have all experienced trial and error learning. Eating behaviors in precocial birds involve trial and error. It is true that the parents will often "show" the young what foods to eat. However, much of their education comes from eating various objects and finding out what is edible and what is not.

Another type of learning is **imprinting**. Generally, imprinting occurs early in the precocial bird's life and its effects are quite strong. There is only a short period of time in which imprinting can take place. The first 24 to 36 hours are critical for the imprinting of many precocial birds. Imprinting of birds has occurred on inanimate objects, as well as humans and other convenient animals.

Precocial birds, such as chickens, ducks, geese, etc., must learn early to follow their parents or they will perish. Imprinting does occur in altricial birds, such as finches and parrots. However, since altricial chicks don't have to follow the parents, imprinting is not as strong, or necessary, as in the precocial birds.

The final type of learning is **insight**, which is primarily associated with higher primates. Insight is the ability to respond correctly to a new situation differently from any previously encountered. In other words, some intellectual analysis of the situation is involved. Most birds do not have good powers of insight. However, I have had cockatoos escape from locked cages that would have foiled even the great Houdini. Trial and error? Maybe.

Motivation is another component of the bird's behavior. We hear a lot about motivation in human behavior. In birds, motivation is commonly referred to as a drive. There are hunger drives, thirst drives, sex drives, attack and defense drives, etc. These drives have their basis in both innate and learned behaviors. For example, we discussed earlier the role of the sex hormones in the initiation of breeding behavior. However, more experienced birds tend to have greater breeding success, implying some learning in the reproductive process.

Another important component of behavior deals with the concept of releasers. Stimuli which are effective in triggering a specific behavior are called "releasing stimuli." The sounds, objects, actions, etc. which give rise to "releasing stimuli" are called releasers.

In chickens, the distress cry of the chick is a strong releaser. The hen will react to the sounds, even if she cannot see the distressed chick. On the other hand, just seeing the chick in distress without hearing the distress cry will not elicit a response from the hen. Defense of the chick is an innate response, brought about by releasers, with few intellectual decisions being made.

One experiment demonstrated releasers in innate behavior very well. A ground nester with one egg in the nest was the subject of this study. The egg was removed from the nest and placed a few inches away. The returning bird rolled the egg back into the nest. This would seem to contradict the innate response. The bird seemed to observe the egg out of the nest, concluded that the egg should be rolled into the nest and finally reacted by rolling the egg (Figure 8.5).

However, if we attach a string to the egg and lift the egg away, while the bird is rolling the egg toward the nest, the bird will continue to roll the "missing" egg to the nest. The egg rolling will continue even though the egg is no longer there. This implies the birds lack of analysis, since it was unable to cope with new circumstances for which it was not innately programmed.

Figure 8.5　Rolling an egg back to nest.

Understanding which releasers are important in breeding behavior is important to the aviculturist. If the breeding behavior is primarily brought about by releasers, rather than a conscious decision such as, "well Polly, I guess its time to have offspring, before we get too old," then breeding behavior will be more predictable.

Learning what these releasers are gives the aviculturist the opportunity to duplicate them. By duplicating these releasers, we may stimulate the desired breeding behavior (see Table 8.1).

Table 8.1   Some breeding behavior releasers.

> rain
> temperature
> food availability
> breeding site availability
> breeding material availability
> breeding behavior of other birds

Unfortunately, we don't know what all of the breeding behavior releasers are for the various species. It is possible that some of the "hard to breed" species are the ones for which we have not yet discovered the breeding behavior releasers. For this reason, field studies of each species of aviculturally significant birds provide important pieces of information. The information in these studies can be used to establish the proper breeding environment for our birds. Reproduction is the one behavior that a bird does not have to engage in to maintain its own health or safety. Therefore, a bird will breed only after its environmental and behavioral needs are met and the breeding behavior releasers are present. We need to know more about what these specific needs are!

Avian communication

Another important component of behavior is communication. Most communication is between birds of the same species, although it is not always restricted to one species. For example, a distress call by one species is often responded to by other species as well. Communication is primarily brought about using the senses of vision, hearing, smell, and even touch.

Imparting information through sound is the most familiar means of communication found in wildlife. The variety and technically sophisticated sounds of birds are unsurpassed in nature. Many people assume that birds sing out of joy or to express love for a mate, etc. These anthropomorphic assumptions are incorrect. Birds sing to communicate more basic types of information.

Bird sound communications are divided into calls and songs (see Table 1.2). Bird calls are used to inform other birds of the discovery of a food source. Or, the call may be used to communicate impending danger, such as the appearance of a hawk or a snake, etc. Some birds use sounds in a way that is similar to the way a dog uses a growl. Cockatiels will often hiss when humans get too close. The hiss, like the growl, often serves to resolve the conflict without any physical violence.

Bird songs are often used as a species recognition signal. Birds also sing to attract a mate, and the song may act as a releaser which brings the female into breeding condition. Songs are often a means of strengthening the pair bond. Some males sing as a means of transmitting information about their territory. Often males who sing the loudest succeed in retaining larger territories.

Bird sounds between parents and chicks may begin before any of the chicks have hatched. This is especially important in the precocial birds' recognition of their parents. These sounds are so unique to each bird, that penguin chicks can pick out their parents in a rookery of thousands of breeding penguins.

There is also communication between the unhatched chicks themselves. The communication of sound between chicks often stimulates the chicks to hatch around the same time. This is important because the parents must leave the nest to show the hatchlings how to find food. If the eggs hatched 3 or 4 days apart, many of the chicks would hatch while the parents are gone from the nest.

Another important means of avian communication is through the use of visual behaviors. The breeding displays of the male peacock and prairie chicken are familiar to most. These signals serve to attract the female and in many cases are also the releasers which bring the female into breeding condition.

Visual displays are also used to communicate other types of information. It is much easier to shake one's head "no" than to take the time to say "I don't want you to do that," or "I don't want to do that." Many species of birds use visual displays as threats to intruders. The young cockatoo in Figure 8.6 attempts to make himself look bigger by fluffing his feathers. Like verbal hissing, visual displays often reduce the chance of actual physical conflict.

Figure 8.6 Visual threat by young cockatoo.

Thalamus & hypothalamus

Another important area of the brain contains the thalamus, and located below it is the hypothalamus. These areas of the brain have control over such things as appetite, temperature control, sleep, water balance, hormonal control, pain, and other important involuntary activities. Since all vertebrates basically perform these involuntary activities in the same way, the thalamus and hypothalamus of birds are not particularly different from those of other vertebrates.

Cerebellum

One area of the brain that is well-developed in birds is the cerebellum. Whether feeding or breeding, birds don't need to make too many intellectual decisions. Most events and behaviors are predictable. However, in the area of defense, the bird needs much more flexibility.

The area of the brain most involved with equilibrium and coordinated muscle contraction is called the cerebellum. Birds have a large, well-developed cerebellum (Figure 8.2). This allows them to be very adept at movements, especially in the air. Anyone who has tried to catch birds on the wing with a net, can attest to the highly developed evasive behaviors of birds.

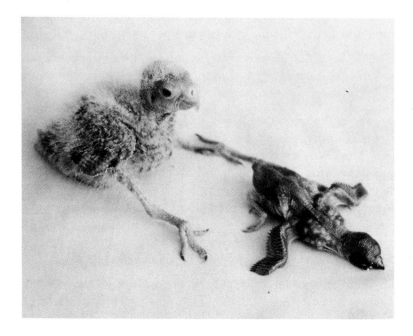

Figure 9.1   Chicks are just beginning to sense the world around them.

9   Sense Organs

Introduction

Birds have the same senses of sight, hearing, smell, taste, and touch as do mammals, but the sensitivity of these senses differ. In addition, there is the possibility that birds have other senses of which we are unaware. An example of a non-human senses is the sonar type of sense used by dolphins to locate objects. Perhaps birds also have some senses which we humans do not possess.

Vision

Vision is the dominant sense organ of man. We even have a saying, "seeing is believing," in spite of all the "wonders" performed by magicians and Hollywood. Birds also have a strong dependence on vision. Physically, the avian eye is unusually large. The eyes of nocturnal birds are proportionally larger than birds who are active during the day.

The eyes of birds, even those who are active during the day, are proportionally larger than the eyes of other vertebrates. The eye of a starling is 15% of its body weight. This is large compared to man, whose eye represents about 1% of his body weight. Ostriches have the largest eye of any land animal, being about two inches in diameter.

Birds, like other vertebrates, have eyelids. Another way the avian eye differs from the human eye is that the avian eye has a third or extra eyelid called the nictitating membrane. The nictitating membrane moves horizontally across the eye starting at the inner corner (Fig. 9.2). This membrane will protect the eye without the necessity of closing the outer eyelids.

Figure 9.2 Nictitating membrane of the avian eye.

In other words, the bird can close the nictitating membrane, thus protecting the eye, without losing vision. Vision through this translucent membrane is not clear, but the bird can at least discern objects. The nictitating membrane may be important when the bird is flying on a windy day with lots of dust, etc. in the air. This membrane also spreads tears (lacrimal fluid) across the eye, thereby ensuring that the eye will remain moist.

It is not only physically that the avian eye is superior, the avian eye is physiologically (functionally) quite sophisticated. Birds cannot problem solve, or perceive solutions, as well as man. Therefore, they need a better "window" to the world around them, so that they may see and react to dangerous stimuli. For example, the avian eye can focus (accommodate) much faster than the human eye, allowing birds to react much faster to danger.

Birds have excellent visual acuity. Visual acuity is the ability to distinguish two distinct points as two distinct points. Having an object in clear focus is important when trying to distinguish the size, location, and distance of that object, especially if it is life threatening.

Accommodation is the ability to change the shape of the lens in order to focus upon an object. There are varying accommodation abilities in birds, but in general birds can accommodate much better than other vertebrates. Generally, birds that must visually follow fast moving objects (i.e. insects or fish in the water) have the ability to focus quickly through a wide range. Owls accommodate very poorly. Therefore, when food is at a close range, they must back away to focus on the food before pouncing on it.

An aspect of vision where birds show a real dominance over human vision is in the amount of area observed, called the field of view. The placement of the avian eyes allows the birds to have a tremendous field of view (Fig. 9.3), much of it is binocular vision. Binocular vision is using two eyes to see.

Binocular vision is important because depth perception is not possible with one eye. With one eye, neither birds nor man can judge distance, except to evaluate distance by the size of the object. This can be quite misleading as many a painting has shown.

Birds, like man, also determine distance by the size of the object and by the size of objects around it. But, if a bird is to accurately judge the distance of an object it must have binocular vision. However, binocular vision is not necessary throughout the full field of vision. One eye is enough to detect movement. The head can then be moved, so that the bird now has binocular vision in that area of the field of view occupied by the object.

Owl has a small field of view, but
has binocular vision in most of it.

Sparrow has a very large
field of view, but less than
20% of it is binocular.

Woodcock has a 360 degree field of view, with
a small binocular field in front and in the rear.

Figure 9.3   Comparative field of view of three bird species.

Birds have color vision and see all colors. However, they see only about 20 different hues, as compared to man, who can perceive about 120 different hues. Given the information imparted to the bird by color, perhaps all those hues simply confuse the issue.

Color undoubtedly plays an important role in the birds choice of food. Aviary birds used to eating green grapes are often reluctant to eat the substitute red grapes. Hummingbirds seem to be attracted to bright red and orange colors. Color seems to play an important role in reproductive behaviors as well.

The retina of birds is one and one-half to two times as thick as the retina of other vertebrates. The retina is the area of the inner eyeball where the photoreceptor cells called rods and cones are found. This increased thickness is due to a greater number of photoreceptor cells. Because of this increase in rods and cones, the visual abilities of birds are much better than those of other vertebrates.

The cones are the photoreceptors used for color and daylight vision. Rods are used for black and white and night vision. In nocturnal birds, there is a significant increase in the proportion of rods to cones. Birds who are most active during the day, have more cones than rods.

Hearing

With the ability to focus clearly and quickly, plus the ability to perceive color and distance, the bird has just about all the information it will need to react to environmental stimuli. But, just in case the bird does not pick up the intruder visually, they have an excellent back up: hearing.

Birds hear very well. They have a hearing range almost comparable to man. Man, at least in youth, can hear from a low of 20 cycles/second (Hertz)to a high of 20,000 cycles/second (Hertz). Most birds don't have a range quite this wide, but some, like the pigeon, can hear at a frequency as low as 0.5 cycles/second (Hertz). Some, such as the chaffinch, can hear as high as 29,000 cycles/second (Hertz). Birds seem to be more sensitive to small pitch changes than does man. Ever think of having your parrot tune your piano?

Sound is much more important, and therefore more refined, to birds, such as owls, who hunt at night, than in a songbird catching flies on the wing. To increase the efficiency of the signal reaching the ear drum (tympanum), many owl species have a soft flap of tissue in front of the ear (Fig. 9.4), which tends to funnel the sound to the tympanum.

The inner ear of birds, like mammals, contains semicircular canals which are involved in equilibrium. There are three semicircular canals, each perpendicular to the others. Each time the head position changes, receptors in the semicircular canals send a signal to the cerebellum. The cerebellum then sends a signal to the muscles necessary to maintain equilibrium. Infections in this area can lead to dizziness.

Touch and smell

Touch and smell don't add much to the bird's ability to perceive its environment. If something is touching the bird it is probably too late for the bird to react, so a high sensitivity to touch is not necessary. Some pet birds tolerate and may even enjoy being touched, but the majority of birds are resistant to being touched.

Although not highly sensitive, birds do have a sense of touch so that they can perceive the environment immediately around themselves. For example, baby birds in the nest huddle together long before their eyes are open, using touch to maintain contact with fellow nest mates. Is mutual preening a "house cleaning" behavior or could it be that birds derive some pleasure from physical contact?

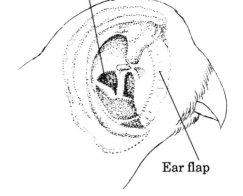

Ear opening

Figure 9.4   Owl ear flap
and
ear opening.

Ear flap

Well developed smell is not of much use for flying birds. This is mainly because smells become so diffuse in the air that they are not very good as indicators of the source of the smell. Some birds do have a highly developed sense of smell. The nocturnal kiwi has poor eyesight, but does have nostrils near the tip of its beak and a well developed sense of smell. The kiwi apparently locates its prey, primarily earthworms, by smell (Fig. 9.5).

Figure 9.5   Kiwi locating earthworm by smell.

It has been proven that vultures are quite capable of locating their prey by smell. Welty describes the time that engineers placed ethyl mercaptan (one of the odors of decaying meat) in a 42 mile natural gas pipeline and were rewarded by the circling of vultures above the previously unlocated leaks.

Taste

The sense of taste is poorly defined in birds. The speed with which they usually dispatch their food suggests as much. Since feeding birds are often on the ground or in other vulnerable positions, they don't have much time for a leisurely meal. They must eat their food quickly, probably tasting very little of it.

Taste is used to advantage by some aviculturists anxious to get their birds to eat new foods. For example, if a bird eats grapes well, but not some other fruit, the aviculturist will scoop out the grape "meat" and replace it with some of the new fruit. Since the bird seems more interested in appearance than taste, the bird may eat the new fruit. Slowly the grape is replaced with more of the new fruit. Since the bird does have some taste sensation, it is hoped that the bird will acquire a taste for the new fruit and continue to eat it without the grape "ruse."

There have been many experiments which show that birds do have some taste sensations. Experiments with chickens showed that they could detect solutions of salt, glycerin, quinine, and acetic acid, but did not respond to sucrose or saccharin. With a few exceptions, similar results were obtained with experiments on pigeons.

Temperature

The reactions of birds to changes in environmental temperature indicates that birds have a well-developed sensitivity to temperature. When temperatures become hot, most birds react by moving to a cooler area, often moving to the cooler ground. Another example of this temperature sensitivity occurs in incubating birds. Sitting hens can detect slight changes in the temperature of the eggs and respond accordingly. This sensitivity is much more well-developed than in man.

Figure 10.1 Feeding young is a hormonally controlled behavior.

10   Endocrine System

Introduction

The major control over growth and metabolism of birds, as in mammals, is exerted by the endocrine system. How well the bird functions is primarily dependent on the functions of the endocrine system. The growth pattern and size of the bird are determined by the this system. Most of the reproductive functions are initiated by and under the control of the endocrine system.

Control

The endocrine system, along with the nervous system, is responsible for the overall control of the bird's body. Although the nervous system and endocrine system often regulate the same organ, they do it in very different ways. The nervous system works by sending nerve impulses as the messengers, while the endocrine system works by sending chemical messengers (hormones) through the blood stream.

The main difference between them is speed. The nervous system is quick to react, but the effects are short-lived, whereas the endocrine system is slow to react and the effects are long-lived. This difference is determined primarily by the longer length of time it takes to release a hormone into the blood stream. It takes time for the hormone to travel through the blood stream. Finally, it takes time for the hormones to travel from the blood stream to the target organ. In comparison, the nerve impulse can travel immediately and quickly, at speeds of up to 250 miles per hour.

A good example of this is the effect that these two control systems have on the heart. A part of the nervous system, called the sympathetic nervous system will, by increasing the number of nerve impulses, speed up the heart rate almost immediately. When the number of nerve impulses decrease, the heart rate will decrease almost immediately.

The endocrine system can also speed up the heart rate through the release of a hormone called adrenalin (epinephrine). Turning this system off, however, takes time. Once the adrenalin is in the blood stream, it will continue to stimulate a heart rate increase until the hormone is removed. This removal of the hormone from the blood takes minutes, not the mere seconds necessary to stop the nervous system effect.

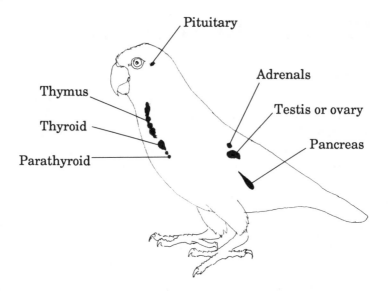

Figure 10.2   Location of endocrine glands.

Pituitary gland

The most important gland of the endocrine system is the pituitary gland (hypophysis). The pituitary is very important because its hormones control the hormone production of the other endocrine glands. It also is one of the prime regulators of growth.

At one time, we called the pituitary the "master gland" because of its control of the other glands. We have since removed the pituitary from this exalted position. This is due primarily to research which indicated that the pituitary is itself controlled by a part of the brain called the hypothalamus. None-the-less, the pituitary is still a dominant endocrine gland.

This relationship between the hypothalamus (brain) and the pituitary gland may cause changes in the normal hormonal balance of the organism. This may be the way in which psychological states, such as fear and stress, affect the breeding behavior of birds. It should be added that this may cause changes in other behaviors as well.

Pituitary hormones

The pituitary produces four hormones which directly affect other endocrine glands. These hormones are TSH (Thyroid stimulating hormone) which stimulates the thyroid gland, thereby affecting our metabolism; ACTH (Adrenocorticotropic hormone) which stimulates the adrenal gland; and LH (Lutenizing hormone) and FSH (Follicle stimulating hormone) which affect the gonads (ovaries and testes). LH and FSH are the prime regulators that initiate reproduction.

Growth hormone

The pituitary also produces GH (growth hormone). In humans, an abnormally high or low level of GH will have serious effects on growth. An abnormally low level will result in a smaller than normal child. An abnormally high level will result in a larger than normal child.

When someone is tall, we like to say "it's in his genes," and in fact, the level of growth hormone is determined by the genes. Size is determined primarily by the level of growth hormone. Very little research has been performed with GH in birds to see how it affects size, but it seems like a reasonable hypothesis that GH levels in birds will have a significant affect on size as it does in mammals.

GH of birds is different from the GH of humans, as well as being different from the GH of other mammals. Researchers have injected these different growth hormones into unusual hosts with some degree of success. For example, GH from a duck was shown to stimulate growth in a rat. However, researchers were not as successful at stimulating growth in a chicken with mammalian GH.

The GH levels in birds, like those in mammals, are primarily determined genetically. Therefore, the hypothesis of breeding two larger birds in order to produce larger offspring is scientifically sound, although, we should add, not always successful. There are other factors, such as nutrition, which affect the growth of birds.

The pituitary also produces MSH (melanocyte stimulating hormone), but the function and chemical nature of this hormone in birds is largely unknown. This hormone is also found in mammals, but here, too, its functions are largely unknown.

Figure 10.3   Growing chicks demonstrate effects of growth hormone.

Pineal gland

A most peculiar gland is the pineal gland, which is located on the lower back part of the brain (upper neck region). It has been researched for many years without yielding many of its secrets. Specific areas currently being actively researched are those which try to understand how the changes that take place in biochemical rhythms, photoperiodism, and reproduction relate to the pineal.

Thyroid gland

The next endocrine gland to be discussed is the thyroid. The paired thyroids are oval shaped with a shiny dark red color. They are located on either side of the trachea. Their size depends on age, sex, environmental conditions, diet, activity, and species.

The primary hormone produced by the thyroid is thyroxine. As in mammals, thyroxine is produced by combining the amino acid tyrosine with iodine. A deficiency of tyrosine or iodine will result in low thyroxine levels. Tyrosine deficiencies are rare, since the bird can produce this amino acid. However, deficiencies of iodine are more common because the bird must acquire iodine in the diet.

If the water supply in an area is deficient in iodine, plant materials in that area will also be iodine deficient. Therefore, the bird will be unable to obtain the necessary amount of this important mineral. This usually results in an enlargement of the thyroid. This enlargement is called a goiter. More importantly, the bird will have a lower than normal level of circulating thyroxine.

A low level of thyroxine is significant because this hormone is the main regulator of metabolism. Hypothyroidism (low thyrosine levels) in chickens results in the same abnormal conditions as seen in mammals. Hypothyroid chickens become obese, mature slowly, and have delayed sexual development.

The main regulator of thyroxine is the hormone TSH, secreted by the anterior pituitary. The pituitary determines the amount of TSH to be released by monitoring the blood level of thyroxine. If the blood thyroxine level is low, the pituitary will release more TSH, thereby stimulating the thyroid to produce more thyroxine. If the thyroxine blood level is too high, then the pituitary will secrete less TSH, thereby resulting in a lower production of thyroxine by the thyroid.

Another factor which has an effect on thyroxine production is the environmental temperature. Higher temperatures tend to decrease thyroxine production, whereas colder temperatures tend to increase thyroxine. This makes sense, when we consider the fact that as the environment temperature gets colder, the heat loss increases. To compensate for this increased heat loss, the bird must increase its heat production. Increasing thyroxine levels is one of the primary ways to increase heat metabolism, hence increasing heat production.

Temperature acclimatization

Increased circulating thyroxine level is an important consideration when moving birds. It is not prudent to take a bird from an indoor situation and place it in an outdoor aviary during the winter. The indoor bird does not have the increased thyroxine levels needed to survive outdoors in the winter. This is true even though the indoor bird may be of the same species as those already in the outdoor aviary. In many cooler areas of the world, this is risky even in the early spring or late fall. Birds that are already outside, as winter nears, are gradually increasing their level of thyroxine. This, along with an increased number of feathers are adaptions to the colder days.

The bird's thyroxine level is also affected by light. Not much is known about the effect that the amount of light (photoperiod) has on the thyroxine level in birds. Some physiologists propose that it may have some effect on breeding. In birds, there is also a much greater interaction between the gonads and thyroxine levels. This again may have an effect on reproduction. For example, it may cause the increased energy level exhibited by males during the breeding season.

There appears to be some relationship between thyroxine level and molting in some birds. One researcher concluded that a peak of thyroxine occurs a few weeks before a molt. This has been shown for passerine birds, but in the case of the chicken, there seems to be no relationship.

Parathyroid glands

Attached to the back surface of the thyroids are four glands called the parathyroids. Regulation of calcium is the primary function of these four small glands. The principle hormone secreted by the parathyroid is called parathormone (PTH).

PTH controls the level of blood calcium in three ways. One is by moving calcium back and forth between the bone and blood. Another way is by controlling the number of carriers which reabsorb the calcium in the kidney. If the calcium blood levels are high, more calcium will be secreted in the urine. The reverse is true if the calcium blood levels are low. The third way is by controlling the amount of calcium absorbed in the digestive tract.

There are other controls of the calcium blood levels in additon to the parathyroids. For example, the sex hormones will influence blood calcium levels. In the female, when the uterus is active, the absorption rate for calcium in the digestive tract increases. Absorption increases from the normal 40% of the ingested calcium to about 70% of the ingested calcium. This increased absorption is required for the added calcium requirements of egg formation.

Normal calcium levels are necessary for strong bones and for the formation of the egg shell. If no external source of calcium is available, a chicken must liberate 10% of its bone calcium to form one egg shell. Calcium is also essential in other ways . Normal blood clotting depends on the availability of calcium. Muscle contraction, cardiac as well as skeletal, requires calcium. The movement of nerve impulses from one nerve to the next won't occur in the absence of calcium.

Another hormone affecting the level of calcium is calcitonin. Calcitonin is secreted from the thyroid of mammals and some birds, but in many birds calcitonin is secreted from the ultimobranchial gland. This gland, unique to birds, is found behind the parathyroids. The calcitonin level in birds does not have the effect on blood calcium that it does in mammals.

Adrenal glands

The paired adrenal glands are located close to the two kidneys. The two major hormones secreted by the adrenal cortex are corticosterone and aldosterone.

The metabolic effects of corticosterone are many. One is to increase the level of glucose in the blood, probably by stimulating the conversion of fats to glucose (gluconeogenesis). Hydrocortisone, which performs this function in mammals, is absent from the avian adrenal gland. Corticosterone also has an effect on fat metabolism and therefore influences body weight. It also causes changes in the white blood cells, and has been shown to decrease the egg laying in chickens.

The role of aldosterone seems to be the same in birds as it is in mammals. Aldosterone is one of the prime regulators of the blood levels of sodium and potassium. These two minerals are important in the contraction of skeletal and cardiac muscles and in the function of the nerve cells.

Adrenalin

The adrenal medulla's secretion of adrenalin (epinephrine) is very important to the survival of the bird. Adrenalin, along with the sympathetic nervous system, prepares the bird for what is called the "fight or flight" response (Figure 10.3). When an organism is presented with an unpleasant or threatening circumstance, it usually responds by trying to change the circumstance (fight) or by trying to get away for the unpleasantness (flight).

To do either, the organism must be physiologically prepared. This preparation includes increasing the heart rate, blood pressure, respirations, blood glucose levels, etc. It is the role of epinephrine and the sympathetic nervous system to initiate these physiological changes.

Figure 10.4   This type of activity increases adrenalin.

Pancreas

Farther up in the abdominal cavity, tucked in a fold of the small intestine just below the stomach, is the pancreas. The pancreas is a true endocrine gland, secreting the two hormones insulin and glucagon. But, it is also an exocrine gland (secretes via a duct), secreting digestive enzymes into the small intestines.

The role of insulin is to facilitate the movement of ingested glucose, from the blood stream, into the body cells. Insulin also facilitates the conversion of glucose to glycogen. Glycogen is the storage form of glucose. Insulin also increases the level of fatty acids in the blood . The role of glucagon in birds is still unknown, although its role in mammals is to elevate blood glucose during fasting.

Thymus gland

Very little is know about thymus gland function in birds. Like the thymus of mammals, the avian thymus gets smaller (atrophies) with age. In medium-sized parrots the thymus atrophies at about four months of age. The thymus is believed to play an important role in the production of antibodies and in the normal function of the immune system.

Gonads

The gonads (ovary of the hen and the testes of the male) are the last two endocrine glands we will discuss. Gonads have two independent functions. One is the production of the sex hormones, estrogen, progesterone, or testosterone. The other is the production of the gametes, either the egg or the sperm cells. Both glands are located in the abdominal cavity.

In almost all bird species, there is only one ovary and one oviduct, both located on the left side. The right ovary and right oviduct are vestigial (non-functioning). Males have a right and left testicle.

The specific role of the ovary is to produce the eggs (ova) and the female sex hormones estrogen and progesterone. The role of the testes is to produce the sperm cells and the male sex hormone testosterone. Both gonads show substantial increases in size during the breeding season (see chapter 2).

Figure 11.1 Western rosella.

11   Circulation

Introduction

The circulatory system of birds is very much like that of other higher vertebrates. This is not too surprising when one considers that the functions and requirements of this system are the same in birds as they are in other vertebrates. We can sum up the function of the circulatory system in one word, transportion. The circulatory system is responsible for transporting nutrients, gases such as oxygen and carbon dioxide, hormones, antibodies, waste products, and heat. The transport of heat is very important in the maintenance of a constant body temperature.

To be efficient, a circulatory system must have passageways, in this case the arteries, veins and capillaries. It must also have a pump to ensure that the blood is moved throughout the system. And finally, the system must have a transporting medium, the blood.

Heart

Let's first take a look at the pump. The heart is a muscle composed of muscle tissue appropriately named cardiac muscle tissue. Like mammals, the heart of a bird has four chambers, two atria and two ventricles. The right side of the heart pumps blood to the lungs to pick up oxygen and to get rid of carbon dioxide. The left side of the heart pumps blood to the head and body, carrying nutrients throughout the vessels of body. Cardiac muscle tissue of the left side of the heart is much thicker than that of the right side. This is due to the greater effort required to move blood throughout the entire body, as compared to the right side which moves blood only to the adjacent lungs.

The heart of a bird is larger and therefore more powerful than that of a mammal of the same weight. The avian heart tends to be about one and one-half times heavier than the heart of a mammal of the same weight. In general, the smaller the bird, the greater the proportional size of the heart. According to Sturkie, the heart of a goose is 0.8% of its body weight, as compared to the hummingbird whose heart is 2.4% of its total body weight. In comparison, the human heart is less than 0.5% of body weight.

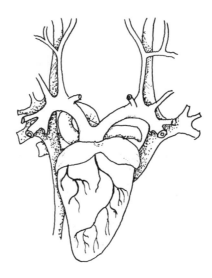

Figure 11.2   Avian heart.

This larger avian heart developed for many reasons. One of the most important is that birds generally have a higher metabolic rate than mammals. Metabolism means all of the chemical reactions occurring in an organism's body. A higher metabolic rate means a faster rate of chemical reactions, which in turn will require more nutrients. Therefore, there is a need for a stronger pump to more efficiently deliver these nutrients.

Another reason for a strong heart relates to the high amount of energy required for flight, especially in takeoff. Low oxygen (hypoxia), found in higher altitudes, is another reason for a strong heart. Birds, such as migrating geese, flying in an environment with less oxygen require a stronger heart to move the reduced supply of oxygen more rapidly.

Body   temperature

Why do birds generally have a higher metabolic rate than do mammals? The answer can be found by looking at body temperature. Birds and mammals are the only two groups of animals which maintain a constant body temperature (homothermic). Avian body temperatures are higher than those of mammals. They vary from a low of 104 F degrees in some species, to a high of 112 F degrees in other species. The average temperature is around 107 F degrees. Table 11.1 lists examples of avian temperatures.

Table 11.1 Body temperatures of selected birds.

Species	Temperature (F)
Hummingbird	111
Canary	110
Mannikin	108
Robin	109
Budgerigar	107.5
Pigeon	105
Duck	106

There are some definite advantages to maintaining a constant body temperature (homothermic). Since chemical reactions are slowed down by a decrease in temperature, it is advantageous to keep the temperature up so that the chemical reactions can occur at an adequate rate.

The main disadvantage of being homothermic is that it requires a lot of energy. For example, it takes a lot more energy to keep the furnace going all night than to turn it off at night. Since both are homothermic, birds and mammals have high energy requirements. However, most birds have a disadvantage, they typically have a higher surface area to volume ratio.

The surface area to volume ratio relates directly to heat loss. In order to maintain a constant body temperature, the organism must produce body heat at the same rate that body heat is lost. Heat production relates to the volume of the organism and to the amount of available energy. This energy is produced by the breakdown (metabolism) of foods such as carbohydrates, fats, and in some cases, protein.

As the environmental temperature drops, birds lose more heat. To compensate for this heat loss, birds must produce more heat. This is done primarily by increasing the metabolism, which will then require the intake of more food, and by the fluffing of body feathers. Other means of maintaining body temperature are described in chapter 12.

Surface area

The loss of heat relates directly to the surface area of the birds. Because of the insulating properties of feathers, birds are able to control their heat loss quite effectively. There is, however, still some heat lost, which is directly proportional to the surface area. However, a peculiar thing happens to the surface area as size decreases, the surface area gets proportionally larger.

We know that the overall surface area decreases as an organism gets smaller. However, if we compare the surface area to the volume, the relative surface area (surface area/volume ratio) increases as the organism gets smaller. This phenomenon is true only when any organism gets smaller and still retains the same basic shape.

Since the relative surface area increases as the bird gets smaller, the smaller bird will have a proportionally greater heat loss. Thus, we have a situation where the heat loss is increasing proportionally, but the volume for the production of this heat is decreasing proportionally. Therefore, the smaller the bird, the greater its proportional heat loss.

To compensate for this increased heat loss, the bird must increase its metabolism. This requires the increased intake of energy providing foods. This increased food intake requires more transport and hence a stronger heart. Therefore, there is a need for a proportionally stronger heart in smaller birds than in larger birds. And also, there is a need for a much stronger heart in birds than in mammals.

The stronger heart isn't the only adaptation by birds to compensate for the increased heat loss. Other important factors include the production of more contour feathers and down feathers, as well as behavioral changes. Behavioral changes would include moving from a cool spot to a warmer one, or the more dramatic change of migrating from a cooler climate to a warmer one.

Heart rate

The heart rate also seems to follow this size pattern. As the bird species gets smaller, the heart rate tends to increase. For example, a chicken's resting heart rate is between 300 and 400 beats per minute, as compared to the hummingbird resting heart rate, which is over 1000 beats per minute. This can also be seen in hatchlings. As the developing chicks increase in size, their heart rate tends to decrease.

Blood pressure

Blood pressure also tends to be higher in birds than in mammals. Blood pressure is measured in millimeters (mm) of mercury (Hg). A typical value for a chicken would be a systolic pressure of 190 mmHg and a diastolic pressure of 150 mmHg (190/150). The systolic pressure is the maximum pressure developed when the heart is actually contracting. Heart contraction is called systole. The diastolic pressure is the lowest pressure reached while the heart is relaxed. Heart relaxation is called diastole.

The pumping force of the heart (pulse pressure) is calculated by subtracting the diastolic pressure from the systolic pressure. In humans, whose blood pressure is typically 120/80, the typical pulse pressure is 40 mmHg (120 mmHg - 80 mmHg = 40 mmHg). Even with the higher blood pressure in the chicken, the pulse pressure (190 mmHg - 150 mmHg = 40 mmHg) is still only 40 mmHg . This results in a pumping force about the same as in humans. However, the chicken has a much shorter distance to pump the blood.

Blood vessels

The efficiency of the heart is determined primarily by the health of the cardiac muscle and the proficiency of the valves. The heart is only effective if there are passageways through which the blood is carried. Arteries and arterioles are vessels with thick walls (to withstand higher blood pressure), which serve as passageways for blood being pumped from the heart. Veins and venules, on the other hand, are thin-walled and serve as passageways for blood returning to the heart.

The final type of blood vessel is the capillary. Capillaries are significant because this is where all exchange takes place between the blood and the tissues. For example, oxygen, glucose, amino acids, minerals and other nutrients pass through the capillary wall, moving from the blood to the tissues. Carbon dioxide, lactic acid and other metabolic waste products pass from the tissue fluids, through the capillary wall to the blood. Capillaries are small, roughly 1 millimeter (about the diameter of a pin head) in length.

Transport

With a strong pump and good clear passageways, we now need a medium which can be pumped through the system without too much resistance. It must also be able to transport all of the blood components. The medium of choice is water. It is known as a polar solvent. Each water molecule carries partial electrical charges. The result is a very weak molecular "magnet" which can draw a wide variety of of blood components into solution. Without this dissolving capability, life as we know it simply would not be possible.

The significance of being a good solvent is that water can transport a greater variety of substances. Also, it can transport these substances in a greater concentration than any other solvent. Other important characteristics of water are that it has a high specific heat and a high heat of vaporization. Because of these two characteristics, water is a most efficient transporter of heat. This is very important because exercising muscles produce large amounts of heat. If this heat is not dissipated, it will incapacitate the enzymes that control chemical reactions.

Blood

Avian blood, like the blood of other vertebrates, contains three types of blood cells. If the blood cells are removed, the remaining clear straw colored liquid is called plasma. Plasma is about 90% water. The remaining 10% contains the substances that are normally transported in the blood. See Table 11.2 for a listing of the more common substances in plasma.

Table 11.2   Common constituents of plasma.

glucose	plasma proteins
amino acids	oxygen
fats	carbon dioxide
vitamins	minerals
hormones	waste products
enzymes	uric acid

Red blood cells

Red blood cells (erythrocytes) are the most common blood cell. There are between 2 and 3 million red blood cells per cubic millimeter of blood, which is about half the number found in human blood. The red blood cells of birds are about 40 to 50% larger than human red blood cells, probably due to the fact that they still have their nucleus and human cells do not (Figure 11.3). They are ovoid in shape and, as in humans, are produced in bone marrow. The life span of avian red blood cells is less than 50 days, resulting in a significant burden on birds to produce high numbers of red blood cells daily.

The primary functions of the red blood cell are to carry oxygen and the waste product carbon dioxide. However, since it is the hemoglobin that is actually the oxygen carrier, the red cells actually exist to produce and carry

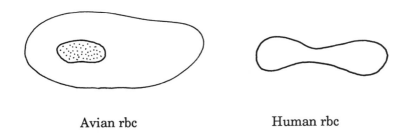

Avian rbc   Human rbc

Figure 11.3   Avian red blood cell compared to human rbc.

the hemoglobin. Although the hemoglobin concentration per cell is slightly-less than in mammals, it is a more efficient carrier of oxygen. As in humans, the hemoglobin content and red blood cell concentration is a little higher in male birds than female birds.

The ostrich has the largest red blood cells of any bird and the humming-bird has the smallest. However, the concentration of these red blood cells is just the opposite. The hummingbird has the greater concentration (5.9 million per cu mm) as compared to a concentration of 1.9 million per cu. mm in the ostrich.

Generally, the more highly evolved birds (hummingbirds) have a smaller red blood cell, but in a higher concentrations than the more primitive birds (ostriches). Table 11.3 compares various factors of a small and large bird. Strong flyers typically have smaller red blood cells.

Here again we see the implications of surface area to the function. The smaller the red blood cell, the greater will be its proportional surface area. Therefore, birds which expend proportionally more oxygen will benefit from the smaller red bloods cell since they will increase the overall surface area for oxygen diffusion. However, the small cell is only advantageous if there is an increase in the number of these smaller red blood cells.

White blood cells

White blood cells (leukocytes) are also quite common in avian blood and are found in twice the concentration present in human blood. Little research has been done on the various types of white blood cells. What little work that has been done indicates functions similar to those white blood cells in mammals. Some have been shown to be phagocytic which means they have the ability to "eat" bacteria and viruses thereby providing protection against these disease causing organisms.

Antibodies

Another important function of the white blood cell is the production of antibodies. Antibodies are proteins produced by the birds against specific bacterial and viral infections. They also serve to protect the body against toxic substances. Antibodies are very specific. In other words, an antibody is produced against one specific microorgansim and won't be effective against any other microorganism. Using a human example to illustrate the point, possessing antibodies (immunity) against the organism that causes mumps does no good when we contact the microorgansim that causes measles.

Birds are not born with most antibodies, but instead will produce them when the specific microorganism is contacted. This "learning" how to produce a specific antibody, along with having that antibody circulating in the blood, is what we call immunity. Since most immunities are developed, rather than inherited, it stands to reason that the younger the organism, the fewer the immunities.

Young children seem to be sick much more than adults. Why? Mainly because they are busy developing their immunities. Any new disease that comes along, children seem to "catch." They then develop antibodies against the new disease. After a few sleepless nights, all is well again, at least until the next "bug" comes along.

This is a natural process and the implications for birds are significant. The younger the birds, the fewer immunities they will have built up, and hence the more susceptible to new diseases they will be. Young children who go off to nursery school often develop many more infections. This is also true of young birds who are exposed to other birds, especially adult birds who may be latent carriers of diseases.

The significant difference in this child vs. young bird analogy is the fact that birds tend to mask their illness and often die before any medical attention is given. It is important to keep young birds away from adult birds as much as possible. It is especially important to keep the young birds away from any adult birds that are suspected disease carriers. This is particularly true if the carriers are stressed, since stress often results in increased disease activity in carrier birds.

Recent studies have indicated that there is some passive immunity in baby birds. Passive immunity is the condition where antibodies produced by the immune parent are passed on to the young, offering the young some temporary immunity. Temporary, that is, until the young can develop their own immunities.

Figure 11.4   Beneficiaries of passive immunity.

Research has shown that antibodies are passed on in both the amniotic fluids and the yolk of the egg. Since birds do not effectively develop their own antibodies for the first month or so after hatching, this passive immunity is very significant in protecting the young against disease.

Obviously, the parent bird cannot pass on antibodies which it has itself not produced. In other words, if the parent bird has not contacted a specific microorganism, then it won't have developed an antibody for that specific organism to pass on.

The loss of chicks in the shell and the loss of young fledged birds is a serious problem in aviculture. Some of this loss is caused by inbreeding or environmental problems, but "many of the problems frequently encountered in clinical avian practice relate directly or indirectly to infectious diseases," so states George V Kollias Jr in *Clinical Avian Medicine and Surgery* by Harrison and Harrison. Much more research, in the area of avian immunity is needed. Until more information is known, caution must be taken, especially with young birds.

Platelets

The third type of blood cell is the platelet (thrombocyte) which is responsible for initiating blood clotting (hemostasis). The circulating level of platelets in birds is much lower than in humans. When bleeding begins, the platelets rupture, stimulating two plasma proteins called prothrombin and fibrinogen to initiate the blood clot. These two plasma proteins are produced by the liver with the assistance of vitamin K. Vitamin K deficiencies are not uncommon in aviary housed birds.

Blood volume

Blood with its plasma and three types of blood cells is called whole blood. This scarlet stream of life is just as important to the birds as it is to man. Sturkie reports an avian blood volume range from 4.8% to 11.3% of body weight. Chickens average 7.8%.

If we assume 8% as a typical average, then a zebra finch weighing about 9 grams would only have 0.7 ml of blood. A large bird such as a macaw weighing 700 grams would have only 56 ml of blood. Since an 8 oz cup is equal to 240 ml, the macaw would have about one-fourth of a cup of blood. We won't even speculate as to how the amount of the zebra's blood relates to the cup.

Humans typically have about 5,000 ml of blood and a loss of 1,000 milliliters (20%) or more becomes life threatening. In the case of our macaw, the bird could lose anly 10 ml (2 teaspoons) of blood without it becoming life threatening. Obviously, concern for any amount of bleeding is paramount in the maintenance of healthy birds.

Comparative physiology

In this chapter comparisons were made between the physiology of different sized birds, especially large birds compared to small birds. In summary, one could make the generalization that the smaller the bird, the faster most things become (Table 11.3). For example, factors such as metabolic rate, heart rate, blood pressure, temperature, growth rate, and the rate of aging (resulting in shorter life spans) increase as the bird species gets smaller. In general, clutch sizes increase as the species gets smaller when large and small psittacines are compared. Hummingbirds and ostriches are both exceptions to this statement.

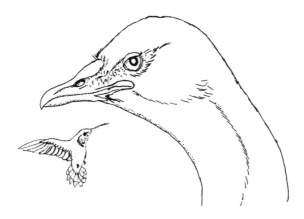

Figure 11.5   Ostrich size compared to a hummingbird.

Table 11.3   Comparison of some physiology of a small bird to that of a large bird and also to a human.

Component	Hummingbird	Ostrich	Man
rbc size (microns)	16 x 10	11 x 6	7 x 2.5
rbc concentration (mm³)	5,900,000	1,800,000	5,000,000
heart rate (minute)	615	65	70
heart weight (% of body wt.)	2.4%	0.1%	0.01%
body temperature (F)	86 - 104	102.5	98.6
life span (aveage in years)	8-10	35-40	70-80

Figure 12.1 Flight requires an efficient respiratory system.

12   **Respiration**

Introduction

The primary function of the respiratory system is to provide oxygen for the cells and to get rid of the waste product carbon dioxide. There are two characteristics that all respiratory systems must have in order to be efficient.

First is a large surface area. The larger the surface area, the greater number of oxygen and carbon dioxide molecules that can be moved in a period of time. It is estimated that the surface area of both human lungs would cover the entire floor of a large room. The surface area of the avian respiratory system would be proportionally even larger.

The other characteristic is that all respiratory structures must be either in water or have an inner coating of water. This is why animals living outside of a water environment have an internal respiratory structure. A dry respiratory system would not be able to slow down the fast moving oxygen and carbon dioxide gases. These gases are slowed down as they move through the water, so that they can now move across the respiratory membrane between the lungs and the blood.

Air sacs

The avian respiratory system is the most efficient respiratory system found in vertebrates. As in most vertebrates, the lung is the primary respiratory structure. However, in birds there is, in addition to the lungs, a system of interconnecting sacs called air sacs (Figure 12.2). These air sacs serve many functions. One function served by having air sacs is a decrease in overall body weight, thereby enhancing flight.

Another more obvious function of air sacs is the significant increase in volume and surface area of the total respiratory system. In man, the lungs occupy about 5% of the total body volume, as compared to only about 2% in the duck. But, when you add in the air sac system of the duck, the total respiratory volume increases to 20% of the total body volume.

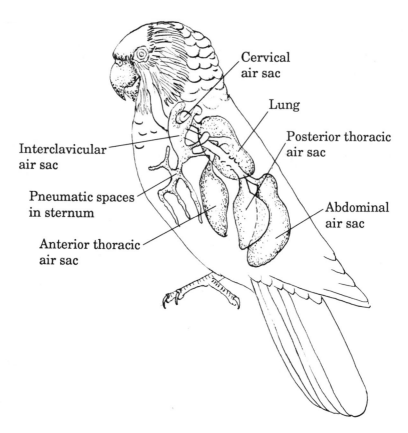

Cervical
air sac

Lung

Posterior thoracic
air sac

Interclavicular
air sac

Abdominal
air sac

Pneumatic spaces
in sternum

Anterior thoracic
air sac

Figure 12.2   Avian air sacs.

The average respiratory volume in most bird species is about 15% of the total body volume. This large respiratory volume allows a much greater oxygen reserve than is possible in mammalian lungs. This is important because birds have a higher metabolic rate and therefore need proportionally more oxygen. This reserve is also important for those birds who spend time at altitudes where oxygen levels are lower.

Not only are the avian lungs smaller than the mammalian lungs, they have more rigid walls. Therefore, when air is taken into the avian lung there is very little change in the total volume of the lungs. This is quite different from the mammalian lung in which there is a significant increase in lung volume during inspiration.

Air passages

Air passes through the mouth cavity and down the trachea. The trachea is a long tube surrounded by cartilaginous rings. These rings keep the trachea open, thereby reducing the pressure needed to move air in and out. The air then passes through the syrinx, a voice box unique to birds, which is found in most species. From the syrinx, air passes into either the right or left bronchi, the two short tubes that lead into the right and left lung. Finally, from the lungs, air can move into the air sacs. Some of these air sacs have segments which project down into the interior of the long bones.

Alveoli

In mammals, the interior of the lung is filled with small grape shaped structures called alveoli. These alveoli greatly increase the functional surface area of the lung. The internal structure of the avian respiratory system is much more complex than this. It is so complex that until recent years we did not even know the how avian respiration occurred.

Inspiration

In mammals, the primary organ responsible for inspiration is a skeletal muscle called the diaphragm. Birds don't have a functional diaphragm, but instead, depend on muscles that attach to the ribs, the intercostal muscles.

During inspiration, the inspiratory intercostal muscles pull the ribs toward the wings. At the same time, the sternum is pulled toward the stomach region and is pulled slightly forward as well. This action of the inspiratory intercostal muscles, increases the volume of the respiratory cavity, causing a decrease in pressure. This decrease in pressure results in an inflow of air into the lungs and air sacs, completing inspiration.

Expiration

Expiration is accomplished by the expiratory intercostal muscles which essentially reverse the action of the inspiratory intercostal muscles, thereby increasing the internal pressure. This increased internal pressure forces air out, completing expiration.

Basically, the respiratory effort occurs in two phases. The first phase moves air into the lungs themselves, and the second phase moves air into the air sacs. Expiration is likewise a two phase process. This is a simplified view of a very complex system, a complete explanation of which is beyond the scope of this book.

The weight of the abdominal organs and the large flight muscles also affect respiration. During inspiration they pull down, aiding inspiration. However, during expiration these structures must be pulled up, resulting in an increased work load during expiration.

One implication of this mechanism is the effect that placing a bird on its back would have on inspiration. While on its back, the bird must now push up on the internal organs and the flight muscles as well. This increased inspiratory burden could be fatal to some birds if kept in this position for any length of time. Likewise, anything wrapped around the bird which restricts the movement of the sternum could be fatal.

Respiratory rate

Birds, on the average, have a faster respiratory rate than man. Yet, when compared to mammals of the same size, the respiratory rate for birds is actually slower. For example, the breathing rate for a 100 gram mammal would be about 100 breaths per minute, as compared to a rate of 28 breaths per minute for the same sized bird.

This again relates to the superiority of the avian respiratory system's ability to move air. The avian respiratory system takes in more air per breath. Therefore, a decreased respiratory rate is required to turn over the same amount of air in a given unit of time.

These deeper breaths in birds are also reflected in the heart rate to breathing ratio. In mammals, a 3 to 1 ratio of heartbeats to breaths taken is common. In birds, the ratio is approximately 7.5 to 1. By way of comparison, the ratio in man is 5 to 1.

Cooling

In birds, the respiratory system serves another important function, that of cooling. Since birds don't have sweat glands, they need another way to dissipate the heat when they are overheated. One way is to increase respirations, thereby blowing off more heat.

Heat production

In the chapter on circulation the surface area/volume ratio and its implications to body temperature, metabolism, and food intake were discussed. Let's look in more detail at the ways that body heat is gained and lost. The primary way for heat gain by the body is metabolism of foods. Therefore, the higher the activity level (flying, walking, etc.), the faster the metabolism, the greater will be the heat production.

Figure 12.3   Keeping warm.

Heat loss

The rate of heat loss is primarily determined by the surface area/volume ratio of the bird. The smaller the bird, the greater the rate of heat loss. Another important factor is insulation. The amount of insulation is principally determined by feathers, but fat may also play a role as an insulator.

If birds experience a drop in body temperature, they must either increase heat production or decrease heat loss. The ideal response would be to do both, thereby stabilizing the body temperature sooner. Increasing metabolism is the primary way to increase heat production. Metabolism can be increased by becoming more active, by shivering, or by increasing the thyroxine hormone levels. Activity changes and shivering are short term solutions. Increasing thyroxine levels takes longer and is a long term solution.

Heat loss can be decreased in many ways. First is by fluffing, which uses trapped air as an insulator. By decreasing its breathing, the bird will retain more heat. Sitting rather than standing will decrease the exposed surface area of the legs. And finally, tucking the head under the wing will reduce heat loss. The head has the greatest proportional blood supply and therefore experiences the greatest heat loss. A long term solution is to increase the production of more feathers.

Heat gain

If birds experience an increase in body temperature they must either decrease heat production or increase heat loss. The fastest temperture reduction would be accomplished by doing both. Heat production can be decreased by decreasing metabolism. This will occur when there is a decrease in thyroxine levels. Decreasing thyroxine is a long term physiologi-cal solution which the bird has no conscious control over. Birds can, however, decrease their activity level, thereby reducing metabolism.

Increasing heat loss can be accomplished by laying body feathers down against the skin, thus eliminating any air pockets. Wing droop will expose more surface area for cooling. Behaviorally, birds can react by going to the ground (generally the coolest area) and also by becoming inactive. Increasing respirations will also increase heat loss. Increased respirations or panting does not indicate thirst in birds, any more than it does in dogs. Since both lack sweat glands, birds and dogs pant in order to get rid of heat faster.

Thermoregulation

Temperature regulation, also called thermoregulation, is quite effective in adult birds, but is poorly developed in some young birds. Precocial birds thermoregulate quite well, however, and after a few days need very little brooding by the parents.

Precocial birds are those birds who are born with their eyes open and their down feathers formed. They also have the ability to move around. Examples of precocial birds are quail, turkeys, ducks, and chickens.

Altricial birds are those birds who are born with their eyes closed, usually have very little feathering, and are completely dependent on the parents. Altricial birds, such parrots and finches, thermoregulate poorly. Therefore, altricial chicks are absolutely dependent on the brooding parents to main-tain their body temperature.

With a small body, resulting in a large proportional surface area, the altricial babies lose heat at a very fast rate. This large surface area, combined with few feathers, results in heat being lost at a rate faster than it can be replaced by the chick. For this reason one of the parents must sit on the nest much of the time, especially at night.

Figure 12.4   Altricial chick (e.g. parrot) compared to a precocial chick (e.g. quail).

It is not uncommon in aviculture for a breeder to discover dead babies in the nest box, with full crops and not a clue as to the cause of their demise. If this occurs in the early spring or fall, the reason may well be that the parents did not sit through the night. There are many possible reasons for this. The most obvious reason is that the birds are being scared off the nest at night. However, quite often young, inexperienced parents will begin to roost at night, long before the young are capable of any effective thermoregulation.

Regardless of why the parents leave the nest early, the survival of the young will be determined by the environmental temperature. Other factors which will determine their survival are the amount of feathers they have, the number of young in the nest, and the heat lost from the nest itself.

A good, thick walled nest will retain heat. The young are more likely to survive because their body heat is retained by the thick nest. Obviously, if there are more young in the nest, more heat will be produced, which will increase the chance of the young surviving cold temperatures. Nests constructed by humans should have thick walls that won't transmit heat readily. The birds should be provided with adequate amounts of nesting material to construct a sound nest with good heat retention qualities.

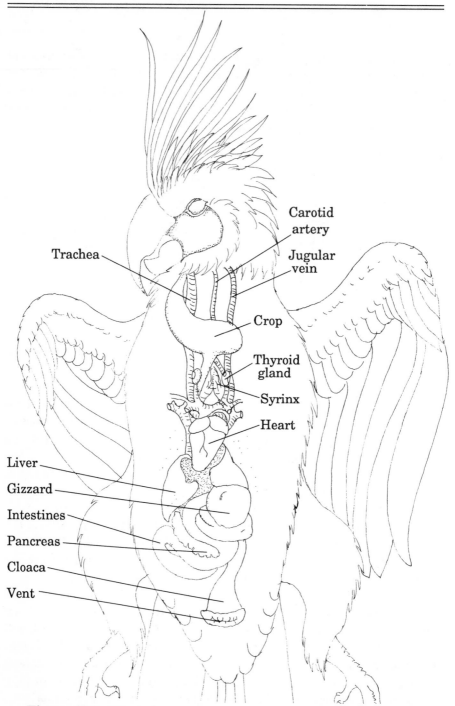

Figure 13.1 Internal organs.

13   Digestion

Hunger

Before beginning a discussion of the digestive system, we should first discuss hunger. What is hunger? Hunger is an internal need to seek food. The hunger center is located in an area of the brain called the hypothalamus. To what stimuli does this critical center respond? If one knew the complete answer to this question, at least in terms of humans, the financial rewards would be great.

Undoubtedly, blood glucose levels and the amount of food in the stomach are two of the physiological factors which affect the hunger center. Other factors, such as the sight and smell of food, availability of food, the bird's activity level and body temperature, to name just a few, are also important. There are other as yet unknown factors affecting the hunger center of birds and mammals.

Most avicultural birds in the United States have a constant supply of seeds available to them. In spite of this, most do not overeat. However, some cage birds do get overweight, but this is probably due more to a lack of exercise than to overeating. This implies that there is some point at which the bird reacts to having had enough to eat (satiety point). We don't understand which physiological factors determine the satiety point. Scientists continue research on this important subject, because the implications are very significant to man, as well as to birds.

Bird feeding preferences seem to be determined primarily by habit. They learn to eat the foods preferred by their parents, or they learn to eat those foods that are readily available. There are also some genetically determined food preferences. For example, hummingbirds don't eat seeds, even when nectar and fruits are unavailable. Because of their inability to crack seeds, hummingbirds with a preference for seeds would not survive and by natural selection would be removed from the gene pool.

Appearance is another determining factor in avian food preferences. Whole seeds are a welcome diet for most birds. However, seeds run through a blender, and placed on feeding stations are unappealing and usually remain uneaten. Another example is spray millet. Spray millet is preferred, by many species of finches, over millet from a hopper. We have no evidence that millet on a spray tastes any better or is more nutritious. Yet, birds have a definite preference for it. Could it be that millet on a spray is preferred by the birds because of its more natural appearance?

Birds are opportunistic feeders, feeding on different foods at different times of the year. They will feed on whatever foods are available, assuming they are physically capable of consuming that food. Hummingbirds, for example, would not be able to take advantage of an abundant harvest of spray millet or a good supply of carrion (decaying flesh).

Sea gulls are a good example of an opportunistic feeder. They are capable of feeding on almost any food. Birds, such as sea gulls, who feed on both plants and animals, are called omnivorous. Birds who feed almost exclusively on plant foods, such as most parrots, are called herbivorous. Those birds that feed only on animals, such as the hawks, are called carnivorous.

Digestive system

The digestive system can be viewed as one long tube with an opening at one end, called the mouth, and an opening at the other, called the anus (Figure 13.4). This true digestive system has food going in one opening and waste products going out the other end. In between, a lot of digestion and absorption will, hopefully, take place. Not only does this system prevent food and waste products from mixing, it also allows for specialization within this long tube. For example, we could enlarge one area for storage (stomach), modify one area with a large surface area for absorption (small intestine), etc.

One more important point about this long modified tube. Any object which is inside of this tube is not really inside of the body. The object is actually in a "hole" (lumen) which passes down through the middle of the body from mouth to anus. In other words, if the food is not digested and absorbed, it won't enter the body. Instead, it will pass out through the anus, undigested in the fecal matter.

This is the situation when a small child swallows a marble or other small objects. Unable to digest or absorb the object, it will be passed in the fecal material a few days later. The point is, the bird must not only efficiently digest its food, but also absorb its food, if nutritional needs are to be met. Whole seeds in the droppings of a cage bird are usually an indication of a potentially serious problem. The bird for some reason is not digesting the seeds it is consuming.

Beak

Digestion must start with the intake of food. The most obvious structure involved is the beak. There are as many different beak shapes as there are food sources to be exploited (Figure 13.2). Over time, those birds with certain beak shapes will be able to exploit a particular food source most successfully.

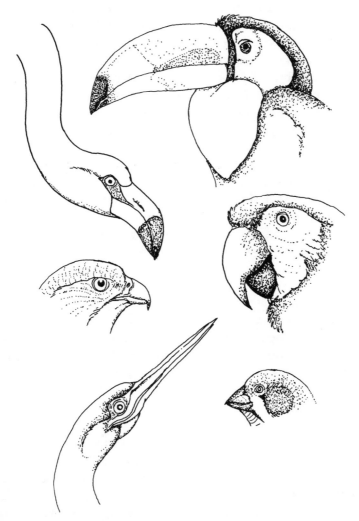

Figure 13.2   Variety of avian beak shapes.

Consuming a food source that others are unable or unwilling to use is a definite advantage. This new food source could eventually result in a larger population. Those birds in the population whose beak shape can best exploit the new food source will prevail. They will be successful in many ways, including breeding, where they pass on this beneficial beak shape to their offspring who then have an increased chance of survival. Over time, many beak types have been naturally selected to exploit a specific food source.

The beak is made from bone and is covered with keratin. Keratin is the same insoluble protein which gives strength to our finger nails and the nails of birds. Since bone is a living, dynamic organ, the beak continues to grow. Normally, edges of the beak are worn away at the same rate that new bone is formed. Therefore, the beak remains the same shape and size. For example, the beak of a budgie grows about three inches a year and it wears away at about three inches a year. There is a tremendous variation in the beak growth rate, depending on the species of bird and its diet.

If a budgie were not able to chew and rub its beak on hard chewable objects, the beak would most likely grow at a faster rate than it is being worn down. This overgrowth would be more severe if the bird were also fed a soft food diet. The beak will then need to be trimmed, or the bird will be unable to feed itself. This trimming should be done early in the overgrowth period, for if it is not, the bird may suffer permanent damage to the beak.

Tongue

The next digestive structure we encounter is the tongue. As mentioned earlier, the tongue can be quite long in some species, such as hummingbirds. Since the ability to taste is not very well developed in most birds, the tongue is probably not too important in food selection. However, it does play a role in the procurement, manipulation, and swallowing of food.

Salivary glands

Birds, like mammals, have salivary glands which produce saliva. The saliva, primarily made of water, has the protein mucin, which is used for lubrication during swallowing. The other important compound is an enzyme (amylase) used to begin the breakdown of starch. Starch is a major constituent of seeds. Some birds, such as the swifts, use their saliva as a cement in nest building. Birds, who use saliva as a cement, exhibit a tremendous increase in the size of their salivary glands during the nesting season.

Esophagus

The esophagus is a small tube running from the back of the throat to the crop. It is primarily a passageway for the movement of food and water into the crop. No digestive enzymes are secreted here, the only secretion being mucous for lubrication. At the base of the esophagus, in many birds, there is an outcropping appropriately called the crop.

Crop

The primary function of the crop, in most birds, is storage. There is a variation in crop size, depending on the species. It also differs in size, depending on the age of the bird. The crop allows birds to eat quite a bit of food in a short period of time. This allows the bird to return quickly to a safer area. The crop is also an important storage organ in baby birds (Figure 13.3). It is thin walled and very distensible, allowing the parents to pass on a lot of food in a short period of time. This allows the parents to return quickly to the field to obtain more food.

Figure 13.3   Avian crop can readily be seen in chick.

Proventriculus

Next is the stomach or in the case of birds, stomaches. Birds typically have two stomaches. The first is a glandular stomach (enzyme secreting) called the proventriculus and the second is a muscular stomach called the gizzard. The proventriculus, like the human stomach, secretes only a few enzymes. The primary enzyme is the protein digesting enzyme pepsin. In flesh eating predatory birds, the proventriculus tends to be the primary stomach. The gizzard is thin walled and weak.

Gizzard

In birds that feed on plant foods (herbivores), the gizzard is a very strong walled structure. The inner layer of the gizzard, in many species, secretes a keratinous material which forms hard ridges. These ridges are important in the grinding type of digestion found here. Many birds also swallow small rocks and pebbles which are also believed to aid digestion.

This brings us to a present controversy in aviculture. Is grit necessary, or even desirable? Not too many years ago, almost everyone in aviculture agreed that cage and aviary birds, parrots and finches, needed grit to digest seed. Then articles began to appear which stated that, not only was grit not necessary, but in some cases resulted in decreased breeding success.

The need for grit in birds who hull their seeds is certainly questionable. With the seed coat removed, the remaining seed softens up quickly in the digestive juices. It seems questionable that grit would aid this process. Many birds have been shown to live normal healthy lives without access to grit.

In birds that eat their seed whole, such as chickens, grit does indeed aid digestion. Experiments have shown that seed digestion in chickens was increased 10% when grit was available.

Some argue that since many birds are shown, at autopsy, to have small pebbles in their stomach, there must be some need for grit in the digestion of seed. Maybe. Many marine birds, such as cormorants and penguins, typically have gizzard stones. But, since they are primarily fish eaters, the stones are obviously not there to grind seed. They undoubtedly serve other purposes, which continue to elude us.

Some breeders claim that grit is, in some way, responsible for poor breeding results and an increase in the number of deformed young (creepers). More data needs to be collected to verify these claims. This does not imply that these claims are not valid, but rather that they alert us to the possibilities and the need for more research in this area.

The muscular gizzard in some species is truly phenomenal. A turkey gizzard can grind up 24 whole walnuts (shell and all) in 4 hours. One turkey was known to swallow and flatten a piece of tubing, which was shown to require a pressure of 80 PSI to flatten.

The gizzard, as well as the proventriculus, is not a static organ, but rather a dynamic organ. Experiments have shown that changes occur in the size and rigidity of the avian stomach when there is a change in diet. When some birds feed on seed, their gizzard is quite hard due to the rigid keratinous plates. But, when the diet changes to insects, the gizzard becomes smaller and softer.

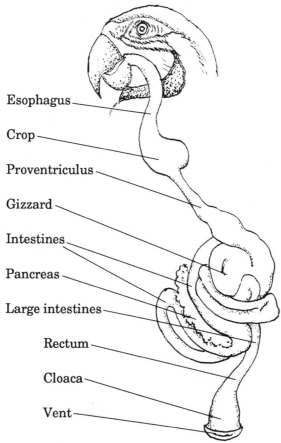

Esophagus
Crop
Proventriculus
Gizzard
Intestines
Pancreas
Large intestines
Rectum
Cloaca
Vent

Figure 13.4   Avian digestive system.

Intestines

When the partially digested food leaves the stomach, it enters the intestines. As in mammals, the intestines are the source of most of the digestive enzymes. Consequently, this is the area where most enzymatic digestion, and absorption take place. There are two reasons why most of the food is absorbed here. One, is that food in the stomach is not yet digested enough to be absorbed, this final process occurring in the intestines. Secondly, most food is absorbed here because of the tremendous surface area of the intestinal lining.

Three glands secrete digestive juices into the intestines. Intestinal glands which line the inner surface of the intestines secrete directly into the intestinal lumen. The pancreas secretes many digestive enzymes, via a duct, into the first part of the intestines. Finally, the liver secretes bile which aids in the digestive process, especially the digestion of fats.

Caeca

Most birds have one or two outcroppings called caeca. Caeca are found in the lower portion of the intestines. The caeca are quite large in ostriches and Gallinaceous birds, such as ducks, geese, and cranes. They serve as areas for the digestion of cellulose and the reabsorption of water.

The digestion of cellulose is worth noting. Cellulose is a long chain of glucose molecules found in plant cell walls. If the cellulose can be digested into glucose, the bird will gain more energy producing food. Otherwise, the undigested cellulose is lost in the fecal material. This is particularly important in herbivores, who normally ingest a lot of cellulose. The problem is that neither birds nor mammals can produce the enzyme cellulase, which breaks down the cellulose.

This is where the caeca are important, they provide "living space" for microorganisms that do produce cellulase. This symbiosis (living together) is found in many living organisms. The microorganisms benefit by having a warm place to live, with food readily provided. The bird benefits from this cellulase production, as well as from vitamins produced by the microorganisms. Neither seems to be affected negatively by this relationship.

When a broad spectrum antibiotic is given to birds, these beneficial microorganisms are usually destroyed. The destruction of the beneficial microorganisms is negative for two reasons. First, the positive benefits of having these normal microorganisms are temporarily lost. And secondly, the lack of these beneficial microorganisms opens the way for disease causing microorganisms to form colonies in the digestive system. Both of these are disadvantages to the host bird.

This is why doctors and veterinarians advise replacing the microorganisms with acidophilus or yogurt after antibiotics. The microorganisms in acidophilus and yogurt are not the same ones destroyed by the antibiotic. Yet, they seem to effectively out compete the harmful microorganisms, such as yeasts, at least until the normal bacterial flora can be restored.

Another important function of the caeca and the latter part of the intestines is the reabsorption of water. Water, consumed in both foods and by drinking, is absorbed in the stomach and the upper part of the intestines. However, many digestive gland secretions are mostly water. If this water is not reabsorbed, it will be lost in the feces resulting in dehydration.

Infections in the digestive tract often result in intestinal materials moving through intestines quite rapidly. This rapid movement causes decreased water reabsorption, resulting in a greater water loss in the feces. This extremely liquid feces is called diarrhea. Although diarrhea is more of a symptom than a disease, it can be very serious. Serious not only in terms of it being an indication of possible health problems, but also in terms of the increased water loss.

In birds, watery droppings don't always mean diarrhea. Unlike mammals, birds excrete their fecal material and urine from the same opening. Therefore, it is more difficult to distinguish between excessive water in the feces or in the urine. Although one should be concerned with diarrhea, watery droppings are not always a cause for concern.

Excess water in the urine can be the normal response to an excessive intake of water. For example, if a bird is eating a lot of watery fruit, the droppings will be wet. This is analogous to you drinking excess water and excreting the excess water. To be sure, there are cases where excess water in the urine is indicative of health problems. However, in many cases, excess water in the urine is simply caused by the excessive intake of water.

Droppings

As stated above, bird droppings contain two components. The first component is the fecal material, which represents undigestible and undesirable waste products being removed from the digestive system. Normal feces are tubular in shape and usually hold this form. The feces normal color ranges from light to dark green or brown, depending on the species and type of food eaten. Because birds don't have the same intestinal bacteria as mammals, the dropping don't have a strong odor.

Surrounding the feces is the urinary system discharge, the urine. To rid themselves of toxic nitrogenous compounds, birds excrete uric acid, rather than the urea found in the urine of mammals. Uric acid requires much less water for its removal. It is also less toxic and so can be stored longer (this is especially important in the egg). This urine discharge, containing primarily water and the urates, forms a white paste-like material.

Droppings can be an important diagnostic tool for your veterinarian. For this reason, the most recent droppings should be collected and taken to your veterinarian along with the ill bird. One way to collect droppings is to place plastic wrap or wax paper on the bottom of the cage, or under the perch if the bird is in an aviary. The paper will serve to collect and wrap the sample. It would also be beneficial to your veterinarian to have an idea of the frequency of droppings. This information should also include whether there have been any changes in the contents or frequency of the droppings.

Figure 13.5 Normal droppings.

Cloaca

The final area of this long, highly modified tube is called the cloaca, which is divided into three areas. The first area receives the waste products (feces) from the digestive system above. The middle area receives the waste products (urine) from the urinary system. It also receives the sperm cells or ova from the genitals.

The last, and the largest, of these three cloacal areas, stores the waste materials mentioned above. They are stored here until a suitable place can be found to dispose of them. This last area of the cloaca posesses strong ejector muscles for expelling the waste. Baby hummingbirds are noted for moving their bottoms up over the edge of the nest and "shooting" the fecal material out with surprising velocity. Some nestlings expel their fecal material in membranous sacs called fecal sacs (Figure 3.9).

Birds have excellent control over fecal expulsion. Nesting birds can accumulate large amount of fecal material, which they expel shortly after leaving the nest. Some people claim to have even "toilet trained" their parrots to expel fecal material only in certain places. Given the somewhat predictability of fecal expulsion, the intelligence of some parrots, and a good positive reward system, this does seem possible.

Birds with large caeca, such as chickens, not only discharge waste material from the cloaca, but also discharge waste from the caeca. In the chicken, there is one caecal discharge for approximately every 10 cloacal discharges. Parrots and finches don't have large caeca and therefore do not exhibit these caecal discharges.

Liver

The liver of birds is composed of many lobes, making it quite large. Only a few species have an accompanying gall bladder. The primary digestive function of the liver is the production of bile.

Very little research has been done on the bile of most species of birds. What research that has been done indicates that many of the functions are similar to those of mammalian bile. One function is the production and secretion of bile salts. Bile salts are important in the digestion and absorption of fats, which includes the absorption of fat (lipid) soluble vitamins.

Another bile function is to act as a vehicle for the excretion of bilirubin. Bilirubin results from the breakdown of old hemoglobin. High levels of bilirubin result in the yellow jaundiced look. Jaundice is not usually a disease, but rather a symptom of some disease relating to the buildup of bilirubin.

For example, a high red blood cell destruction rate would result in elevated bilirubin. More commonly, damage to the liver results in a decrease in the liver's ability to excrete bilirubin. This often results in an elevated bilirubin level.

Other functions of the liver include the production of some important proteins, such as those involved in blood clotting. The liver also plays a role in the production of cholesterol. In spite of its poor reputation, cholesterol in birds, as in mammals, is a very important compound. It is the compound from which many other important compounds, such as steroid hormones and bile salts are formed. The liver is also an important blood filter. It is quite effective at removing toxic substances from the blood.

Because so many diseases affect the liver, changes in it are diagnostically important. For example, the disease Psittacosis results in an enlarged, fragile liver with yellow discoloration and rounded edges, among other changes.

14   **Nutrition**

Introduction

Writing a chapter on nutrition is a most difficult task. Difficult not so much because the subject itself is difficult, but because there has been so little research done on the nutrition requirements of most bird species. At this time, the chicken has been the bird with enough commercial value to receive most avian nutritional research money. Universities, such as the University of California, Davis, have done some research, but they are limited by the minimal funds available to them.

Therefore, almost everything written in this chapter will be based on research done on chickens, some parrots and mammals, including humans. There is no doubt that the nutritional requirements of the different species of birds differ from one another. Unfortunately, we have too little data indicating what these differences might be.

For some reason, many people treat all seed eating birds as though they all have the same nutritional requirements. If we were to apply this same thought process to mammals, we would feed dogs, cats, and apes the exact same diet. Research has shown that there are similarities in the nutritional requirements of these three mammals. Yet, each has its own individual nutritional requirements and therefore requires a different diet. This is undoubtedly true with the different bird species as well.

With these limitations in mind, we will take a look at nutrition as we presently understand it. We hope that much of what we know is applicable to the various bird species. The diets that we feed avicultural birds are undoubtedly adequate, as evidenced by the fact that these birds are thriving and breeding.

However, more research would identify which specific components of these diets provide the necessary nutrition. Then we would be better prepared to provide the necessary nutrition for the various avian species. Unfortunately, we have not identified many of these specific avian nutritional requirements. Thus, we continue to feed birds a varied diet, hoping to provide the nutrients necessary for the various species. This chapter will explain the basics of what we do know about vertebrate nutrition.

Nutrition

The word nutrient refers to those substances which the organism needs for maximal health but cannot produce, or cannot produce in adequate amounts, for its own needs. Water is an example of this. During some metabolic processes water is produced, but not enough water is produced to sustain the organism. Therefore, the organism must get water from an outside source. Therefore, water should be considered a nutrient. We don't usually think of water as a nutrient, probably because it is so readily available.

Water

For cage and aviary birds, water is rarely limited. However, fresh, clean cool water may be. It is important that birds have fresh, clean water daily. The containers for this water should also be clean and sanitary. To avoid heating up the water, the containers should be placed in a area which is not exposed to sunlight.

Figure 14.1 Dove at a water hole.

One southern California breeder was known to tell his workers "if you won't drink out of the container, don't expect my bird to." This may seem a bit much, but many people are much too casual about cleaning the water containers. One often sees water containers lined with green algae. The algae is not usually a health threat to the birds, but its presence can indicate how often the water container is being cleaned.

The water supply to the home is treated with chloramines and chlorine and therefore is rarely contaminated. However, the water delivery system in the aviary is a potential source of problems. This is especially true where old hoses or self-watering systems are used. While these systems are a definite benefit to the aviculturist, they provide a conduit for spreading contaminants. This is especially true in systems that have been in place for many years.

Running nutrients through these self watering systems greatly accentuates this problem. While this is an efficient way to get water soluble nutrients to the birds, it is also provides nutrients for the growth of microorganisms such as bacteria. Without proper monitoring this method of delivering nutrients could be deadly.

Adding supplemental nutrients to the water container is an acceptable way to provide these nutrients for the birds. The nutrients in the water will provide additional nutritional benefits to the birds, but these nutrients will also will be a stimulus for the growth of microorganisms in the container. Because of this growth, you will need to wash the water container more frequently to avoid contamination.

Organic materials

The major organic materials necessary for normal health and growth in birds, as in mammals, are the carbohydrates, amino acids (protein), lipids (fats), and vitamins. The fifth type of organic matter, the nucleic acids (chromosomes) will be discussed in the chapter on heredity.

Carbohydrates

Birds, like mammals, use carbohydrates almost exclusively as an energy source. Because carbohydrates are used for energy, rather than being incorporated into organic materials, they are sometimes referred to as "empty calories." This is a real misnomer since energy is very important in the formation of compounds.

For example, energy is as necessary in the formation of a protein, as are the amino acids which make it up. Probably, the main reason that we refer to carbohydrates as "empty calories" is that we consume too many of them. One then wonders what a "full calorie" would be. Maybe an examination of what a calorie is, will help answer this question.

Calorie

Many people mistakenly think that a calorie is a component of food similar to carbohydrates, proteins, and lipids. It is not. Instead, a calorie is a unit used to measure energy, analogous to using degrees as a measurement of heat energy. When you drink coffee that is at 110 degrees, you are not drinking degrees, but rather coffee at a certain temperature (energy) level.

A calorie is not a thing (matter), but a unit measuring the energy level of compounds. When you eat a food containing 90 calories, you are not really eating calories. Instead you are eating a certain amount of a food, which when metabolized will release a certain amount of energy, measured in calories. This energy can then be used to "power" all of the body functions which require energy.

It is obvious that energy is just as important as any vitamin or any of the other nutrients. The problem with most calories is not so much that they are "empty," but that we usually consume more energy than we utilize at one time. This additional energy intake, unfortunately, is efficiently stored for later use, as fat.

Monosaccharides

There are many forms of carbohydrates. The carbohydrates that we will discuss here are those that are made of six carbon atoms, or multiples of six carbon atoms. These six carbon sugars are called monosaccharides. The "saccharide" refers to the six carbon sugar unit. "Mono," "di" and "poly" refer to the number of these six carbon units in the carbohydrate. For example a "mono" (one) "saccharide" is a carbohydrate with only six carbons and is therefore called a simple sugar.

There are three common simple sugars (monosaccharides). They are glucose (dextrose), fructose (levulose), and galactose. To be absorbed from the digestive tract, all carbohydrates must be in the form of simple sugars, otherwise they are too large to enter the blood. Regardless of the form in which the simple sugar is ingested, almost all ot them end up as glucose. In other words, if you take in fructose and galactose they will be converted by the liver to glucose. Glucose is the main circulating blood sugar of birds, as well as mammals.

glucose   **fructose**   **galactose**

Figure 14.2   Symbols which will be used in this chapter to
represent monosaccharides.

Disaccharides

If we take two of these monosaccharides and bond them together, we produce what is called a disaccharide. There are three common disaccharides. Sucrose, called table sugar, is the most common. It results from combining one glucose molecule with one fructose molecule. Sucrose is produced primarily by sugar cane and sugar beets. Regardless of its source, sucrose is the same whether produced by the sugar cane or sugar beets. Nor does color matter. Sucrose is sucrose whether it is in white table sugar or brown sugar or any other color for that matter.

Table 14.1   Disaccharides and their components. Symbols represent
the monosaccharides and the line between them a bond.

Common name	Source	Components	Disaccharide
table sugar	beet or cane	glucose + fructose	sucrose
malt sugar	starch	glucose + glucose	maltose
milk sugar	milk	glucose + galactose	lactose

Sucrose has developed a bad reputation in recent years, because of the role it plays in tooth decay and the fact that it provides those nasty "empty calories." Other than its obvious association with tooth decay, there is nothing intrinsically bad about sucrose. Its most damning characteristic is that because it tastes so good, we consume too much of it.

Its other limitation is that in table sugar form, it does not provide any other nutrients. This is not good, but does not make sucrose intrinsically bad. Brown sugar does provide some nutrients along with the sucrose. However, if we had to depend on brown sugar for any of our nutritional requirements, we would not survive.

The same is true for honey. We can get our glucose and fructose in honey in a more "natural" form. Sucrose is just as natural. It is also stated that honey contains nutrients not found in table sugar. Very true, but the nutrients found in honey are in such low concentrations as to be inconsequential to health. Honey has also been found to contain spores of the infection causing molds in the genus *Aspergillus*. These molds have been a problem in the feeding of honey water to hummingbirds.

The next disaccharide is maltose. Maltose consists of two glucose molecules bonded together. It is formed primarily in the breakdown of starch which is a long chain of glucose molecules. If you break starch apart, two glucose units at a time, you will produce maltose. This typically occurs when a germinating seed, in need of energy, is breaking down the stored starch to glucose.

The third disaccharide is lactose, the sugar found in milk. It is formed by combining one glucose molecule with one galactose molecule. Lactose is produced primarily by nursing mammals for consumption by their young. After weaning, mammals rarely consume lactose in their diet. The exceptions are man and pets of man, mainly cats and dogs.

Although milk is an excellent food, many adults don't produce enough of the enzyme lactase to breakdown the lactose. The result is a problem called "lactose intolerance." Young birds in the wild never consume lactose. Therefore, they would not be expected to produce the enzyme lactase. Will birds develop a "lactose intolerance" if fed milk?

Sturkie in *Avian Physiology* discusses studies showing both lactose and galactose problems in the birds studied. "Feeding diets varying in quantities of the disaccharide lactose, as well as of the pentoses l-arabonose or d-xylose to chickens, results in marked depression of growth, diarrhea, reduced egg production and feed efficiency, retardation of liver and intestine size and cellularity, and depletion of liver and skeletal muscle glycogen levels."

With regard to galactose he states, "Dietary levels of galactose below 10% are innocuous, physiologically, in domestic fowl; above 10% dietary galactose induces a central nervous system disorder characterized by epileptiform convulsions." Aviculturists using milk, as one of the components of a handfeeding formula, many want to note these potential dangers.

Polysaccharide

If we take many of these glucose molecules and bond them together, we form the third major group of carbohydrates called the polysaccharides. "Poly" is the Greek word for many and "saccharide" refers to the six carbon unit, so the polysaccharides says, many six carbon units. All polysaccharides are chains of glucose. There are four common polysaccharides: starch, glycogen, cellulose and chitin.

Starch is a long chain of glucose produced by plants. During the day, and long summer months, plants use energy from the sun in a process called photosynthesis. One of the main products of photosynthesis is the energy bearing compound, glucose. To store much of this glucose for future use, the glucose is bonded in long chains to form starch.

Glycogen is also a long chain of glucose. It is the way most animals store glucose for later use. Therefore, glycogen could be called "animal starch," because of the similarities. Most glycogen is stored in the liver and muscles, which have a limited amount of storage space. Once these glycogen reserves are full, the excess glucose is converted to fat and stored in adipose (fat) cells.

Cellulose is another polysaccharide of plant origin. It is a long chain of glucose similar to starch. The cellulose bonding is different, and requires a different enzyme (cellulase) to break it down. This enzyme, discussed in the chapter on digestion, is not produced by birds or mammals. Therefore, if birds are to obtain any glucose from cellulose, they must depend on microorganisms in their digestive system to digest it for them.

As stated earlier it does not matter whether the ingested sugar is fructose, galactose, sucrose, maltose, lactose, starch, glycogen or cellulose, the ultimate end product will be glucose. It is glucose that birds use as the energy source for most of their reactions. Glucose in long chains called glycogen is the carbohydrate stored by the bird for later use.

If a bird is not eating, the blood glucose level will drop, and the bird becomes weak. Weak birds are often unable to eat and will surely die if steps are not taken to increase glucose quickly. Tube feeding is one way to save a weak bird, but many aviculturists are reluctant to perform this procedure.

Another possibility for raising the glucose level is to give the bird some water with glucose in it. Since honey is high in glucose, a little honey water will help. Or, one of the "thirst aid" drinks on the market may help. Be sure to read the label to make sure it contains glucose instead of sucrose. It takes time to digest sucrose to the simple sugars glucose and fructose. A weak bird may not be able to afford the time required for this breakdown to occur. Of course, one does not want to forget to give attention to the problem (illness, etc.) that caused the weakness in the first place. The glucose will, hopefully, build up the bird's strength until a diagnosis of the problem is ascertained.

Anytime something is placed in the mouth of a bird, care must be taken. The bird is generally unaware that we are going to place a liquid in its mouth and will continue breathing as usual. If you place water in the back of the mouth, the bird will likely aspirate (breath into the lungs) the water. This could result in death. The best technique is to place a small amount of the liquid in the front portion of the beak area. Then wait, allowing the bird to swallow on its own. Much of the liquid will be lost this way but it is a safer method.

What are some good sources of carbohydrates for healthy birds? Fruits are good sources of simple sugars. While almost all foods have some carbohydrates in them, the grass and grain seeds are a good source of starch. Table 14.2 lists the seeds high in starch.

Table 14.2 Table of Starch (carbohydrate) seeds.

White millet	Oats	Corn
Yellow millet	Wheat	Rice
Spray millet	Buckwheat	
Canary	Milo	

Proteins

The second major group of organic materials is the proteins, which form many important compounds. Examples of these protein compounds can be seen in Table 14.3. Proteins make up approximately 20 to 25% of the total organic matter of the bird. The protein found in the birds feathers make up almost one-third of all the protein found in the bird's entire body.

It goes without saying that the ability to produce all necessary protein is critical to the health of birds. It's not the actual dietary proteins themselves which are so important, but rather the amino acids of which they are composed. Amino acids are used by birds to form their own protein compounds, which are determined by the genetic material.

Table 14.3   Important compounds made of protein.

Compound	Function
enzymes	speed up chemical reactions
hemoglobin	carry oxygen
antibodies	fight disease
hormones	chemical messengers
keratin	component of feathers, nails, beak
actin & myosin	contractile proteins of muscle
structural protein	component of all cell membranes
collagen	holds cells together, gives strength to ligaments & tendons

Amino acids

In birds, as in mammals, proteins consumed in the diet are too large to be absorbed through the digestive wall into the blood. They must first be digested into their individual components, the amino acids. Amino acids are small enough to be absorbed throught the wall. For example, let's look at a bird consuming some protein keratin in its diet. The bird will have to digest the keratin into the individual amino acids, before they can be absorbed.

This seems like a very inefficient system, since the bird needs keratin for its beak, feathers and nails. Why not absorb the keratin and reuse it? This would be very efficient, but it is not possible because the proteins in the diet are too large to be absorbed.

Consider one disadvantage of the direct use of ingested proteins. We would literally be what we eat. If this were the case, most people would look more like a cow than a human, given the amount of beef in the human diet. Adding some beef muscle to our body doesn't sound too bad, but who wants to look like a tomato? In spite of the popular phrase, we are not what we eat, nor are birds.

Again, it is not the proteins in the diet which are important, but rather the amino acids they contain. These amino acids will then be utilized by the birds to form their own proteins. There are over 20 different amino acids commonly found in protein (See Table 14.4). Every living thing, from microorganisms to whales, from algae to the largest trees, uses these same amino acids, but in different amounts and sequences.

Table 14.4   Amino acids commonly found in nature.

Alanine	Threonine	Glycine
Histidine	Tryptophan	Hydroxylysine
Isoleucine	Valine	Hydroxyproline
Leucine	Alanine	Proline
Lysine	Aspartic acid	Serine
Methionine	Cystine	Tyrosine
Phenylalanine	Glutamic acid	

If all organisms use the same amino acids, why then do we look so different? It is the different combinations of ways (sequence) these amino acids are put together that determines the individual look of each species. And, it is the slight differences in these sequences that determines the uniqueness of each individual within the species.

To understand how so many different proteins can be produced from a pool of only 20 amino acids, we need only to look as far as the alphabet. Using only 26 letters we can produce an almost infinite number of words. Specifically, using 20 different amino acids to produce proteins which are only six amino acids long would result in 64,000,000 different proteins. Most proteins are 100 amino acids in length or longer.

Non-essential amino acids

Amino acids have been divided into two groups. One group, the non-essential amino acids, are those amino acids that birds can synthesize for themselves. These amino acids are called non-essential amino acids because they are non-essential in the diet, not because they are non-essential in protein synthesis.

Essential amino acids

The second group, the essential amino acids, are those amino acids that birds cannot synthesize and therefore must get in the diet (Table 14.5). Because of the dependence on external sources for getting essential amino acids, they are often the limiting factors in protein synthesis. Since the non-essential amino acids are synthesized by birds, they are rarely a limiting factor in protein synthesis.

Table 14.5 Essential amino acids.

Known to be required for all species of higher animals.

Isoleucine	Phenylalanine
Leucine	Threonine
Lysine	Tryptophan
Methionine	Valine

Required for growth of many avian species.

Histidine	Arginine

May be required* during rapid growth or injury repair.

Cystine	Tyrosine
Glycine	Proline

*There is some disagreement here.

Complete proteins

The avian diet should contain foods which make available all the essential amino acids. There are foods, called "complete proteins," which contain all of the essential amino acids in them. All these "complete proteins" are of animal origin, such as milk and eggs. If milk and eggs are being fed, one could be assured that the birds are getting all the essential amino acids. However, it is not practical to feed birds milk. And, as an earlier discussion suggests (see lactose), this may be harmful in some ways.

It is obvious that the egg is a complete protein for birds. The developing chick grows from one cell to a hatchling, using only the essential amino acids stored in the egg. Actually, the only compound necessary for growth, that is not in the egg, is oxygen. Many aviculturists feed hard boiled egg to their birds with good success. One must be cautious, however, to feed only the amount of egg that will be consumed in a short period of time, since the egg will spoil quickly.

Most birds eat foods of plant origin. There are very few plant species which have adequate levels of all the different essential amino acids. Therefore, a variety of plant foods must be eaten to achieve the essential amino acid requirements.

For example, common millet, *Panicum miliaceum*, is low in tryptophan and spray millet, *Setaria italica*, is low in arginine. Canary seed, *Phalaris canariensis*, is low in methionine, but is a good source of arginine and histidine. Therefore, canary seed and millet seeds complement each other in these amino acid deficiencies.

Wheat is low in lysine, whereas corn is low in tryptophan. By consuming both in the diet, tryptophan can be obtained from the wheat and lysine can be obtained from the corn. Each makes up for the deficiency of the other.

The "oil seeds" such as, sunflower, niger, rape, flax, etc. have a higher protein content than the "starch seeds" such as, millet, canary and grain seeds. Safflower and sunflower seeds are a good source of essential amino acids, as well as some minerals and vitamins. Unfortunately, some birds have a decided preference for sunflower seeds and will eat them to the exclusion of other seeds. The result is a lack of nutritional variety in their diet, and a propensity to get fat.

Table 14.6 shows a comparison of the nutritional constituents of sunflower and safflower seeds. The comparisons are based on the data that is available. There is no evidence that safflower seeds are nutritionally better than sunflower seeds. In fact, sunflower seeds are nutritionally superior to safflower in all categories. The essential amino acid levels are significantly higher as are vitamins, calcium, and the essential fatty acid, linoleic acid.

However, the total fat content in sunflower seeds is 28.8% higher than in safflower seeds. Since birds tend to overeat sunflower seeds, it should be somewhat limited, to prevent obesity. Birds don't have the propensity to overeat safflower seeds (maybe because of the bitter taste!).

In spite of information circulated by some aviculturists in recent years, there is no evidence at this time to indicate that sunflower seed contain a narcotic causing addiction in birds. For this reason, there is no basis for excluding sunflower seed from a good seed mix. There is basis for decreasing the amount of sunflower seed in the mix, but to eliminate it altogether means the loss of a reasonably nutritious seed.

Table 14.6   Nutritional comparison of safflower and sunflower seeds.
(Amount in 100 grams, edible portion {dried})*

Nutrient	Safflower	Sunflower
Food energy	517.0 Calories	570.0 Calorie
Total fat	38.5 grams	49.6 grams
Total carbohydrate	34.3 grams	18.8 grams
Total protein	16.2 grams	22.8 grams
Essential amino acids:		
Tryptophan	183.0 mg	348.0 mg
Leucine	1,154.0 mg	1,659.0 mg
Lysine	534.0 mg	937.0 mg
Methionine	284.0 mg	494.0 mg
Phenylalanine	806.0 mg	1,169.0 mg
Isoleucine	717.0 mg	1,139.0 mg
Valine	1,025.0 mg	1,315.0 mg
Threonine	586.0 mg	928.0 mg
Saturated fats and unsaturated fatty acids:		
Saturated fats	3.7 grams	5.2 grams
Oleic acid	4.8 grams	9.4 grams
Linoleic acid	28.1 grams	32.6 grams
Linolenic acid	0.11 grams	0.07 grams
Selected vitamins:		
Thiamine	1.2 mg	2.3 mg
Riboflavin	0.4 mg	0.25 mg
Niacin	2.3 mg	4.5 mg
Selected minerals:		
Calcium	78.0 mg	116.0 mg
Phosphorus	644.0 mg	705.0 mg

Sources: Handbook of the Nutritional Contents of Foods,
U.S. Dept. of Agriculture Handbook #8-12. Composition
of Foods: Nut & Seed Products. 1984.

Maximal health depends on a daily intake of these essential amino acids, since very few of them are stored. If any one of these essential amino acids is absent, the proteins containing them could not be produced (synthesized) at that time.

An analogy would be, trying to write a letter without using the letter "e". Almost impossible. And, getting to use the "e" tomorrow, won't do you any good, if tomorrow you cannot use the letter "i". To write you must have every letter every day. The same thing is true for the essential amino acids. If the birds are to make all of the important proteins listed in Table 14.3, then they must have all the essential amino acids every day.

The stimulus for the production of these important proteins comes, not from the availability of these amino acids, but rather from a need for that particular protein. For example, the stimulus for producing more of the oxygen-carrying hemoglobin comes from tissue hypoxia (low oxygen). Eating excessive amounts of amino acids won't stimulate the production of more hemoglobin. The only way to stimulate more hemoglobin is to create some tissue hypoxia, by performing some form of exercise, or going to high altitudes, etc.

The point is, that increasing your amino acid intake will not, in itself, increase your protein synthesis. You don't increase your muscle proteins by eating more protein (amino acids), but rather you increase your muscle proteins by exercise. A deficiency of amino acids could decrease the synthesis of muscle proteins, but it does not go the other way. Again, an increase in amino acid levels above normal will not, by itself, increase muscle protein synthesis.

Lipids

The third group of organic materials to be considered here is the lipids. The lipids can be placed into three categories:

Triglycerides - energy storage (stored in fat cells).

Phospholipids - structural component of the cell membranes.

Steroids - functional lipids such as hydrocortisone,
testosterone, estrogen, etc.

Triglycerides

The triglycerides, also called neutral fats, are made up of four components. One is a small compound called glycerol. The other three are called fatty acids. We categorize fatty acids into two categories, the saturated and the unsaturated. The saturated fatty acids are typically found in animal tissues and are usually a semi-solid. The fat on a pork chop is a good example of a saturated fat. Unsaturated fatty acids are typically found in plants and are usually liquid. Corn oil is a good example of this (Table 14.7).

Table 14.7 List of saturated and unsaturated fatty acids.

Saturated fatty acids	Unsaturated fatty acids
Lauric acid	Palmitoleic acid
Palmitic acid	Oleic
Stearic acid	Linoleic acid
Arachidic acid	Linolenic acid
	Arachidonic acid

Essential fatty acids

Essential fatty acids (EFA) are those fatty acids which are necessary for the normal growth and metabolism of the bird but cannot be synthesized. The unsaturated fatty acids linoleic and arachidonic are both essential fatty acids in birds. Therefore, they must be acquired in the diet.

Table 4 shows that both safflower and sunflower seeds are a good source of linoleic acid. Since birds can convert linoleic to arachidonic, the only fatty acid that birds must get in their diet is linoleic. Deficiencies in linoleic have been shown to produce smaller eggs in hens, and decreased fertile capacity in males. The "oil seeds" mentioned earlier are, in general, good sources of linoleic acids (Table 14.8).

Table 14.8 Table of seeds high in oil.

Sunflower	Rape	Sesame
Safflower	Flax	Hemp
Peanuts	Poppy	

Phospholipids

Phospholipids are compounds similar to triglyceride in that they are made up of glycerol and fatty acids. However, unlike the triglycerides which have three fatty acids, the phospholipids have only two fatty acids. The third position contains choline and phosphate instead of the fatty acid. The significance of choline and phosphate is that they cause the phospholipid to become polarized. The polarized phospholipids are important structural components of the cell membrane.

Steroids

As we have seen, the triglycerides represent energy storage and the phospholipids represent structural lipids. The steroids, on the other hand, represent functional lipids (Table 14.9). The common denominator of all steroids is that they are all produced from cholesterol.

Cholesterol has gotten a bad name in recent years, but in fact it is an essential compound. Cholesterol is needed as the begining compound (precursor) for the synthesis of the steroids listed in Table 14.9. It is also an important structural component in the formation of the cell membrane. As you would guess, a compound of such importance is synthesized by the bird, specifically in the liver.

Table 14.9　Steroids

Steroid name	Steroid function
Cholesterol	Precursor for other steroids.
Bile acids (salts)	Digestion of lipids. Absorption of lipid-soluble vitamins.
Estrogen	Female sex hormone.
Progesterone	Female sex hormone.
Testosterone	Male sex hormone.
Cortisone	Important during physical stress. Stimulates healing.
Aldosterone	Regulates sodium and potassium.

Minerals

Although all minerals are a link in the chain of health, calcium is undoubtedly the most important link in that chain. Calcium has many essential functions as indicated in Table 14.10).

Table 14.10   Functions in which Calcium is essential.

Formation of bones
Contraction of muscles
Transmission of nerve impulses
Blood clotting
Egg shell formation

Unfortunately, seeds are not a good source of calcium. Therefore, birds must get their calcium in other ways, such as, in foods like leafy green vegetables or in supplementation. Table 14.11 lists some forms of calcium supplements:

Table 14.11   Calcium supplement sources.

Cuttlebone
Calcium blocks
Crushed chicken egg shells (sterilized)
Crushed oyster shells
Powder supplements

There are many other minerals that are important to the health of birds. No mineral can be synthesized by the body and so all minerals must be obtained in the diet. Minerals are placed in two nutritional categories. Major minerals are those which the organism needs a large amount of. The trace minerals, on the other hand, are needed in small amounts, but are just as important to health as are the major minerals. Table 14.12 lists these minerals and some good sources for them.

Table 14.12   Major minerals.

Mineral	Functions	Sources
Phosphorus	Important structural component of bone. Important in most metabolic reactions.	Nuts, whole grains, cereals, milk legumes.
Potassium	Important in nerve con-, duction, muscle contraction. Maintain osmotic pressure in cell.	Avocados, dried apricots, nuts, potatoes, banana.
Sodium	Important in nerve conduction, muscle contraction. Maintain osmotic pressure outside of cell.	Table salt, salted foods, salt blocks.
Sulfur	Essential part of some amino acids, and other important organic materials.	Meats, milk, eggs, legumes.
Chlorine	Important in maintaining osmotic pressure outside of cells. Important in pH.	Same as sodium.
Magnesium	Abundant in bones. Needed in many metabolic reactions.	Dairy products, legumes, nuts, leafy greens.

In addition to needing relatively large amounts of these major minerals, birds also need what are called trace minerals. These trace minerals are just as important as the major minerals, but the amounts needed for metabolism are much less. Table 14.13 lists these trace minerals and gives some of the sources for each.

Table 14.13   Trace Minerals.

Trace mineral	Function	Sources
Iron	Part of hemoglobin. Important in the release of energy.	Liver, lean meats, rasins, apricots, legumes enriched whole grains.
Manganese	Important in the formation of fatty acids and cholesterol.	Nuts, legumes, whole grains, leafy greens & fruits.
Copper	Important in forming bone, hemoglobin, melanin and myelin.	Nuts, whole grains, legumes.
Iodine	Essential component of thyroid hormones.	Iodized table salt, amount varies in food & water, depending on geographical location.
Cobalt	Component of cyano-cobalamin. Involved in enzyme synthesis.	Found primarily in animal products.
Zinc	Constituent of enzymes involved in digestion, respiration, bone & liver metabolism. Important in healing.	Seafoods, meats, cereals, legumes, nuts, vegetables.

None of the minerals, major or trace, can be formed or synthesized by the body. The only source of minerals is the diet, or from the release of minerals when old body cells die and rupture. There is no scientific evidence that the cells can take one mineral and convert it to another.

A good varied diet will provide these minerals. There are powder supplements, which will provide the birds with more of these minerals during times of stress. These supplements are also important when a varied diet is not possible, such as in the case of birds who eat only one food (i.e. sunflower seeds). Trace mineral salt blocks are also good means of supplementation.

Vitamins

The last nutritional group that we will consider are the vitamins. Early in nutritional research it was discovered that a group of compounds, called amines, were essential for normal health. These were called "vital amines." Later research showed that not all of these essential compounds were amines. The name was then contracted to the present term, vitamins.

For humans and other mammals, vitamins are organic compounds needed to assist in various chemical reactions in the body. What sets these compounds apart, from other assisting compounds in the body, is the fact that we cannot produce them. So, vitamins are organic compounds which assist chemical reactions, but cannot be synthesized by the body.

Vitamins are typically made by plants for their own metabolism. Since the plant can produce the vitamins, they don't fit the definition, "cannot be made by the body." Therefore a vitamin, although essential to the plant, is not really a vitamin to the plant.

How many of these "human vitamins" can birds produce, and how many are required in their diet? No doubt birds use the same vitamins that man uses. The question is, which ones can they produce? There is evidence that some birds can produce vitamin C. Again, we face the problem of very little research. The safest thing, for an aviculturist, is to assume that the birds do need the same vitamins and then to provide a diet that will make these vitamins available.

Lipid soluble vitamins

Vitamins are classed into two groups depending on whether they are water soluble or lipid (fat) soluble. Vitamins A, D, E, & K are fat (lipid) soluble. Being lipid soluble means that these vitamins can be stored in the fatty tissues. This is quite positive, because, over a period of time, the bird will store a reserve of these lipid soluble vitamins. The negative side of storing the lipid soluble vitamins is that they can then reach toxic levels. For sources of these lipid soluble vitamins see Table 14.14.

Table 14.14 Lipid soluble vitamins.

Vitamin	Characteristics	Functions	Sources
A	Synthesized from carotenes, stored in liver; stable in heat, acids and alkalis; unstable in light.	Synthesis of visual pigments; normal bone development.	Fish liver oils, milk, eggs, green leafy vegetables, yellow & orange fruits & vege- tables.
D-3	Resistant to heat, oxidation, acids, alkali; stored in liver, skin, brain spleen & bones.	Promotes absorp- tion of calcium and phosphorus.	Produced in skin that's exposed to UV light; egg yolk fish liver & oils.
E	Resistant to heat and visible light; unstable in oxygen &UV light; stored in muscles and fat.	Prevents oxidation of vitamin A and polyunsaturated fatty acids.	Cereal seed oils; salad oils, fruits; vegetables.
K	Occurs in different forms; resistant to heat but destroyed by acids, alkali and light; stored in liver.	Required by the liver to synthesize blood clotting agent prothrombin.	Leafy green vegetables, egg yolk, soy oil, tomatoes, cauliflower.

Lipid soluble vitamins require fats in the diet to assist their absorption from the digestive system into the blood. If the diet were completely deficient of fats, the lipid soluble vitamins would not be absorbed. This would result in a deficiency of these vitamins.

Feeding high levels of vitamins to birds is not beneficial. Some avicultur- ist claim that supplementation of vitamin E increases their breeding suc- cess. This would be true only if the bird was deficient in vitamin E to begin with. Increasing the vitamin levels above the normal storage levels does no good, and in time could kill the birds due to toxicity.

There is a lot of controversy about vitamin supplementation in both human health and bird health. If a bird is vitamin deficient, then additional vitamins will be beneficial. However, the addition of vitamins above the normal level, imparts no nutritional or health benefit to the bird. As an analogy, putting twice as much gasoline in your car won't make it run any better or faster, but it won't run without it.

Water soluble vitamins

The other group of vitamins are the water soluble vitamins, represented by vitamin C and the B complex vitamins. These vitamins, being water soluble, are not stored. Therefore, the regular intake of these vitamins is essential. The positive side of not being able to store water soluble vitamins is that it is much harder to reach toxic levels. So, the health of birds is threatened less by overzealous vitamin supplementers. For the sources of water soluble vitamins see Table 14.15.

Table 14.15   Water soluble vitamins.

Vitamin	Characteristics	Functions	Sources
Thiamine (B-1)	Destroyed by heat and oxygen.	Coenzyme in oxidation of glucose and in synthesis of ribose.	Liver, eggs, whole grains,, vegetables, legumes.
Riboflavin (B-2)	Stable to heat, acids & oxidation; destroyed by heat & light.	Coenzyme for oxidation of glucose and fatty acids.	Dairy products, leafy green vegetables, whole grain cereals.
Niacin (Nicotinic Acid)	Stable to heat, acids & alkalis; converted to niacinamide; made from tryptophan.	Coenzyme for oxi-oxidation of glucose & synthesis of pro-, teins, fats, nucleic acids.	Liver, lean, meats, poultry peanuts, corn, whole grains.
Pyridoxine (B-6)	Group of three compounds; stable to heat and acids; destroyed by oxi-, dation, alkalis, and UV light.	Coenzyme for synthesis of many amino acids, for converting typytophan to niacin, for production of antibodies & nucleic acids.	Bananas, avocados, beans, peanuts, whole grain cereals, egg yolk.
Cyano-cobalamin (B-12)	Cobalt-containing; Stable to heat; Inactivated by light, strong acids and alkalis; stored in liver.	Coenzyme in synthesis of nucleic acids and metabolism of carbohydrates; plays a role in rbc production.	All plants are low in this vitamin; eggs, insects and vitamin supplements.

Table 14.15   Water soluble vitamins. (Cont)

Vitamin	Characteristics	Functions	Sources
Panto-thenic Acid	Destroyed by heat, acids and alkali.	Coenzyme for oxidation of carbohydrates & fats.	Whole grains, legumes, fruits, vegetables.
Folic acid	Occurs in several forms; destroyed by oxidation in acidity or by heat or in alkalinity; stored in liver.	Coenzyme in metabolism of some amino acids and for synthesis of DNA; stimulates the production of red blood cells.	Leafy green vegetables, whole grain, cereals, and legumes.
Biotin	Stable to heat, acids and light; destroyed by oxidation and alkalis.	Coenzyme in the metabolism of some amino acids, fatty acids and nucleic acid synthesis.	Egg yolk, nuts, legumes, mushrooms.
Ascorbic acid (Vit C)	Stable in acids, but destroyed by oxidation, heat, light and alkalis.	Needed for making collagen, metabolism of some amino acids, promotes absorption of iron, and stimulates the synthesis of hormones from cholesterol.	Citrus juices & fruits, cabbage, potatoes, leafy greens, and fresh fruits.

Figure 15.1 Although it appears to be drinking, this flamingo is actually filter feeding.

15   Excretion

Introduction

The excretory system is one of the most misunderstood of the body's systems. Most of us tend to think of the kidneys as some kind of biological garbage disposal. While it is true that the kidneys get rid of many waste products through the urine, the primary function of the kidney is as a regulator. It is the role of the kidneys to maintain normal levels of body substances. Some of the regulated substances are water, minerals such as sodium, potassium and calcium, hydrogen ions (pH) and uric acid.

Water regulator

The kidney is a very efficient regulator. One of the most important compounds to be regulated is water. The amount of water in the cells, and the amount of water surrounding the cells (interstitial fluids), is very important. Too little body water will result in dehydration and too much water will result in edema.

Controlled by a pituitary hormone called Anti-diuretic Hormone (ADH), the kidneys will excrete or reabsorb more water. The amount of ADH will depend on the amount of body water. If water levels are not normal, the cells will have too much water causing them to burst. Too little water will cause them to shrivel up and function improperly. Failure of this water regulatory system could result in death regardless of whether external water is or is not available.

Mineral regulator

The kidney is also important in regulating many minerals such as sodium, potassium, and calcium. As in the case of water, the amount of minerals that are excreted or reabsorbed is controlled by the hormones. As in the case of water, regulation of these minerals is so critical, that in the absence of kidney function, death follows very quickly. For example, low levels of calcium can cause the abnormalities listed in Table 15.1.

Table 15.1 Abnormalities cause by a calcium deficiency.

Soft egg shells	Impaired muscle contraction
Soft bones (ricketts)	Inefficient nerve conduction
Poor blood clotting	

Some other examples of poor regulation would be abnormally high or low levels of potassium, which can cause cardiac problems. High levels of nitrogenous waste products, such as uric acid, could cause serious toxicity. If the blood pH (acid and base balance) is not regulated and maintained in a normal range, the enzymes of the body won't function properly.

Kidney

The avian kidney is generally a less efficient organ than its mammalian counterpart. It is structurally more similar to a reptilian kidney than to a mammalian kidney. Because of the high metabolic rate of birds, the avian kidney is proportionally twice as large as the mammalian kidney. The two kidneys are located in a bony depression on each side of the fused pelvis.

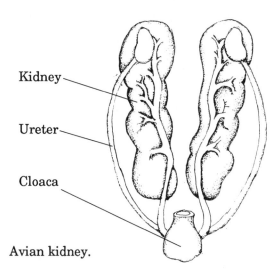

Kidney

Ureter

Cloaca

Figure 15.2 Avian kidney.

As blood flows through the kidneys, the waste products are removed. The kidney also removes substances in excess (e.g. minerals whose levels are above normal). The beneficial substances are reabsorbed back into the blood and continue to circulate through the body. The waste products and excess substances, along with excess water, form the urine. Once formed, the urine must be disposed of.

The urine leaves the kidney through a right and left ureter. There is no urinary bladder, again another concession to flight. Water weighs about 8 pounds per gallon, and most of urine is water. Because of this weight, a bird does not want to carry around a lot of water in a bladder.

In most birds, the ureters empty directly into the upper portion of the cloaca. Here the urine is temporarily stored and then excreted. Some water reabsorption does occur from the cloaca. Research into how much is reabsorbed is inconclusive.

Nephron

The functional units of the kidney are called nephrons. This is where the blood substances are filtered and regulated. These microscopic units actually perform the work of the kidney. The avian kidney has some simple nephrons, similar to those in the reptilian kidney, and some more sophisticated nephrons, similar to those of the mammalian kidney, but smaller.

A mammalian kidney will have around 15 nephrons per cubic millimeter of tissue. Birds will have anywhere from 90 to 500 nephrons in one cubic millimeter of kidney tissue. The number varies with the environmental conditions in which the species lives. Such conditions include whether the birds live around salt water, on the dry desert, or in a tropical rain forest.

Nitrogenous waste products

Metabolic reactions in the body produce many waste produces some of which contain nitrogen. One important characteristic of these nitrogenous waste products is that they are very toxic. For this reason, it is important to convert them to a less toxic form and to get them out of the body as soon as possible.

One of the main differences between the avian and mammalian kidney functions is the excretion of nitrogenous (nitrogen) waste products. Table 15.2 shows that the primary way mammals excrete their nitrogenous waste is in the form of urea. By comparison, the avian method of getting rid of nitrogenous waste is in the form of uric acid.

Table 15.2   Nitrogenous waste products.

	Chicken	Mammal
Uric acid	75-80	0.4-2.2%
Ammonia	10-15%	2.7-8.0%
Urea	2-10%	68.0-88.0%
Creatine	1-5%	3.6-10.0%
Amino acids	2.0%	?

Uric acid

Getting rid of nitrogenous waste as uric acid, rather than urea, is significantly different. It takes much more water to get rid of urea than to get rid of uric acid. About 60 ml. of water is required to excrete 1 gram of urea, as compared to only about 3 ml. of water to excrete 1 gram of uric acid. This results in a considerable conservation of water, thereby decreasing the need for the bird to drink as frequently.

Also, birds can excrete a good deal of nitrogenous waste, without losing a lot of body water. More importantly, birds can excrete a good deal of nitrogenous waste without having to carry around a lot of extra water in the urine. Because of the weight of water, this is a definite advantage during flight.

Because there is less water, bird urine is normally in the form of a paste. This paste-like urine is quite different from the more familiar liquid urine produced by mammals. Bird urine can be liquid. Following excess water intake by the bird, the droppings (urine portion) will be liquid, and this is normal (see "droppings" in digestion).

The significance of uric acid becomes obvious when we look at the egg. Normally, the only exchange between the egg and the outside world is gases, such as oxygen and carbon dioxide. Consequently, the nitrogenous waste products must be stored in the egg throughout the incubation period.

If these nitrogenous wastes were stored as ammonia or urea, toxicity would quickly develop. This toxicity would retard normal chick development and could ulitmately cause death to the chick. However, uric acid, being relatively insoluble, can be stored in a membranous structure within the egg, without being toxic to the embryo.

Salt glands

In addition to the kidney, some birds have another way of controlling body salts. Many marine birds have the ability to excrete salt via salt glands in the nasal region (Figure 15.2). These glands are located primarily in the head. They allow the birds to consume salt water and then rapidly remove and excrete the excess salts. This process, referred to as extrarenal salt excretion, allows marine birds to utilize salt water to supply some of their water needs.

Figure 15.3   Petrel excreting salt crystals.

Figure 16.1   Scarlet-chested parakeet (*Neophema spendida*)

16   Taxonomy

Introduction

Taxonomy is defined as the science of classification. Many of us have the impression that taxonomy involves a lot of uninteresting names, requiring a lot of time to memorize. And, in fact, there may be something to these impressions. However, this need not be so. We don't need to memorize a lot of scientific names to make use of taxonomy. All we need to do is understand the taxonomic system, so that we can make it useful to us.

Understanding the basis for scientific naming and classification of organisms is very important. One of the most important reasons for understanding this system is to eliminate the confusion caused by using various common names for the same organism.

Do you know what a dust bin is? If you live in England, this is where you throw your rubbish. In the United States we call this a waste basket and it holds our trash. We speak the same language, but it is obvious that there could be some misunderstandings, when we use different terms for the same thing.

A good biological example is a small Australian finch kept by many aviculturists called the "double bar" in Australia, "Bicheno's finch" in England, and the "owl finch" in the United States. Because of the popularity of this bird, many people in aviculture are familiar with these different names. However, there are many other birds with various common names that are unfamiliar to most of us.

Scientific Name

To avoid the problems associated with many common names, taxonomists have come up with a unique name, called the scientific name, for each organism. For example, our double bar/Bicheno/owl finch has the scientific name *Poephila bichenovii*. No other bird, animal, or plant has this scientific name.

Therefore, if you were to use the scientific name, *Poephila bichenovii* there would be no confusion as to which bird you were talking about. This would occur, regardless of where in the world you mention this name. The only confusion would come from a lack of familiarity with this scientific name. However, this confusion can be eliminated by looking up the scientific name in a taxonomy book.

This is not to imply that you should get out the books and memorize the scientific names of those birds in which you are interested. There is no need to memorize these names. You need only refer to them when communicating about these birds to others who may not be familiar with the common names used in your area.

Let's take a closer look at the scientific name. The scientific name is made up of two categories, the Genus and Species. When the Genus and Species are written together as the scientific name, they are always written in either one of two ways. One is to write them in italics . The other is to <u>underline</u> them.

The Genus is always capitalized and the species always begins with a lower case letter. The reason we write the scientific name in this very specific way is so that it will stand out and not be confused with some foreign language phrase.

Most of the scientific names are derived either from Latin or Greek. Again, this relates to the need to use terminology that is close to universal. At one time in the history of man, these were the universal languages.

A closer look at the scientific name shows that the names are not abstract words meant to confuse, but rather names which have some specific meaning. Using Latin and Greek terms for some characteristic of the bird reveals some important information about the bird.

The well known mocking bird, *Mimus polyglottos,* is a good example of this. The scientific name relates to the bird's well known ability to mimic sounds. This genus Mimus is derived from the Latin "mimus" which means to mimic. The species name has two derivations. "Poly" comes from the Greek work "polus" which means many. The "glottos" means the tongue. Therefore, the scientific name *Mimus polyglottos* translates to a "mimic with many tongues."

The Australian finch, *Poephila bichenovii*, mentioned earlier also has a very descriptive name. The word "poa" is Greek for grass and "philos" is Latin for loved or pleasing. Therefore, Poephila is very descriptive of these grass finches who spend a lot of time on the ground, among the seeding grasses.

The species name of bichenovii was derived in honor of J. E. Bicheno an English secretary of the Linnaen Society. This practice of using peoples names in the scientific name is now in disfavor. Using a persons name in the scientific name discloses very little information about the organism.

Figure 16.2   Owl finch (*Poephila bichenovii*).

One final example is the masked lovebird, *Agapornis personata*. The word "agape" is Greek for love and "ornis" is Greek for bird. The Latin word "personatus" means masked. This scientific name says "lovebird with a mask." Again, we do not need to study Latin and Greek to use these words. If the derivations are interesting to you, simply pick up a dictionary of word roots. You will be surprised how uncomplicated scientific names can be.

Figure 16.3 Lovebird (*Agapornis personata*).

Taxonomic categories

What is the relationship of the scientific name to the overall taxonomic scheme of organisms? Although there are many subcategories, the main categories are kingdom, phylum, class, order, genus and species. This hierarchy of classification is listed in Table 16.1.

Table 16.1 The classification hierarchy.

Actual	Analogy
Kingdom	Country
Phylum	State
Class	County
Order	City
Family	Street
Genus	Number
Species	Apartment

The kingdom is probably the easiest taxonomic category to understand. We can separate the plants into one kingdom (Plantae) and the animals into another kingdom (Animalia). Taxonomists recognize more kingdoms than these, but it does not serve our purposes to go into that here.

Phylum

We will now ignore the Plantae kingdom and concentrate on the kingdom Animalia. The next task is to organize the animals into different phyla (plural for phylum). This is done by putting those organisms which are most similar in the same phylum. For example, a bird, a jellyfish and a crab would each be in a different phylum. All Birds are in the phylum Chordata. Because of the presence of vertebrae, they are in a subphylum called vertebrata.

Class

By organizing animals with vertebrae into the phylum Chordata, we will eliminate most of the animals without backbones . However, we still have a tremendous number of different animals to organize. So we need another category. The next category is the Class. All birds are in the class Aves. There are two primary distinguishing characteristics of the class Aves. One is that they have feathers, and the other is that their forelimbs have been modified for flight.

We are talking here of having feathers, but notice that we are not listing flight as a unique characteristic of Aves. Not all birds fly, and there are animals in other groups that can fly. Bats can fly and they are in the class Mammalia. House flies can fly and they are in a totally different phylum, the Arthropoda.

Order

The class Aves has over 8,500 species of birds. So, we must sort them out into still another category called the Order. The order contains those birds with somewhat similar characteristics. For example, hawks are grouped with falcons, or ducks are grouped with geese. The list of orders and the typical birds found in them are described in the next chapter.

Family

The order also contains too many birds to be practical. Therefore, we use another category, called the family. All birds in an order have characteristics in common. Although birds in an order are similar, birds in each family share even more similar characteristics. An example of some families of birds can be seen in the next chapter.

Genus

The family is broken down into even smaller groups, called genus. Now, we are getting back to the scientific name. The genus is a group of birds with very similar characteristics, such as the lovebirds of the genus Agapornis. Finally, the birds in a genus are broken down into individuals called the species.

Species

The definition of species has changed some over time. Basically, the species is defined as that group of animals capable of breeding and producing young very similar to themselves. We are continually learning more about all species of animals. That is why taxonomists have developed a new category, the subspecies. The subspecies contains those organisms within a given species that could easily interbreed, but due to conditions, such as geographical isolation, do not.

This classification of animals allows us to relate more readily to the differences and similarities of organisms. It also allows us to establish "taxonomic keys." These "keys" are used to more easily identify organisms.

One can imagine the horror of looking at a book with 100,000 plants listed and having in your hand one red flowering plant that you want to identify. However, if we group the 100,000 plants into categories such as color of flower, number of petals, size of petals, height of plant, size of leaves, and color of leaves, we could save ourselves a tremendous amount of time.

Table 16.2 shows the interrelationship of the categories that we have been discussing. The first example will demonstrate the application of these principles. See if you can figure out some of the characteristics which sort out the organisms in this taxonomic example:

Table 16.2   Classification of selected species of animals.

Kingdom	U.S.	Animalia	Animalia	Animalia	Animalia
Phylum	Calif.	Chordata	Chordata	Chordata	Chordata
Class	San Jose	Mammalia	Avies	Avies	Avies
Order	Oak St	Primates	Psittaciformes	Passeriformes	Passeriformes
Family	1015	Hominidae	Psittacidae	Estrildidae	Estrildidae
Genus	*Apt.*	*Homo*	*Agapornis*	*Poephila*	*Poephila*
Species	*C*	*sapien*	*personata*	*guttata*	*bichonevii*
Common Name	Home	Man	Lovebird	Zebra finch	Owl finch

Figure 16.4   Crested seriema (*Cariama cristata*).

17   Avian Orders

Introduction

The purpose of this chapter is to give a brief overview of the avian orders. In the class Aves there are 26 orders. These 26 orders, and the types of birds found in each, are listed in Table 17.1. No pretense is made here at presenting a survey of the avian orders. For those interested, the orders are covered in depth in some of the refrence books listed in the bibliography.

Table 17.1   Avian orders and the type of birds in each.

Struthioniformes (Ostriches)
Rheiformes (Rheas)
Casuariiformes (Cassowaries and Emus)
Apterygiformes (Kiwis)
Tinamiformes (Tinamous)
Sphenisciformes (Penguins)
Gaviiformes (Loons)
Podicipediformes (Grebes)
Procellariiformes (Albatrosses, Shearwaters, and Petrels)
Pelecaniformes (Pelicans, Boobies, and Cormorants)
Ciconiiformes (Herons, Storks, Ibises, Spoonbills, Flamingoes)
Anseriformes (Ducks, Geese, and Swans)
Falconiformes (Vultures, Hawks, and Eagles)
Galliformes (Grouse, Quail, Pheasants, Turkeys, and Fowl)
Gruiformes (Buttonquails, Cranes, Rails, and Coots)
Charadriiformes (Gulls, Terns, Auks, and Shorebirds)
Columbiformes (Pigeons, Doves, and Sandgrouse)
Psittaciformes (Lories, Parrots, Cockatoos, and Macaws)
Cuculiformes (Cuckoos, Roadrunners, and Touracos)
Caprimulgiformes (Goatsuckers, Nightjars, and Frogmouths)
Apodiformes (Swifts and Hummingbirds)
Coliiformes (Mousebird)
Trogoniformes (Trogons)
Coraciiformes (Kingfishers, Rollers, and Hornbills)
Piciformes (Barbets, Toucans, and Woodpeckers)
Passeriformes (Perching and Song Birds)

Struthioniformes: (Ostriches)

The first four orders are groups of flightless birds called the ratites. Ostriches are large African ground dwelling birds. There is only one living species of ostrich, but there are five different subspecies. At one time they were found in Asia as well. However, at the present time, they are found in the wild (feral), only in Africa.

As with all ratites, ostriches are incapable of flight because they lack a breastbone for the attachment of flight muscles and they have such a heavy body. They are fast runners with a strong kick, which they are none too reluctant to use. Ostriches have been successfully captive-bred in many areas of the world.

Rheiformes: (Rheas)

There are only two species of rheas, both of which are found exclusively in South America. The common rhea, *Rhea americana*, standing about four and one half feet tall is the largest American bird and is sometimes called the American ostrich. The other species is Darwin's rhea, *Pterocnemia pennata*, which stands about 3 feet tall and is found at high altitudes. Although they superficially look somewhat alike, the rhea and ostrich are quite different. For example, the ostrich has two toes whereas the rhea has three. Like the ostrich, the rhea is a fast runner, a distinct advantage to a flightless bird.

Casuariiformes: (Cassowaries & Emus)

There are three living species of cassowaries, found mostly in Australia and New Guinea. Although they are ratites like the rheas and ostriches, the cassowaries are primarily forest dwellers. As a group, they are smaller than the previous ratites. Another characteristic of this order is that two of the three species has a conspicuous wattle. They have extremely sharp claws and have been known to attack and cause serious injury to humans.

There is one species of Emu, found only in Australia. Somewhat resembling the ostrich, the emu is only about two-thirds the size and has a much better disposition. They are successfully bred in captivity around the world.

Apterygiformes: (Kiwis)

There are two or three species of kiwis, all of whom are found in New Zealand. Their soft feathers make them appear almost mammalian. These birds differ from the other ratites in that they are small birds with a long bill. The long bill has nostrils at the end. Kiwis have a very acute sense of smell, a most unusual characteristic for a bird. Being nocturnal birds with small eyes may explain the need for this highly developed sense of smell. They represent the last of the four orders of ratites.

Tinamiformes: (Tinamous)

There are about 50 species of tinamous, all of whom are found in Central and South America. The tinamous are small birds, about the size of a typical game bird. Some authorities consider them to be the most primitive birds alive. They have a keeled breastbone (for attachment of flight muscles) and although strong flyers for short distances, they are very poor distant flyers. Although not ratites, they spend most of their time on the ground. They also nest on the ground. This is due to the fact that they don't have the grasping toes necessary for perching.

Figure 17.1   Double-wattled cassowary (*Casuarius casuarius*).

Sphenisciformes: (Penguins)

There are 17 species of penguins, all of whom are found in the southern hemisphere. Most are found in the antarctic, but some get as close to the equator as the Galapagos Islands. They are flightless birds, although there is evidence that this was not always so. Now, they are the most marine of all birds. Their wings are modified as strong flippers and their feet are webbed. The body has an insulating layer of fat. They also feathers which are overlapping and scale-like covering the entire body.

Gaviiformes: (Loons)

There are four species of loons, most nest in Eurasia and America, and winter at sea. They are strong divers, with many adaptations for life at sea. The three front toes are webbed, and their legs are adapted for swimming rather than walking. Although they have some trouble taking off from the water, once airborne, they are strong flyers.

Figure 17.2   Brown pelican (*Pelecanus occidentalis*).

Podicipediformes: (Grebes)

There are 18 to 20 species of grebes found worldwide. There are representatives of this order on all continents and large islands of the world. Like the loons, the grebes are aquatic, but each toe is lobed, rather than being webbed, and they don't dive as well. They have an unusual behavior of picking and feeding their own feathers to their young.

Procellariiformes: (Albatrosses, Shearwaters, Petrels)

This order of sea birds is characterized by having their external nostrils modified into a tube. The group is often referred to as the "tube-noses." Their beaks are noticeably hooked at the end and are covered with horny plates. The three front toes are webbed and the plumage is tight and oily. The largest birds in the group are the albatrosses, of which there are 13 species, found mainly around the southern oceans. They are renown for their ability to glide for long distances, a definite advantage when ranging far out to sea.

Shearwaters, fumers, and petrels contain 82 species of birds, found on all the oceans of the world. The exception to this are the diving petrels, found only in the south temperate and south polar seas. This group contains the smallest marine birds, the storm petrels, a bird who is active throughout most of the 24 hour day.

Pelecaniformes: (Pelicans, boobies, cormorants)

The most unique characteristic of this order is the webbing between all four toes (totipalmate foot). All have a gular (throat) pouch, although it is much larger in some. In fact, the gular pouch of pelicans is so large that it holds twice as much food as their stomach. The gular pouch is an adequate storage area for birds "fishing" at sea.

There are three species of tropicbirds. Tropicbirds spend much of their time in the air over southern waters. They are distinguished by central tail feathers, which are a foot longer than the other tail feathers.

The most obvious and well known birds in this order are the pelicans, of which there are eight species. These birds are found worldwide, except for the polar extremes. They are strong flyers and dive into the water from 10 to 20 feet above the surface.

There are seven species of boobies and gannets who are found on all oceans, except the polar oceans. They are well known for their dives, which can start as high as 100 feet from the ocean surface.

Although not the largest in size or reputation, the cormorants dominate this order with 30 species. Except for the central Pacific, northern Asia, and inland areas of north America, the cormorants are found in fresh and salt water areas, all over the world. Because of their superb fishing skills, they have been tamed and trained for this task by fishermen in the Orient.

There are four species known as darters, or snake birds. They are called snake birds because they often swim with their body submerged, thus only their head and neck are seen on the surface. Darters enter the water usually to feed. This group is found on all continents.

The last group in this order is the Frigatebirds (Man-o-war), of which there are five species. They are found in the temperate and tropical oceans. Since they have poor waterproofing, they spend little time in or on the ocean. The group is distinguished by the presence of a red throat pouch in the males, which can be inflated during mating displays, even in flight.

Ciconiiformes: (Herons, Storks, Ibises, Spoonbills, Flamingoes)

This order is made up of a large group of long-legged waders. They are characterized by a long neck, often folded in flight. Except for the flamingos, they have unwebbed toes. The group feeds primarily on fish and is found along shores and marshes through out the world.

There are 66 species of herons, egrets and bitterns in one family. They are characterized by a long straight bill and an extremely long neck, with a "kink" in it. The second largest family contains 28 species of ibises and spoonbills, found worldwide. Storks and wood ibises make up a family of 17 species, found worldwide. This order also contains three families with one species each, the whale-headed stork, boat-billed heron and hammerkop.

The final family in this order contains six species of flamingoes. The flamingo, with its long legs and its beak down-turned at the midpoint, is probably the most recognized bird in this order. Flamingos have a peculiar method of feeding because they are filter feeders. They immerse their heads, turning the bill upside down to eat. The flamingos are members of what is believed to be the oldest known family of birds. Some experts believe that they may be an evolutionary link between the two orders, Ciconiformes and Anseriformes.

Anseriformes: (Ducks, Geese, Swans)

One of the obvious common denominators of the birds in this order are their adaptations to an aquatic environment. Especially notable are the webbed feet and a dense undercoating of down feathers. One exception to the group is the three species of birds called screamers.

The three species called screamers are aptly named, because of their propensity to make noise at all hours of the day or night. Although they look more like a game bird, and fly like a bird of prey, the screamers have more in common with waterfowl than either game birds or birds of prey. These similarities are more internal than external and so are not so obvious to the casual ornithologist.

The duck family has 150 species and is found worldwide. Their bill is typically flat, broad, and rounded at the end and has small plates (lamellate). They tend to be gregarious. Most fly, but a few are flightless. Many are aquatic divers, diving in search of food or to escape enemies. There are quite a few birds of avicultural interest in this order, most of whom are bred by aviculturists who are called "game breeders".

Figure 17.3   Hammerhead or Hammerkop (*Scopus umbretta*).

Falconiformes: (Vultures, Hawks, Eagles)

This is the order of diurnal (of the daytime) birds of prey. All have a proportionally large hooked beak and wings with a large surface area for strong flight. The symbol of the United States, the bald eagle, is a member of this family.

The first family in this order (Carthartidae) contains 6 species. They are known as the New World Vultures, since they are found only in South America and North America to Canada. Two of the largest birds that fly, the Andean and California condors, are in this group. Like many birds of prey, these magnificent birds are being threatened by man's intentional and unintentional encroachment on their environment. Most require very large territories to survive.

The next family (Accipitridae) contains the eagles, hawks, kites, harriers, and the Old World Vultures, numbering 217 species found worldwide. Eagles and hawks have strong beaks, claws, and feet used to capture their prey. They are generally distinguished from the falcons by their unnotched upper mandibles and broader wings. Most species in this family feed on live animals, but the vultures are opportunistic feeders, feeding primarily on dead meat (carrion).

The true falcons (Falconidae) number 61 species and are also found worldwide. Although looking similar to the casual observer, hawks and falcons are quite different. The notched upper mandible and other differences are not as noticeable when the bird is in flight. Falcons are aerial wizards striking their prey with lightning speed.

The osprey is in a family by itself and there is only one species. They are found almost worldwide, and always near a body of water because they feed primarily on fish. Unlike the marine birds that dive for fish, the osprey dive feet first into the water often coming out with a large fish almost too heavy to carry. They differ from the Old World Vultures primarily in the structure of the foot and toe bones. Ospreys are more closely related to the eagles.

The odd-ball bird in this order is the strange looking secretary bird. There is only one species of this large bird and its range is confined to Africa, south of the Sahara. This bird has long legs and webbing between the three front toes, with a one small rear toe. They can fly very well, but rarely do. This bird certainly does not look like it belongs in the order with hawk type birds, but with its hawk-like bill and talons, it probably fits in this order better than in any other order.

Figure 17.4   Blue-eared pheasant (*Crossoptilon auritum*).

Galliformes: (Grouse, Quail, Pheasants, Turkeys, Fowl)

This order is comprised of "hen-like" birds, with small beaks, small wings, and heavy feet, as typified by the domestic chicken. Most of the birds in this order would probably resent the use of the domestic chicken as their typical representative. Never-the-less, the domestic chicken is a descendent of one of their own, the Asian jungle fowl.

These small-winged birds are adapted more for walking than flying. They have a well developed crop, a muscular gizzard, and a caecum, allowing a greater variety of food sources to be used. This order of birds, more than any other, has the greatest impact on the dinner table and economics of man.

The first family in this order is made up of the megapodes or mound builders. This family numbers 10 species, all found in Australia or the surrounding islands. A unique behavior of this group is the incubation of their eggs with heat created by rotting vegetation rather than body heat.

Next, is the family of the curassows, of which there are 44 species. These birds live from Texas, south through Central and South America. These birds have long tails and erectile crests. Curassows tend to be arboreal (tree dwellers).

The grouse family has only 18 species and is found only in the Northern Hemisphere. Their most distinguishing feature is that they have feathered nostrils. Some species have feathers covering the legs down to the toes. One member of this family is the prairie chicken. The male prairie chicken puts on one of the most entertaining and beautiful displays of any bird, including the more well known peacock.

The pheasant family is by far the largest in this order. There are 177 species found mostly in the Old World. The exception to this are the New World quail. This is the family, within the order Galliformes, that represents the birds having the most economic impact on man.

In this family we find the pheasant, peacock, partridge, quail, peafowl, jungle fowl, and the chicken. Many species of this group have spurs on their lower legs. Anyone who has encountered an enraged rooster can attest to the power with which these birds can contact one's leg with their spurs.

The smallest of all the gallinaceous birds, *Excalfactoria chinensis*, is in this family. This bird, called a "buttonquail" in the United States, is quite commonly kept in aviaries. It is popular because of its beauty and compatibility with other birds, especially finches. Here is a classic example of the problems associated with using common names. This "buttonquail" is actually a painted quails from Asia and is not one of the buttonquails which are found in the order Gruiformes.

The Guinea fowl comprise a small family. There are seven species found only in Africa and Madagascar. They are competent flyers, who usually prefer to run. These birds have bare necks, which are usually colored, and often have wattles or hackles.

The turkey family has only two wild (feral) species. One is found in Mexico and the other in the United States. One of these species, the Wild Turkey, is the ancestor of the domestic turkey. The other, the Ocellated Turkey, has an especially beautiful luster to the feathers.

The final family in this order contains only one species, the Hoatzin. This is a primitive bird found in wooded river banks of northern South America. Hoatzins are arboreal birds who produce young with claws on their wings, which are lost when they maturity.

Gruiformes: (Buttonquails, Cranes, Rails, Coots)

This order is often referred to as the "marsh" birds. Most do live in marshes; however some are prairie dwellers. The categorizing of the birds in this order is quite nebulous. Taxonomists may have grouped these birds in one order, rather than create different orders for this diverse group.

There are over 180 species in this order, including representatives of Roaletos, buttonquails (Turnix quails), cranes, liumpking, trumpeters, rails, coots, gallinules, finfoots, sunbitterns, seriemas, and bustards.

The largest family in this order is made up of the rails and coots. There are 138 species in this family of birds, representatives of whom are found worldwide. Most of these birds are found in swampy habitats. In fact, one of the common names for the coot is the mudhen.

The cranes have 14 species in their family and are probably the most recognizable of this order. They are tall birds; some are five feet tall. Cranes, generally, have an elaborate courtship display. Because of the anatomical relationship of the breastbone and collarbone, they are able to utter loud, penetrating calls.

Charadriiformes: (Gulls, Terns, Auks, Shorebirds)

Over 320 species of birds are found in this order. Most have webbed toes, compact plumage, and are strong fliers. These are characteristics of birds who spend most of their life around water. A list of the common names of the families and the numbers of species appears in Table 17.2.

Table 17.2   Family members of the order Charadriiformes.

Jacanas	7 species	Pratincoles	17 species
Painted snipe	2 species	Seed-snipes	4 species
Oystercatcher	6 species	Sheathbills	2 species
Plovers	63 species	Sandgrouse	16 species
Sandpipers	82 species	Skuas, Jaegers	4 species
Avocets, Stilts	7 species	Gulls terns	85 species
Phalaropes	3 species	Skimmers	3 species
Crab-plover	1 species	Auks, murres,	
Thick-knees	9 species	puffins	21 species

Place yourself near any body of water in the world and you would be almost assured of seeing some representative of this order during your stay. Because of the specialized habitats and feeding pattern, few of the birds in this order are kept in aviculture.

Columbiformes: (Pigeons, Doves, Sandgrouse)

The least known family in this order are the sandgrouses of which there are 16 species. They are found in the desert regions of southern Europe, Asia, and Europe. The name is indicative of their close resemblance to the grouse, but they are not related.

The only other present day family in this order are the pigeons. There are 316 species, found in most areas of the world. There is no distinction, at least to the ornithologist, between a pigeon and a dove. The names are often used interchangeably.

Most are strong flyers and tend to be gregarious. They produce "pigeon milk" in their crop, which is fed to the young. This regurgitated food is not the same as mammal's milk. This is one group of birds which has adapted well to the civilization of man. The keeping of pigeons and doves is an important part of aviculture, which goes back as far as recorded history.

Psittaciformes: (Lories, Parrots, Cockatoos, Macaws)

This order is characterized by birds with a hooked beak, an upper mandible which is hinged to the skull, and a fleshy tongue. They are also characterized by brightly colored plumage and feet with two toes projecting forward and two projecting backward.

There are over 330 species, all placed in the same family because of similarities. Most of the species are found in the more tropical areas of Central and South America, Australia, and Asia. There are about 15 species of this order in Africa and none presently in Europe or the United States. The thick-billed parrot (*Rhynchopsitta pachyrhyncha*) was the last psittacine to be found naturally in the United States. Thick-bills were regular winter visitors to the mountains of southern Arizona and New Mexico.

There was one hookbill, the Carolina parakeet (*Conuropsis carolinensis*) that was a year-round native to the United States. The last known specimen died at the Cincinnati Zoo in 1918, but the species was doomed many years before that. The birds were not popular with farmers because of their propensity for crop destruction. Flying in flocks made them an easy target for a revengeful or protective farmer.

However, no one is sure farmers were to blame for their disappearance. Hunters were probably not to blame, since the Carolina parakeets were not hunted as game birds. It is not believed that the development of the land was so great by 1900 as to completely eliminate a species of bird. What caused the decline of this population is a big mystery. Man was probably responsible, but we don't know how.

This order undoubtedly has more avicultural interest than any other avian order. This interest is reflected by the fact that the greatest number of avicultural birds bred each year are from this order. This order has also produced the greatest variety, in terms of different species bred in aviculture. For this reason and the fact that all the hookbills are in one family, we will take a closer look at each of the subfamilies and genera in the family Psittacidae in Table 17.3.

Table 17.3   Subfamilies and genera of the family Psittacidae.

Parrots of the Pacific:

Genus	Type of hookbill	Number of species
Loriidae (subfamily)		
Chalcopsitta	Lories	4
Eos	Lories	6
Pseudos	Dusky Lory	1
Trichoglossus	Small to medium Lories	10
Lorius	Lories	8
Phigys	Collared Lory	1
Vini	Small Lories	5
Glossopsitta	Lorikeets	3
Charmosyna	Lorikeets	14
Oreopsittacus	Whiskered Lorikeet	1
Neopsittacus	Lorikeet	2
Cacatuidae (subfamily)		
Probosciger	Palm Cockatoo	1
Calyptorhynchus	Black Cockatoos	3
Callocephalon	Gang-gang Cockatoo	1
Eolophus	Galah Cockatoo	1
Cacatua	"white" Cockatoos	11
Nymphicinae (subfamily)		
Nymphicus	Cockatiel	1
Nestorinae (subfamily)		
Nestor	Kea &Kakas	3

Table 17.3 (cont)

Genus	Type of hookbill	Number of species
Micropsittinae (subfamily)		
Micropsitta	Pygmy Parrots	6
Psittacinae (subfamily)		
Opopsitta	Fig Parrots	2
Psittaculirostris	Fig Parrots	3
Bolbopsittacus	Guaiabero	1
Psittinus	Blue-rumped Parrot	1
Psittacella	New Guinea mountain parrots	4
Geoffroyus	Parrots	3
Prioniturus	Rack-tailed Parrots	6
Tanygnathus	Great-billed Parrots	5
Eclectus	Eclectus Parrot	1
Psittrichas	Pesquet's Parrot	1
Prosopeia	Shining Parrots	2
Alisterus	King Parrots	3
Aprosmictus	Red-winged Parrots	2
Polytelis	Princess Parrots	3
Purpureicephalus	Red-capped Parrot	1
Barnardius	Aust. Ring-necked Parrots	2
Platycercus	Rosella Parrots	8
Psephotus	Many-colored Parrots	5
Cyanoramphus	Kakariki Parrots	6
Emymphicus	Horned Parakeet	1
Neophema	Grass parakeets	7
Lathamus	Swift Parrot	1
Melopsittacus	Budgerigar	1
Pezoporus	Ground Parrot	1
Geopsittacus	Night Parrot	1
Strigopinae (subfamily)		
Strigops	Kakapo	1

Parrots of the Afro-Asian Distribution:

Psittacinae (subfamily)		
Lophopsittacus	Broad-billed Parrot	1
Necropsittacus	Rodrigues Parrot	1
Mascarinus	Mascarene Parrot	1

Table 17.3 (cont)

Genus	Type of hookbill	Number of species
Coracopsis	Vasa/Black Parrots	2
Psittacus	Grey Parrot	1
Poicephalus	Senegal/Meyers Parrot Group	9
Agapornis	Lovebirds	9
Loriculus	Hanging Parrots	10
Psittacula	Afro-Asian Ringneck Parrots	15

Parrots of the South American Distribution:

Psittacinae (subfamily)

Genus	Type of hookbill	Number of species
Anodorhynchus	Hyacinth Macaw	3
Cyanopsitta	Spix's Macaw	1
Ara	Macaws	15
Aratinga	true Conures	19
Nandayus	Nanday Conure	1
Leptosittaca	Golden-plumed Conure	1
Ognorhynchus	Yellow-cared Conure	1
Rhynchopsitta	Thick-billed Parrot	1
Conuropsis	Carolina Parakeet	1
Cyanoliseus	Patagonian Conure	1
Pyrrhura	Conures	18
Enicognathus	Austal/Slender-billed Conures	2
Myiopsitta	Monk Parakeet	1
Bolborhynchus	Mountain Parakeets	5
Forpus	Parrotlets	7
Brotogeris	Bee-bee parrots	7
Nannopsittaca	Tepui Parrotlet	1
Touit	rare Parrotlets	7
Pionites	Caiques	2
Pionopsitta	Parrots	6
Gypositta	Vulturine Parrot	1
Hapalopsittaca	Black-winged Parrot	2
Graydidascalus	Short-tailed Parrot	1
Pionus	Pionus Parrots	8
Amazona	Amazon Parrots	27
Deroptyus	Hawk-headed Parrot	1
Triclaria	Purple-bellied Parrot	1

Cuculiformes: (Cuckoos, Roadrunners, Touracos)

There are about 150 species in this order, and representatives are found on all continents. One unique characteristic of this group is that the outer rear toe can be moved forward or backward.

The largest family in this order contains the cuckoos and roadrunners. Because of Hollywood's use of the roadrunner in cartoons, they are the most recognizable members of this order. The cuckoos have a dubious reputation because of their practice of brood parasitism which is the replacing of other birds eggs' with their own. However, this behavior is not common to all the cuckoo species.

The other family contains 20 species of touracos. These brightly colored birds possess pigments unique to all of these birds called turacin or tura-coverdin. Many ornithologists place the touracos in their own order, the Musophagiformes.

Strigiformes: (Owls)

There are about 145 species of owls found worldwide. These nocturnal birds of prey are familiar to almost everyone. Although not related, we could think of the owls as night hawks. A large head with large eyes, large external ear openings, and soft, fluffy feathers for silent flight are a few of the adaptations which make the owl a very efficient nocturnal hunter. They vary in size from as a small as a sparrow to as large as an eagle.

Caprimulgiformes: (Goatsuckers, Nightjars, Frogmouths)

Birds in this group tend to have owl-like heads and plumage, as well as disproportionately large eyes. They also share with the owls a nocturnal habit. However, their beaks and legs are not proportionally as heavy as those of the owls. These birds also have an exceptionally large gape.

There are five families in this order, containing 95 species. Few of these species are found in the United States. One of the more well know is called the whip-or-will, because of its curious call. Their nocturnal nature probably explains their lack of recognition

Apodiformes: (Swifts, Hummingbirds)

This order contains some of our fancier flyers. They tend to be small birds with small feet and short legs. Wings tend to be long and narrow. The flight muscles are proportionally quite large, up to a third of the body weight in some species.

There are two families of swifts with a total of 79 species. The swifts are probably better adapted for aerial life than any other group of birds. They collect nesting material, mate, feed and sometimes even sleep in the air. Swifts are found in both the Old and New World.

The hummingbird family contains over 320 species, all of whom are found exclusively in the New World. The smallest birds on earth are found in the hummingbird family. The Cuban bee hummingbird is around 2 inches and the Giant hummingbird is about 8 inches. Most hummingbirds are between these two sizes. Because of their beautiful iridescent coloration, amazing acrobatic skills, and apparent trust of man, these are one of the most enjoyable groups of birds. Actually, trust is not involved, more likely, they simply have no great fear of man. This lack of fear most likely relates to their ability to move rapidly in almost any direction.

Figure 17.5   Coral-billed ground cuckoo (*Carpococcyx renauldi*).

Coliiformes: (Mousebirds)

This order has only one family and one genus with six species, all of whom are found in Africa. They are sparrow sized, with a long tail and a crest. In addition, they possess the ability to move the rear toes forward. These gregarious birds feed primarily on fruits and vegetables. Because of their brown to gray coloration, they were given the name mousebirds. A large flock of mousebirds can be very destructive to fruit or vegetable gardens.

Trogoniformes: (Trogons)

The order of the trogons is another "one family" order, but there are nine genera and 34 species, all of whom are presently found in the tropics. This group is known for its predominantly rich green, iridescent plumage and small flat beak. They also have a long tail and small feet, with the first and second toes pointed backward. Insects and fruit, are both taken on the wing.

Coraciiformes: (Kingfishers, Rollers, Hornbills)

Ten families and over 190 species make this a very diverse order. The common characteristics of the birds in this group are the rather large head, disproportionally large bill, colorful plumage, and third and fourth toes joined at the base.

Representatives of the kingfisher family are found worldwide. With long narrow pointed beak, they display a well known profile. Because of poorly developed legs, the large beak plays an important role in obtaining their carnivorous diet. Table 17.4 shows the other families in this order.

Table 17.4   Other families in the order Coraciiformes.

Toides	5 species
Motmots	8 species
Bee-eaters	24 species
Cuckoo-roller	1 species
True and Ground Rollers	16 species
Hoopoe	1 species
Wood-hoopoes	6 species

The last family is the most peculiar of all. The hornbill family has 46 species found from tropical Africa and Asia to the Solomon Islands. They are distinguished by a large curved bill, and many have a large casque (helmet) on top. While advantageous to the fruit eating habits of this bird, one wonders how the bird can support such a structure projecting from the body. The casque is mostly hollow and the bill is honeycombed, resulting in a surprisingly light-weight structure.

Piciformes: (Barbets, Toucans, Woodpeckers)

There are six families in this order, each which have specialized beaks. Most have two toes forward and two back. With the exception of the Jacamar family, the young are born naked without any down feathers.

The Jacamar family has 16 species and is found in Central and South America. Another family from these same regions is the Puffbirds (32 species), so called because of the propensity to fluff their feathers. There are 78 species of the tropical Barbet family. Barbets tend to stay in one place for a long time and have a "song" composed of few notes, which they repeat for long periods of time.

Figure 17.6   Great hornbill (*Buceros bicornis*).

The family of Honeyguides has 16 species and they are found in the Old World tropics. All are brood parasites, laying eggs in other birds' nests, to be raised by the unsuspecting host. They get their name from the behavior, by some members of the species, of attracting man and other animals to stores of honey.

The Toucan family is found only in the New World tropics and numbers some 40 species. Like the hornbill, the toucan is conspicuous because of a very large bill. The toucan is a fruit eater, but it will also eat small critters, including small exotic finches kept in an aviary with them.

The largest family in this order is the woodpeckers. Representatives of the 213 species of this order are found almost worldwide. Most are found in the tropic and subtropical forests. These birds have a strong chisel-like bill, a long retractable tongue, strong neck muscles, and strong legs and feet. These adaptations permit these birds to make a multitude of holes in a tree in a very short time.

Figure 17.7   Rothschild's mynah (*Leucopsar rothschildi*).

Passeriformes: (Perching & Song Birds)

With more than 5,000 species, this order has more birds than all the other avian orders combined. There are more families (66) than there are species in some of the other avian orders. In other words, over half of all birds species living today are in this order.

As the name suggests, these birds are adapted for perching. The most important adaptation for this purpose is the presence of three toes forward and one well developed back toe. Another characteristic is a well developed syrinx, thereby permitting melodious songs to be sung by many of these birds. All their young are hatched naked, helpless, and with their eyes closed.

Along with the Psittaciformes, this is the order with the most avicultural interest. More specifically, the families of Fringillidae, Estrildidae, and Ploceidae contain the birds primarily kept by aviculturists. Chapter 18 lists the scientific names of the birds in these three families which are of the most interest to aviculturists.

The sheer number of families in this order precludes any discussion of them here. Instead, Table 17.5 lists the families and the type of bird in each, including the number of species:

Table 17.5 Families and number of species of the order Passeriformes.

Family	Type of birds	Number of species
Eurylaimidae	Broadbills	14
Dendrocolaptidae	Woodcreepers	50
Furnariidae	Ovenbirds	217
Formicariidae	Antbirds	230
Conopophagidae	Antpittas	8
Rhinocryptidae	Tapaculos	29
Cotingidae	Cotingas	79
Pipridae	Manakins	53
Tryannidae	Tyrant flycatchers	362
Oxyruncidae	Sharpbills	1
Phytotomidae	Plantcutters	3
Pittidae	Pittas	26
Acanthisittidae	New Zealand wrens	3
Philepittidae	Asities	4

Table 17.5 (cont)

Family	Type of birds	Number of species
Menuridae	Lyrebirds	2
Atrichornithidae	Scrub-birds	2
Alaudidae	Larks	76
Hirundinidae	Swallows, martins	74
Motacillidae	Wagtails, pipits	55
Campephagidae	Caterpillar birds	72
Pycnonotidae	Bulbuls	18
Irenidae	Fairy bluebirds, leafbirds	14
Laniidae	Shrikes	79
Vangidae	Vangas	13
Bombycillidae	Waxwings	8
Dulidae	Palmchat	1
Cinclidae	Dippers	4
Troglodytidae	Wrens	59
Mimidae	Mockingbirds, thrashers	30
Prunellidae	Hedge sparrows	13
Turdidae	Thrushes	304
Timaliidae	Babblers	252
Sylviidae	Old World warblers	339
Maluridae	Aust. fairy wrens	29
Acanthizidae	Australian warblers	59
Muscicapidae	Old World flycatchers	360
Remizidae	Penduline tits	9
Aegithalidae	Long-tailed tits	7
Paridae	Titmice	46
Sittidae	Nuthatches	21
Climacteridae	Australian treecreepers	6
Certhiidae	Creepers	6
Dicaeidae	Flowerpeckers	58
Nectariniidae	Sunbirds	118
Zosteropidae	White-eyes	79
Ephthianuridae	Australian chats	5
Meliphagidae	Honey-eaters	169
Emberizidae	Buntings, Am. sparrows	233

Table 17.5 (cont)

Family	Type of bird	Number of species
Parulidae	Amer. wood warblers	120
Drepanididae	Hawaiian honeycreepers	15
Vireonidae	Vireos	39
Icteridae	Am. blackbirds, orioles	92
Fringillidae	**Chaffinches, linnets**	126
Estrildidae	**Waxbills**	124
Ploceidae	**Typical weavers**	150
Sturnidae	Starlings	106
Oriolidae	Old World orioles	28
Dicruridae	Drongos	20
Callaeidae	Wattlebirds	3
Grallinidae	Mudnest-builders	4
Artamidae	Wood-swallows	10
Craticidae	Bell-magpies	11
Ptilonorhynchidae	Bowerbirds	17
Paradisaeidae	Birds of paradise	40
Corvidae	Crow, jays, magpies	103

Figure 17.8 Inca tern (*Larosterna inca*).

18   Avian Species

Introduction

Many times we hear a common name or a scientific name and are not sure to which bird it refers. Listed in the following tables are those bird species of most avicultural interest. The parrot-type birds are listed by common name (Table 18.1), and then by scientific name (Table 18.2). Then, three families of finch-type birds (Estrildidae, Fringillidae and Ploceidae) are listed by both common names (Table 18.3) and scientific names (Table 18.4).

The chapter on taxonomy provided a sense of how organisms are classified. The chapter on avian orders provided a sense of the classification of birds, at least down to order and family. The purpose of this chapter is to become more familiar with the genus and species names of specific birds, and to provide lists of names of avicultural birds that will be of value in the identification of birds by name.

Identifying the names of avicultural birds can be very important. The type of information provided in these tables is normally placed in an appendix. However, since the identification of birds by genus and species relates directly to the previous two chapters, this information is given a chapter of its own.

Table 18.1   Common names of parrot-type birds.

Common name	Genus	species
Adelaide rosella	Platycercus	adelaidae
African Grey parrot	Psittacus	erithacus
Alexandrine parakeet	Psittacula	eupatria
Amboina king parrot	Alisterus	amboinensis
Andean parakeet	Bolborhynchus	orbygnesius
Antipodes green parakeet	Cyanoramphus	unicolor
Austral conure	Enicognathus	ferrugineus
Australian king parrot	Bolborhynchus	scapularis
Barraband's Parrot	Pionopsitta	barrabandi
Barred parakeet	Bolborhynchus	lineola
Black cockatoo	Calyptorhynchus	funereus
Black lory	Chalcopsitta	atra
Black parrot	Coracopsis	nigra

Common name	Genus	species
Black-billed amazon	Amazona	agilis
Black-capped conure	Pyrrhura	rupicola
Black-capped lory	Lorius	lory
Black-cheeked lovebird	Agapornis	nigrigenis
Black-collared lovebird	Agapornis	swindeniana
Black-fronted parrot	Cyanoramphus	zealandicus
Black-headed caique	Pionites	melanocephala
Black-lored parrot	Tanygnathus	gramineus
Black-winged lory	Eos	cyanogenia
Black-winged lovebird	Agapornis	taranta
Black-winged parrot	Hapalopsittaca	melanotis
Blaze-winged conure	Pyrrhura	devillei
Blossom-headed parakeet	Psittacula	roseata
Blue and gold macaw	Ara	ararauna
Blue-bonnet	Psephotus	haematogaster
Blue-cheeked amazon	Amazona	dufresniana
Blue-collared parrot	Geoffroyus	simplex
Blue-crowned conure	Aratinga	acuticaudata
Blue-crowned hanging par.	Loriculus	galgulus
Blue-crowned lory	Vini	australis
Blue-crowned racket-tailed parrot	Prioniturus	discurus
Blue-eared lory	Eos	semilarvata
Blue-eyed cockatoo	Cacatua	ophthalmica
Blue-fronted amazon	Amazona	aestiva
Blue-fronted lorikeet	Charmosyna	oxopei
Blue-headed macaw	Ara	couloni
Blue-headed parrot	Pionus	menstruus
Blue-naped parrot	Tanygnathus	lucionensis
Blue-rumped parrot	Psittinus	cyanurus
Blue-streaked lory	Eos	reticulata
Blue-thighed lory	Lorius	tibialis
Blue-throated conure	Pyrrhura	cruentata
Blue-winged parakeet	Neophema	chrysostoma
Blue-winged parrotlet	Forpus	xanthopterygius
Blyth's parakeet	Psittacula	caniceps
Bourke's parakeet	Neophema	bourkii
Brehm's parrot	Psittacella	brehmii
Broad-billed parrot	Lophopsittacus	mauritianus

Common name	Genus	species
Bronze-Winged parrot	Pionus	chalcopterus
Brown-backed parrotlet	Touit	melanonota
Brown-breasted conure	Pyrrhura	calliptera
Brown-headed parrot	Poicephalus	cryptoxanthus
Brown-hooded parrot	Pionopsitta	haematotis
Brown-throated conure	Aratinga	pertinax
Budgerigar	Melopsittacus	undulatus
Buff-faced pygmy parrot	Micropsitta	pusio
Buffon's macaw	Ara	ambigua
Buru racket-tailed parrot	Prioniturus	mada
Cactus conure	Aratinga	cactorum
Caica parrot	Pionopsitta	caica
Canary-winged parakeet	Brotogeris	versicolorus
Caninde macaw	Ara	caninde
Cape parrot	Poicephalus	robustus
Cardinal lory	Chalcopsitta	cardinalis
Carolina parakeet	Conuropsis	carolinensis
Celebes hanging parrot	Loriculus	stigmatus
Ceylon hanging parrot	Loriculus	beryllinus
Chattering lory	Lorius	garrulus
Chestnut-fronted macaw	Ara	severa
Cobalt-winged parakeet	Brotogeris	cyanoptera
Cockatiel	Nymphicus	hollandicus
Collared lory	Phigys	solitarius
Crimson (Pennant) rosella	Platycercus	elegans
Crimson-bellied conure	Pyrrhura	rhodogaster
Cuban amazon	Amazona	leucocephala
Cuban conure	Aratinga	euops
Cuban macaw	Ara	tricolor
Derbyan parakeet	Psittacula	derbiana
Desmarest's fig parrot	Psittaculirostris	desmarestii
Double-eyed fig parrot	Opopsitta	diophthalma
Duchess lorikeet	Charmosyna	margarethae
Ducorp's cockatoo	Cacatua	ducorpsii
Dusky lory	Pseudeos	fuscata
Dusky parrot	Pionus	fuscus
Dusky-headed conure	Aratinga	weddellii
Duvenbode's lory	Chalcopsitta	duivenbodei
Eastern rosella	Platycercus	eximius

Common name	Genus	species
Grey-headed lovebird	Agapornis	cana
Ground parrot	Pezoporus	wallicus
Guaiabero	Bolbopsittacus	lunulatus
Hawk-headed parrot	Deroptyus	accipitrinus
Hispaniolan amazon	Amazona	ventralis
Hispaniolan conure	Aratinga	chloroptera
Hoffman's conure	Pyrrhura	hoffmanni
Horned paraakeet	Eunymphicus	cornutus
Hyacinth macaw	Anodorhynchus	hyacinthinus
Illiger's macaw	Ara	maracana
Imperial amazon	Amazona	imperialis
Intermediate parakeet	Psittacula	intermedia
Iris lorikeet	Trichoglossus	iris
Jandaya conure	Aratinga	jandaya
Jardine's parrot	Poicephalus	gulielmi
Johnstone's lorikeet	Trichoglossus	johnstoniae
Josephine's lorikeet	Charmosyna	josefinae
Kaka	Nestor	meridionalis
Kakapo	Strigops	habroptilus
Kea	Nestor	notabilis
Kuhl's lory	Vini	kuhlii
Lear's macaw	Anodorhynchus	leari
Lesser sulphur-crested	Cacatua	sulphurea
Lilac-crown (Finsch's) amazon	Amazona	finschi
Little corella	Cacatua	sanguinea
Little lorikeet	Glossopsitta	pusilla
Long-billed corella	Cacatua	tenuirostris
Long-tailed parakeet	Psittacula	longicauda
Madarasz's parrot	Psittacella	madaraszi
Major Mitchell's cockatoo	Cacatua	leadbeateri
Malabar parakeet	Psittacula	columboides
Mallee ringneck parrot	Barnardius	barnardi
Maroon-bellied conure	Pyrrhura	frontalis
Maroon-tailed conure	Pyrrhura	melanura
Mascarene parrot	Mascarinus	mascarinus
Masked lovebird	Agapornis	personata
Masked shining parrot	Prosopeia	personata
Mauritius parakeet	Psittacula	echo

Common name	Genus	species
Eclectus parrot	Eclectus	roratus
Edward's fig parrot	Psittaculirostris	edwardsii
Elegant parakeet	Neophema	elegans
Emerald lorikeet	Neopsittacus	pullicauda
Emerald-collared parakeet	Psittacula	calthorpae
Fairy lorikeet	Charmosyna	pulchella
Festive amazon	Amazona	festiva
Fiery-shouldered conure	Pyrrhura	egregia
Finsch's conure	Aratinga	finschi
Finsch's pygmy parrot	Micropsitta	finschii
Fischer's lovebird	Agapornis	fischer
Galah	Eolophus	roseicapillus
Gang-gang cockatoo	Callocephalon	fimbriatum
Geelvink pygmy parrot	Micropsitta	geelvinkiana
Glaucous macaw	Anodorhynchus	glaucus
Glossy cockatoo	Calyptorhynchus	lathami
Goffin's cockatoo	Cacatua	goffini
Golden conure	Aratinga	guarouba
Golden-capped conure	Aratinga	auricapilla
Golden-mantled racket-tailed parrot	Prioniturus	platurus
Golden-plumed conure	Leptosittaca	branickii
Golden-shouldered parrot	Psephotus	chrysopterygius
Golden-tailed parrotlet	Touit	surda
Golden-winged parakeet	Brotogeris	chrysopsopterus
Goldie's lorikeet	Trichoglossus	goldei
Great-billed parrot	Tanygnathus	megalorynchos
Greater. sulphur-crested cockatoo	Cacatua	galerita
Green conure	Aratinga	holochlora
Green hanging parrot	Loriculus	exilis
Green racket-tailed parrot	Prioniturus	luconensis
Green rosella	Platycercus	caledonicus
Green-cheeked amazon	Amazona	viridigenalis
Green-cheeked conure	Pyrrhura	molinae
Green-rumped parrotlet	Forpus	passerinus
Green-winged king parrot	Alisterus	chloropterus
Green-winged macaw	Ara	chloroptera
Grey-cheeked parakeet	Brotogeris	pyrrhopterus

Common name	Genus	species
Mealy amazon	Amazona	farinosa
Meek's lorikeet	Charmosyna	meeki
Meek's pygmy parrot	Micropsitta	meeki
Mexican parrotlet	Forpus	cyanopygius
Meyer's parrot	Poicephalus	meyeri
Military macaw	Ara	militaris
Mitred conure	Aratinga	mitrata
Modest parrot	Psittacella	modesta
Moluccan hanging parrot	Loriculus	amabilis
Monk parakeet	Myiopsitta	monachus
Mountain parakeet	Bolborhynchus	aurifrons
Mountain racket-tailed p.	Prioniturus	montanus
Moustached parakeet	Psittacula	alexandri
Mulga (manycolor) parrot	Psephotus	varius
Muller's parrot	Tanygnathus	sumatranus
Musk lorikeet	Glossopsitta	concinna
Musschenbroek's lorikeet	Neopsittacus	musschenbroekii
Nanday conure	Nandayus	nenday
New Caledonian lorikeet	Charmosyna	diadema
Newton's parakeet	Psittacula	exsul
Niam-Niam parrot	Poicephalus	crassus
Night parrot	Geopsittacus	occidentalis
Norfolk Island kaka	Nestor	productus
Northern (Brown's) rosella	Platycercus	venustus
Nyasa lovebird	Agapornis	lilianae
Olive-throated conure	Aratinga	nana
Orange-fronted hanging p.	Loriculus	aurantiifrons
Orange-bellied paraakeet	Neophema	chrysogaster
Orange-breasted fig parrot	Opopsitta	gulielmiterti
Orange-chinned parakeet	Brotogeris	jugularis
Orange-fronted conure	Aratinga	canicularis
Orange-fronted parrot	Cyanoramphus	malherbi
Orange-winged amazon	Amazona	amazonica
Ornate lory	Trichoglossus	ornatus
Pacific parrotlet	Forpus	coelestis
Painted conure	Pyrrhura	picta
Painted parrot	Psittacella	picta
Pale-headed (blue) rosella	Platycercus	adscitus
Palm cockatoo	Probosciger	aterrimus

Common name	Genus	species
Palm lorikeet	Charmosyna	palmarum
Papuan lory	Charmosyna	papou
Paradise parrot	Psephotus	pulcherrimus
Patagonian conure	Cyanoliseus	patagonus
Peach-faced lovebird	Agapornis	roseicollis
Peach-fronted conure	Aratinga	aurea
Pearly conure	Pyrrhura	perlata
Perfect lorikeet	Trichoglossus	euteles
Pesquet's parrot	Psittrichas	fulgidus
Philippine hanging parrot	Loriculus	philippensis
Pileated parakeet	Pionopsitta	pileata
Plain parakeet	Brotogeris	tirica
Plum-crowned parrot	Pionus	tumultuosus
Plum-headed parakeet	Psittacula	cyanocephala
Ponape Lory	Trichoglossus	rubiginosus
Port Lincoln Parrot	Barnardius	zonarius
Princess parrot	Polytelis	alexandrae
Puertro Rican amazon	Amazona	vittata
Purple-bellied lory	Lorius	hypoinochrous
Purple-bellied parrot	Triclaria	malachitacea
Purple-crowned lorikeet	Glossopsitta	porphyrocephala
Purple-naped lory	Lorius	domicellus
Rainbow lory	Trichoglossus	haematodus
Red and Blue lory	Eos	histrio
Red lory	Eos	bornea
Red shining parrot	Prosopeia	tabuensis
Red-bellied macaw	Ara	manilata
Red-bellied parrot	Poicephalus	rufiventris
Red-billed parrot	Pionus	sordidus
Red-breasted pygmy par.	Micropsitta	bruijnii
Red-capped parrot	Purpureicephalus	spurius
Red-cheeked parrot	Geoffroyus	geoffroyi
Red-chinned lorikeet	Charmosyna	rubrigularis
Red-eared conure	Pyrrhura	hoematotis
Red-faced lovebird	Agapornis	pullaria
Red-flanked lorikeet	Charmosyna	placentis
Red-fronted conure	Aratinga	wagleri
Red-fronted kakariki par.	Cyanoramphus	novaezelandiae
Red-fronted macaw	Ara	rubrogenys

Common name	Genus	species
Red-lored amazon	Amazona	autumnalis
Red-masked conure	Aratinga	erythrogenys
Red-necked amazon	Amazona	arausiaca
Red-rumped parakeet	Psephotus	haematonotus
Red-shouldered macaw	Ara	nobilis
Red-spectacled amazon	Amazona	pretrei
Red-spotted lorikeet	Charmosyna	rubronotata
Red-spotted racket-tailed par.	Prioniturus	flavicans
Red-tailed amazon	Amazona	brasiliensis
Red-tailed cockatoo	Calyptorhynchus	magnificus
Red-throated lorikeet	Charmosyna	amabilis
Red-vented cockatoo	Cacatua	haematuropygia
Red-winged parrot	Aprosmictus	erythropterus
Red-winged parrotlet	Touit	dilectissima
Regent parrot	Polytelis	anthopeplus
Ringneck (Rose-ringed) p.	Psittacula	krameri
Rock parakeet	Neophema	petrophila
Rodriguez parrot	Necropsittacus	rodericanus
Rose-crowned conure	Pyrrhura	rhodocephala
Rose-face parrot	Pionopsitta	pulchra
Rufous-fronted parakeet	Bolborhynchus	ferrugineifrons
Rufous-tailed parrot	Tanygnathus	heterurus
Ruppell's parrot	Poicephalus	rueppellii
Rusty-faced parrot	Hapalopsittaca	amazonina
Saffron-headed parrot	Pionopsitta	pyrilia
Salmon-crested cockatoo	Cacatua	moluccensis
Salvadori's fig parrot	Psittaculirostris	salvadorii
Santa Marta conure	Pyrrhura	viridicata
Sapphire-rumped parrotlet	Touit	purpurata
Scaly-breasted lorikeet	Trichoglossus	chlorolepidotus
Scaly-headed parrot	Pionus	maximiliani
Scaly-naped amazon	Amazona	mercenaria
Scarlet macaw	Ara	macao
Scarlet-chested parakeet	Neophema	splendida
Scarlet-shouldered parrotlet	Touit	huetii
Sclater's parrotlet	Forpus	sclateri
Senegal parrot	Poicephalus	senegalus
Seven-colored parrotlet	Touit	batavica
Seychelles parakeet	Psittacula	wardi

Common name	Genus	species
Short-tailed parrot	Graydidascalus	brachyurus
Sierra parakeet	Bolborhynchus	aymara
Singing parrot	Geoffroyus	heteroclitus
Slaty-headed parakeet	Psittacula	himalayana
Slender-billed conure	Enicognathus	leptorhynchus
Society parakeet	Cyanoramphus	ulietanus
Spectacled parrotlet	Forpus	conspicillatus
Spix's macaw	Cyanopsitta	spixii
Spot-winged parrotlet	Touit	stictoptera
St. Croix macaw	Ara	autocthones
St. Lucia amazon	Amazona	versicolor
St. Vincent amazon	Amazona	guildingii
Stephen's lory	Vini	stepheni
Stresemann's lory	Lorius	amabilis
Striated lorikeet	Charmosyna	multistriata
Sun conure	Aratinga	solstitialis
Superb parrot	Polytelis	swainsonii
Swift parrot	Lathamus	discolor
Tahitian lory	Vini	peruviana
Tepui parrotlet	Nannopsittaca	panychlora
Thick-billed parrot	Rhynchopsitta	pachyrhyncha
Timor red-winged parrot	Aprosmictus	jonquillaceus
Tucuman amazon	Amazona	tucumana
Tui parakeet	Brotogeris	sanctithomae
Turquoisine parakeet	Neophema	pulchella
Ultramarine lory	Vini	ultramarina
Varied lorikeet	Trichoglossus	versicolor
Vasa parrot	Coracopsis	vasa
Vernal hanging parrot	Loriculus	vernalis
Vinaceous amazon	Amazona	vinacea
Violet-necked lory	Eos	squamata
Vulturine parrot	Gypopsitta	vulturina
Wallace's hanging parrot	Loriculus	flosculus
Western (Stanley's) rosella	Platycercus	icterotis
Whiskered lorikeet	Oreopsittacus	arfaki
White cockatoo	Cacatua	alba
White-bellied caique	Pionites	leucogaster
White-capped parrot	Pionus	senilis
White-eared conure	Pyrrhura	leucotis

Common name	Genus	species
White-eyed conkre	Aratinga	leucophthalmus
White-fronted amazon	Amazona	albifrons
White-headed parrot	Pionus	seniloides
White-naped lory	Lorius	albidinuchus
White-necked conure	Pyrrhura	albipectus
Wilhelmina's lorikeet	Charmosyna	wilhelminae
Yellow and green lorikeet	Trichoglossus	flavoviridis
Yellow rosella	Platycercus	flaveolus
Yellow-bibbed lory	Lorius	chlorocercus
Yellow-billed amazon	Amazona	collaria
Yellow-capped pygmy par.	Micropsitta	keiensis
Yellow-collared macaw	Ara	auricollis
Yellow-eared conure	Ognorhynchus	icterotis
Yellow-faced amazon	Amazona	xanthops
Yellow-faced parrot	Poicephalus	flavifrons
Yellow-faced parrotlet	Forpus	xanthops
Yellow-fronted kakariki p.	Cyanoramphus	auriceps
Yellow-headed amazon	Amazona	ochrocephala
Yellow-lored amazon	Amazona	xantholora
Yellow-shouldered amazon	Amazona	barbadensis
Yellow-sided conure	Pyrrhura	hypoxantha
Yellow-streaked lory	Chalcopsitta	sintillata
Yellow-throated hanging p.	Loriculus	pusillus

Table 18.2 Scientific names of parrot-type birds.

Genus	species	Common name
Agapornis	cana	Grey-headed lovebird
Agapornis	fischeri	Fischer's lovebird
Agapornis	lilianae	Nyasa lovebird
Agapornis	nigrigenis	Black-cheeked lovebird
Agapornis	personata	Masked lovebird
Agapornis	pullaria	Red-faced lovebird
Agapornis	roseicollis	Peach-faced lovebird
Agapornis	swinderniana	Black-collared lovebird
Agapornis	taranta	Black-winged lovebird
Alisterus	amboinensis	Amboina king parrot

Genus	species	Common name
Alisterus	chloropterus	Green-winged king par.
Alisterus	scapularis	Australian king parrot
Amazona	aestiva	Blue-fronted amazon
Amazona	agilis	Black-billed amazon
Amazona	albifrons	White-fronted amazon
Amazona	amazonica	Orange-winged amazon
Amazona	arausiaca	Red-necked amazon
Amazona	autumnalis	Red-lored amazon
Amazona	barbadensis	Yellow-shouldered amaz.
Amazona	brasiliensis	Red-tailed amazon
Amazona	collaria	Yellow-billed amazon
Amazona	dufresniana	Blue-cheeked amazon
Amazona	farinosa	Mealy amazon
Amazona	festiva	Festive amazon
Amazona	finschi	Lilac-crowned (Finsch's) amazon
Amazona	guildingii	St. Vincent amazon
Amazona	imperialis	Imperial amazon
Amazona	leucocephala	Cuban amazon
Amazona	mercenaria	Scaly-naped amazon
Amazona	ochrocephala	Yellow-headed amazon
Amazona	pretrei	Red-spectacled amazon
Amazona	tucumana	Tucuman amazon
Amazona	ventralis	Hispaniolan amazon
Amazona	versicolor	St. Lucia amazon
Amazona	vinacea	Vinaceous amazon
Amazona	viridigenalis	Green-cheeked amazon
Amazona	vittata	Puerto Rican amazon
Amazona	xantholora	Yellow-lored amazon
Amazona	xanthops	Yellow-faced amazon
Anodorhynchus	glaucus	Glaucous macaw
Anodorhynchus	hyacinthinus	Hyacinth macaw
Anodorhynchus	leari	Lear's macaw
Aprosmictus	erythropterus	Red-winged parrot
Aprosmictus	jonquillaceus	Timor red-winged parrot
Ara	ambigua	Buffon's macaw
Ara	ararauna	Blue and gold macaw
Ara	auricollis	Yellow-collared macaw
Ara	autocthones	St. Croix macaw

Genus	species	Common name
Ara	caninde	Caninde macaw
Ara	chloroptera	Green-winged macaw
Ara	couloni	Blue-headed macaw
Ara	macao	Scarlet macaw
Ara	manilata	Red-bellied macaw
Ara	maracana	Illiger's macaw
Ara	militaris	Military macaw
Ara	nobilis	Red-shouldered macaw
Ara	rubrogenys	Red-fronted macaw
Ara	severa	Chestnut-fronted macaw
Aratinga	tricolor	Cuban macaw
Aratinga	acuticaudata	Blue-crowned conure
Aratinga	aurea	Peach-fronted conure
Aratinga	auricapilla	Golden-capped conure
Aratinga	cactorum	Cactus conure
Aratinga	canicularis	Orange-fronted conure
Aratinga	chloroptera	Hispaniolan conure
Aratinga	erythrogenys	Red-masked conure
Aratinga	euops	Cuban conure
Aratinga	finschi	Finsch's conure
Aratinga	guarouba	Golden conure
Aratinga	holochlora	Green conure
Aratinga	jandaya	Jandaya conure
Aratinga	leucophthalmus	White-eyed conkre
Aratinga	mitrata	Mitred conure
Aratinga	nana	Olive-throated conure
Aratinga	pertinax	Brown-throated conure
Aratinga	solstitialis	Sun conure
Aratinga	wagleri	Red-fronted conure
Aratinga	weddellii	Dusky-headed conure
Barnardius	barnardi	Mallee ringneck parrot
Barnardius	zonarius	Port Lincoln Parrot
Bolbopsittacus	lunulatus	Guaiabero
Bolborhynchus	aurifrons	Mountain parakeet
Bolborhynchus	aymara	Sierra parakeet
Bolborhynchus	ferrugineifrons	Rufous-fronted parakeet
Bolborhynchus	lineola	Barred parakeet
Bolborhynchus	orbygnesius	Andean parakeet
Brotogeris	chrysopsterus	Golden-winged parakeet

Genus	species	Common name
Brotogeris	cyanoptera	Cobalt-winged parakeet
Brotogeris	jugularis	Orange-chinned parakeet
Brotogeris	pyrrhopterus	Grey-cheeked parakeet
Brotogeris	sanctithomae	Tui parakeet
Brotogeris	tirica	Plain parakeet
Brotogeris	versicolorus	Canary-winged parakeet
Cacatua	alba	White cockatoo
Cacatua	ducorpsii	Ducorp's cockatoo
Cacatua	galerita	Greater sulphur-crested cockatoo
Cacatua	goffini	Goffin's cockatoo
Cacatua	haematuropygia	Red-vented cockatoo
Cacatua	leadbeateri	Major Mitchells cockatoo
Cacatua	moluccensis	Salmon-crested cockatoo
Cacatua	ophthalmica	Blue-eyed cockatoo
Cacatua	sanguinea	Little corella
Cacatua	sulphurea	Lesser sulphur-crested cockatoo
Cacatua	tenuirostris	Long-billed corella
Callocephalon	fimbriatum	Gang-gang cockatoo
Calyptorhynchus	funereus	Black cockatoo
Calyptorhynchus	lathami	Glossy cockatoo
Calyptorhynchus	magnificus	Red-tailed cockatoo
Chalcopsitta	atra	Black lory
Chalcopsitta	cardinalis	Cardinal lory
Chalcopsitta	duivenbodei	Duvenbode's lory
Chalcopsitta	sintillata	Yellow-streaked lory
Charmosyna	amabilis	Red-throated lorikeet
Charmosyna	diadema	New Caledonian lorikeet
Charmosyna	josefinae	Josephine's lorikeet
Charmosyna	margarethae	Duchess lorikeet
Charmosyna	meeki	Meek's lorikeet
Charmosyna	multistriata	Striated lorikeet
Charmosyna	palmarum	Palm lorikeet
Charmosyna	papou	Papuan lory
Charmosyna	placentis	Red-flanked lorikeet
Charmosyna	pulchella	Fairy lorikeet
Charmosyna	rubrigularis	Red-chinned lorikeet
Charmosyna	rubronotata	Red-spotted lorikeet

Genus	species	Common name
Charmosyna	toxopei	Blue-fronted lorikeet
Charmosyna	wilhelminae	Wilhelmina's lorikeet
Conuropsis	carolinensis	Carolina parakeet
Coracopsis	nigra	Black parrot
Coracopsis	vasa	Vasa parrot
Cyanoliseus	patagonus	Patagonian conure
Cyanopsitta	spixii	Spix's macaw
Cyanoramphus	auriceps	Yellow-fronted kakariki
Cyanoramphus	malherbi	Orange-fronted parrot
Cyanoramphus	novaezelandiae	Red-fronted kakariki
Cyanoramphus	ulietanus	Society parakeet
Cyanoramphus	unicolor	Antipodes green para.
Cyanoramphus	zealandicus	Black-fronted parrot
Deroptyus	accipitrinus	Hawk-headed parrot
Eclectus	roratus	Eclectus parrot
Enicognathus	ferrugineus	Austral conure
Enicognathus	leptorhynchus	Slender-billed conure
Eolophus	roseicapillus	Galah
Eos	bornea	Red lory
Eos	cyanogenia	Black-winged lory
Eos	histrio	Red and Blue lory
Eos	reticulata	Blue-streaked lory
Eos	semilarvata	Blue-eared lory
Eos	squamata	Violet-necked lory
Eunymphicus	cornutus	Horned paraakeet
Forpus	coelestis	Pacific parrotlet
Forpus	conspicillatus	Spectacled parrotlet
Forpus	cyanopygius	Mexican parrotlet
Forpus	passerinus	Green-rumped parrotlet
Forpus	sclateri	Sclater's parrotlet
Forpus	xanthops	Yellow-faced parrotlet
Forpus	xanthopterygius	Blue-winged parrotlet
Geoffroyus	geoffroyi	Red-cheeked parrot
Geoffroyus	heteroclitus	Singing parrot
Geoffroyus	simplex	Blue-collared parrot
Geopsittacus	occidentalis	Night parrot
Glossopsitta	concinna	Musk lorikeet
Glossopsitta	porphyrocephala	Purple-crowned lorikeet
Glossopsitta	pusilla	Little lorikeet

Genus	species	Common name
Graydidascalus	brachyurus	Short-tailed parrot
Gypopsitta	vulturina	Vulturine parrot
Hapalopsittaca	amazonina	Rusty-faced parrot
Hapalopsittaca	melanotis	Black-winged parrot
Lathamus	discolor	Swift parrot
Leptosittaca	branickii	Golden-plumed conure
Lophopsittacus	mauritianus	Broad-billed parrot
Loriculus	amabilis	Moluccan hanging par.
Loriculus	aurantiifrons	Orange-fronted hanging parrot
Loriculus	beryllinus	Ceylon hanging parrot
Loriculus	exilis	Green hanging parrot
Loriculus	flosculus	Wallace's hanging parrot
Loriculus	galgulus	Blue-crowned hanging p.
Loriculus	philippensis	Philippine hanging par.
Loriculus	pusillus	Yellow-throated hanging parrot
Loriculus	stigmatus	Celebes hanging parrot
Loriculus	vernalis	Vernal hanging parrot
Lorius	albidinuchus	White-naped lory
Lorius	amabilis	Stresemann's lory
Lorius	chlorocercus	Yellow-bibbed lory
Lorius	domicellus	Purple-naped lory
Lorius	garrulus	Chattering lory
Lorius	hypoinochrous	Purple-bellied lory
Lorius	lory	Black-capped lory
Lorius	tibialis	Blue-thighed lory
Mascarinus	mascarinus	Mascarene parrot
Melopsittacus	undulatus	Budgerigar
Micropsitta	bruijnii	Red-breasted pygmy par.
Micropsitta	finschii	Finsch's pygmy parrot
Micropsitta	geelvinkiana	Geelvink pygmy parrot
Micropsitta	keiensis	Yellow-capped pygmy p.
Micropsitta	meeki	Meek's pygmy parrot
Myiopsitta	monachus	Monk parakeet
Nandayus	nenday	Nanday conure
Nannopsittaca	panychlora	Tepui parrotlet
Necropsittacus	rodericanus	Rodriguez parrot

Genus	species	Common name
Neophema	bourkii	Bourke's parakeet
Neophema	chrysogaster	Orange-bellied paraa.
Neophema	chrysostoma	Blue-winged parakeet
Neophema	elegans	Elegant parakeet
Neophema	petrophila	Rock parakeet
Neophema	pulchella	Turquosine parakeet
Neophema	spendida	Scarlet-chested parakeet
Neopsittacus	musschenbroekii	Musschenbroek's lorikeet
Neopsittacus	pullicauda	Emerald lorikeet
Nestor	meridionalis	Kaka
Nestor	notabilis	Kea
Nestor	productus	Norfolk Island kaka
Nymphicus	hollandicus	Cockatiel
Ognorhynchus	icterotis	Yellow-eared conure
Opopsitta	diophthalma	Double-eyed fig parrot
Opopsitta	gulielmiterti	Orange-breasted fig par.
Oreopsittacus	arfaki	Whiskered lorikeet
Pezoporus	wallicus	Ground parrot
Phigys	solitarius	Collared lory
Pionites	leucogaster	White-bellied caique
Pionites	melanocephala	Black-headed caique
Pionopsitta	barrabandi	Baraband's parrot
Pionopsitta	caica	Caica parrot
Pionopsitta	haematotis	Brown-hooded parrot
Pionopsitta	pileata	Pileated parrot
Pionopsitta	pulchra	Rose-face parrot
Pionopsitta	pyrilia	Saffron-headed parrot
Pionopsitta	chalcopterus	Bronze-Winged parrot
Pionus	fuscus	Dusky parrot
Pionus	maximiliani	Scaly-headed parrot
Pionus	menstruus	Blue-headed parrot
Pionus	senilis	White-capped parrot
Pionus	seniloides	White-headed parrot
Pionus	sordidus	Red-billed parrot
Pionus	tumultuosus	Plum-crowned parrot
Platycercus	adelaidae	Adelaide rosella
Platycercus	adscitus	Pale-headed(blue)rosella
Platycercus	caledonicus	Green rosella
Platycercus	elegans	Crimson(Pennant)rosella
Platycercus	eximius	Eastern rosella
Platycercus	flaveolus	Yellow rosella
Platycercus	icterotis	Western(Stanley's)rosella
Platycercus	venustus	Northern(Brown's)rosella
Poicephalus	crassus	Niam-Niam parrot
Poicephalus	cryptoxanthus	Brown-headed parrot
Poicephalus	flavifrons	Yellow-faced parrot
Poicephalus	gulielmi	Jardine's parrot
Poicephalus	meyeri	Meyer's parrot
Poicephalus	robustus	Cape parrot
Poicephalus	rueppellii	Ruppell's parrot
Poicephalus	rufiventris	Red-bellied parrot
Poicephalus	senegalus	Senegal parrot
Polytelis	alexandrae	Princess parrot
Polytelis	anthopelus	Regent parrot
Polytelis	swainsonii	Superb parrot
Prioniturus	discurus	Blue-crowned racket-tailed par.
Prioniturus	flavicans	Red-spotted racket-tailed parrot
Prioniturus	luconensis	Green racket-tailed p.
Prioniturus	mada	Buru racket-tailed p.
Prioniturus	montanus	Mountain racket-tailed parrot
Prioniturus	platurus	Golden-mantled racket-tailed par.
Probosciger	aterrimus	Palm cockatoo
Prosopeia	personata	Masked shining parrot
Prosopeia	tabuensis	Red shining parrot
Psephotus	chrysopterygius	Golden-shouldered par.
Psephotus	haematogaster	Blue-bonnet
Psephotus	haematonotus	Red-rumped parakeet
Psephotus	pulcherrimus	Paradise parrot
Psephotus	varius	Mulga (manycolor) par.
Pseudeos	fuscata	Dusky lory
Psittacella	brehmii	Brehm's parrot
Psittacella	madaraszi	Madarasz's parrot
Psittacella	modesta	Modest parrot
Psittacella	picta	Painted parrot

Genus	species	Common name
Psittacula	alexandri	Moustached parakeet
Psittacula	calthorpae	Emerald-collared para.
Psittacula	caniceps	Blyth's parakeet
Psittacula	columboides	Malabar parakeet
Psittacula	cyanocephala	Plum-headed parakeet
Psittacula	derbiana	Derbyan parakeet
Psittacula	echo	Mauritius parakeet
Psittacula	eupatria	Alexandrine parakeet
Psittacula	exsul	Newton's parakeet
Psittacula	himalayana	Slaty-headed parakeet
Psittacula	intermedia	Intermediate parakeet
Psittacula	krameri	Ringneck (Rose-ringed) parakeet
Psittacula	longicauda	Long-tailed parakeet
Psittacula	roseata	Blossom-headed para.
Psittacula	wardi	Seychelles parakeet
Psittaculirostris	desmarestii	Desmarest's fig parrot
Psittaculirostris	edwardsii	Edward's fig parrot
Psittaculirostris	salvadorii	Salvadori's fig parrot
Psittacus	erithacus	African Grey parrot
Psittinus	cyanurus	Blue-rumped parrot
Psittrichas	fulgidus	Pesquet's parrot
Purpureicephalus	spurius	Red-capped parrot
Pyrrhura	albipectus	White-necked conure
Pyrrhura	calliptera	Brown-breasted conure
Pyrrhura	cruentata	Blue-throated conure
Pyrrhura	devillei	Blaze-winged conure
Pyrrhura	egregia	Fiery-shouldered conure
Pyrrhura	frontalis	Maroon-bellied conure
Pyrrhura	hoematotis	Red-eared conure
Pyrrhura	hoffmanni	Hoffman's conure
Pyrrhura	hypoxantha	Yellow-sided conure
Pyrrhura	leucotis	White-eared conure
Pyrrhura	melanura	Maroon-tailed conure
Pyrrhura	molinae	Green-cheeked conure
Pyrrhura	perlata	Pearly conure
Pyrrhura	picta	Painted conure
Pyrrhura	rhodocephala	Rose-crowned conure
Pyrrhura	rhodogaster	Crimson-bellied conure

Genus	species	Common name
Pyrrhura	rupicola	Black-capped conure
Pyrrhura	viridicata	Santa Marta conure
Rhynchopsitta	pachyrhyncha	Thick-billed parrot
Strigops	habroptilus	Kakapo
Tanygnathus	gramineus	Black-lored parrot
Tanygnathus	heterurus	Rufous-tailed parrot
Tanygnathus	lucionensis	Blue-naped parrot
Tanygnathus	megalorynchos	Great-billed parrot
Tanygnathus	sumatranus	Muller's parrot
Touit	batavica	Seven-colored parrotlet
Touit	dilectissima	Red-winged parrotlet
Touit	huetii	Scarlet-shouldered parrotlet
Touit	melanonota	Brown-backed parrotlet
Touit	purpurata	Sapphire-rumped parrotlet
Touit	stictoptera	Spot-winged parrotlet
Touit	surda	Golden-tailed parrotlet
Trichoglossus	cholorolepidotus	Scaly-brested lorikeet
Trichoglossus	euteles	Perfect lorikeet
Trichoglossus	flavoviridis	Yellow and green lorikeet
Trichoglossus	goldiei	Goldie's lorikeet
Trichoglossus	haematodus	Rainbow lory
Trichoglossus	iris	Iris lorikeet
Trichoglossus	johnstoniae	Johnstone's lorikeet
Trichoglossus	ornatus	Ornate lory
Trichoglossus	rubiginosus	Ponape Lory
Trichoglossus	versicolor	Varied lorikeet
Triclaria	malachitacea	Purple-bellied parrot
Vini	australis	Blue-crowned lory
Vini	kuhlii	Kuhl's lory
Vini	peruviana	Tahitian lory
Vini	stepheni	Stephen's lory
Vini	ultramarina	Ultramarine lory

Table 18.3   Common names of seceeted finch-type birds.

Estrildidae:

Common name	Genus	species
Abyssinian crimson-wing	Cryptospiza	salvadorii
Alpine munia	Lonchura	monticola
Anambra waxbill	Estrilda	poliopareia
Ant-pecker	Parmoptila	woodhousei
Arabian waxbill	Estrilda	rufibarba
Arfak munia (mannikin)	Lonchura	vana
Aurora finch	Pytilia	phoenicoptera
Bamboo parrot-finch	Erythrura	hyperythra
Bar-breasted firefinch	Lagonosticta	rufopicta
Beautiful firetail	Emblema	bella
Bibfinch	Lepidopygia	nana
Black munia (mannikin)	Lonchura	stygia
Black-bellied firefinch	Lagonosticta	rara
Black-bellied seed-cracker	Pyrenestes	ostrinus
Black-cheeked waxbill	Estrilda	erythrononotos
Black-chinned quail-finch	Ortygospiza	gabonensis
Black-crowned waxbill	Estrilda	nonnula
Black-faced firefinch	Lagonosticta	vinacea nigricollis
Black-headed nun	Lonchura	atricapilla
Black-headed waxbill	Estrilda	atricapilla
Black-lored waxbill	Estrilda	nigriloris
Black-tailed lavender waxbill	Estrilda	perreini
Blue-billed mannikin	Lonchura	bicolor
Blue-breasted waxbill	Uraeginthus	angolensis
Blue-capped waxbill	Uraeginthus	cyanocephala
Blue-faced parrot-finch	Erythrura	cucullata
Brown firefinch	Lagonosticta	nitidula
Brown ricebird (sparrow)	Lonchura	fuscata
Brown twinspot	Clytospiza	monteiri
Cherry (Plum head) finch	Aidemosyne	modesta
Chestnut-breasted mannikin	Lonchura	castaneothorax
Chestnut-breasted negro-finch	Nigrita	bicolor
Cinderella waxbill	Estrilda	thomensis

Common name	Genus	species
Cordon-bleu	Uraeginthus	bengalus
Crimson (Blood) finch	Neochmia	phaeton
Crimson seed-cracker	Pyrenestes	sanguineus
Cut-throat	Amadina	fasciata
Dark firefinch	Lagonosticta	rubricata
Diamond sparrow	Emblema	guttata
Dusky crimson-wing	Cryptospiza	jacksoni
Dusky munia	Lonchura	fuscans
Dusky twinspot	Euchistospiza	cinereovinacea
Dybowski''s twinspot	Euchistospiza	dybowskii
Fawn-breasted waxbill	Estrilda	paludicola
Firefinch	Lagonosticta	senegala
Five colored munia	Lonchura	quinticolor
Forbes' munia (mannikin)	Lonchura	forbesi
Goldbreasted waxbill	Amandava	subflava
Gouldian finch	Chloebia	gouldiae
Grand valley munia	Lonchura	teerinki
Grant's blue-bill	Spermophaga	poliogenys
Gray-headed negro-finch	Nigrita	canicapilla
Great-billed munia	Lonchura	grandis
Green (Schlegel's) twinspot	Mandingoa	nitidula
Green avadavat	Amandava	formosa
Grey-headed munia	Lonchura	caniceps
Grey-headed olive-back	Nesocharis	capistrata
Grey-headed silverbill	Lonchura	griseicapilla
Hill munia	Lonchura	kelaarti
Hunstein's munia	Lonchura	hunsteini
Jameson's firefinch	Lagonosticta	rhodopareia
Java (rice) sparrow	Lonchura	oryzivora
Java munia (mannikin)	Lonchura	leucogastroides
Kulikoro firefinch	Lagonosticta	virata
Landana firefinch	Lagonosticta	landanae
Lavender waxbill	Estrilda	caerulescens
Lesser seed-cracker	Pyrenestes	minor
Locust-finch	Ortygospiza	locustella
Magpie mannikin	Lonchura	fringilloides
Manila parrot-finch	Erythrura	viridifacies
Masked firefinch	Lagonosticta	larvata
Masked grassfinch	Poephila	personata

Common name	Genus	species
Silverbill, Indian	Lonchura	malabarica
Snow mountain munia	Lonchura	montana
Society (Bengalese) finch	Lonchura	striata
Spice finch	Lonchura	punctulata
St. Helena waxbill	Estrilda	astrild
Star finch	Neochmia	ruficauda
Strawberry finch(Avadavat)	Amandava	amandava
Streak-headed munia	Lonchura	tristissima
Swee waxbill	Estrilda	melanotis
Sydney waxbill	Aegintha	temporalis
Thick-billed munia	Lonchura	melaena
Tri-colored nun (mannikin)	Lonchura	malacca
Tri-colored parrot-finch	Erythrura	tricolor
Vinaceous firefinch	Lagonosticta	vinacea vinacea
Violet-eared waxbill	Uraeginthus	granatina
White-backed munia	Lonchura	striata
White-bellied munia	Lonchura	leucogastra
White-breasted negro-finch	Nigrita	fusconota
White-collared olive-back	Nesocharis	ansorgei
White-crowned munia	Lonchura	nevermanni
White-hooded nun	Lonchura	maja
White-spotted munia	Lonchura	leucosticta
Yellow-rumped finch	Lonchura	flaviprymna
Yellow-winged pytilia	Pytilia	hypogrammica
Zebra finch	Poephila	guttata

Fringillidae:

Common name	Genus	species
Alario finch	Serinus	alario
Black and Yellow grossbeak	Coccothraustes	icteroides
Black-faced canary	Serinus	capistrata
Black-headed siskin	Carduelis	magellanicus
Blue chaffinch	Fringilla	teydea
Brambling	Fringilla	montifringilla
Bullfinch	Pyrrhula	pyrrhula

Common name	Genus	species
Melba finch	Pytilia	melba
Mindanao parrot-finch	Erythrura	coloria
Mollucan munia	Lonchura	molucca
New Britain munia	Lonchura	spectabilis
Orange-cheeked waxbill	Estrilda	melpoda
Orange-winged pytilia	Pytilia	afra
Owl (Bicheno) finch	Poephila	bichenovii
Painted finch	Emblema	picta
Pale-fronted negro-finch	Nigrita	luteifrons
Pale-headed munia	Lonchura	pallida
Papuan parrot-finch	Erythrura	papuana
Parson finch	Poephila	cincta
Peale's parrot-finch	Erythrura	pealii
Peters' twinspot	Hypargos	niveoguttatus
Pictorella finch	Lonchura	pectoralis
Pin-tailed nonpareil	Erythrura	prasina
Pink-bellied-parrot finch	Erythrura	kleinschmidti
Pink-belly blackcheek waxbill	Estrilda	charmosyna
Purple Grenadier	Uraeginthus	ianthinogaster
Quail-finch	Ortygospiza	atricollis
Red-billed aurora finch	Pytilia	lineata
Red-breasted blue-bill	Spermophaga	haematina
Red-eared firetail	Emblema	oculata
Red-eared waxbill	Estrilda	troglodytes
Red-faced crimson-wing	Cryptospiza	reichenovii
Red-fronted ant-pecker	Parmoptila	rubrifrons
Red-headed blue-bill	Spermophaga	ruficapilla
Red-headed finch	Amadina	erythrocephala
Red-headed parrot finch	Erythrura	psittacea
Red-sided mountain finch	Oreostruthus	fuliginosus
Rosy twinspot	Hypargos	margaritatus
Rosy-rumped waxbill	Estrilda	rhodopyga
Royal parrot-finch	Erythrura	cyaneovirens
Shaftail (Long-tailed) grassfinch	Poephila	acuticauda
Shelley's crimson-wing	Cryptospiza	shelleyi
Shelley's olive-back	Nesocharis	shelleyi
Silverbill, African	Lonchura	cantans

Common name	Genus	species
Canary	Serinus	canarius
Chaffinch	Fringilla	coelebs
Chinese green finch	Carduelis	sinica
Chinese hawfinch	Coccothraustes	migratoria
Citril finch	Serinus	citrinella
Common crossbill	Loxia	curvirostra
Common rosefinch	Carpodacus	erythrina
Evening grossbeak	Coccothraustes	vespertina
Goldfinch	Carduelis	carduelis
Green singing finch	Serinus	mozambicus
Greenfinch	Carduelis	chloris
Grey singing finch	Serinus	leucopygius
Hawfinch	Coccothraustes	coccothraustes
Himalayan greenfinch	Carduelis	spinoides
Hooded siskin	Carduelis	cucullatus
House finch	Carpodacus	mexicanus
Linnet	Acanthis	cannabina
Natal linnet	Serinus	scotops
Pine grossbeak	Pinicola	enucleator
Pink-browed rosefinch	Carpodacus	rhodopeplus
Purple finch	Carpodacus	purpureus
Red-fronted serin	Serinus	pusillus
Red-headed bullfinch	Pyrrhula	erythrocephala
Redpoll	Acanthis	flammea
Serin	Serinus	serinus
Siskin	Carduelis	spinus
St. Helena seed-eater	Serinus	flaviventris
Sulphury seed-eater	Serinus	sulphuratus
Tibetan siskin	Carduelis	tibetanus
Trumpeter bullfinch	Rhodopechys	githaginea
Twite	Acanthus	flavirostris
Yellow-rumped serin	Serinus	atrogularis

Ploceidae:

Common name	Genus	species
Baya weaver	Ploceus	philippinus
Benguela sparrow	Passer	jagoensis
Black-headed weaver	Ploceus	melanocephalus
Bush petronia	Petronia	dentata
Cape saprrow	Passer	melanurus
Cinnamon sparrow	Passer	cinnamoneus
Crimson-crowned bishop	Euplectes	hordeacea
Dinemelli's weaver	Dinemellia	dinemelli
Fire-fronted bishop	Euplectes	diademata
Golden sparrow	Passer	luteus
Grey-headed sparrow	Passer	griseus
Half-masked weaver	Ploceus	vitellinus
House sparrow	Passer	domesticus
Jackson's whyday	Euplectes	jacksoni
Little masked weaver	Ploceus	luteola
Long-tailed whydah	Euplectes	progne
Madagascar weaver	Foudia	madagascariensis
Napolean weaver	Euplectes	afra
Orix bishop	Euplectes	orix
Paradise whydah	Steganura	paradisea
Pintailed whydah	Vidua	macroura
Queen whydah	Vidua	regia
Red-billed weaver	Quelea	quelea
Red-collared whydah	Euplectes	ardens
Red-shouldered whydah	Euplectes	axilliaris
Reichenow's weaver	Ploceus	reichenowi
Rock sparrow	Petronia	petronia
Rufous-necked weaver	Ploecus	cucullatus
Scaly-crowned weaver	Sporopipes	squamifrons
Senegal combassou	Hypochera	chalybeata
Southern masked weaver	Ploceus	velatus
Spanish sparrow	Passer	hispaniolensis
Tree sparrow	Passer	montanus
Vieillot's black weaver	Ploceus	nigerrimus
White-winged whydah	Euplectes	albonatus
Yellow-rumped bishop	Euplectes	capensis
Yellow-shouldered whydah	Euplectes	macrourus

Table 18.4   Scientific name of selected finch-type birds.

Estrildidae:

Genus	species	Common name
Aegintha	temporalis	Sydney waxbil
Aidemosyne	modesta	Cherry (Plum head) fin.
Amadina	erythrocephala	Red-headed finch
Amadina	fasciata	Cut-throat
Amandava	amandava	Strawberry finch
Amandava	formosa	Green avadavat
Amandava	subflava	Goldbreasted waxbill
Chloebia	gouldiae	Gouldian finch
Clytospiza	monteiri	Brown twinspot
Cryptospiza	jacksoni	Dusky crimson-wing
Cryptospiza	reichenovii	Red-faced crimson-wing
Cryptospiza	salvadorii	Abyssinian crimsonwing
Cryptospiza	shelleyi	Shelley's crimson-wing
Emblema	bella	Beautiful firetail
Emblema	guttata	Diamond sparrow
Emblema	oculata	Red-eared firetail
Emblema	picta	Painted finch
Erythrura	coloria	Mindanao parrot-finch
Erythrura	cyaneovirens	Royal parrot-finch
Erythrura	hyperythra	Bamboo parrot-finch
Erythrura	kleinschmidti	Pink-bellied-parrot finch
Erythrura	papuana	Papuan parrot-finch
Erythrura	pealii	Peale's parrot-finch
Erythrura	prasina	Pin-tailed nonpareil
Erythrura	psittacea	Red-headed parrot finch
Erythrura	tricolor	Tri-colored parrot-finch
Erythrura	trichroa	Blue-faced parrot-finch
Erythrura	viridifacies	Manila parrot-finch
Estrilda	astrild	St. Helena waxbill
Estrilda	atricapilla	Black-headed waxbill
Estrilda	caerulescens	Lavender waxbill
Estrilda	charmosyna	Pink-belly black-cheek waxbill
Estrilda	erythrononotos	Black-cheeked waxbill
Estrilda	melanotis	Swee waxbill
Estrilda	melpoda	Orange-cheeked waxbill
Estrilda	nigriloris	Black-lored waxbill
Estrilda	nonnula	Black-crowned waxbill
Estrilda	paludicola	Fawn-breasted waxbill
Estrilda	perreini	Black-tailed lavender waxbill
Estrilda	poliopareia	Anambra waxbill
Estrilda	rhodopyga	Rosy-rumped waxbill
Estrilda	rufibarba	Arabian waxbill
Estrilda	thomensis	Cinderella waxbill
Estrilda	troglodytes	Red-Eared waxbill
Euchistospiza	cinereovinacea	Dusky twinspot
Euchistospiza	dybowskii	Dybowski''s twinspot
Hypargos	niveoguttatus	Peters' twinspot
Hypargos	margaritatus	Rosy twinspot
Lagonosticta	landanae	Landana firefinch
Lagonosticta	larvata	Masked firefinch
Lagonosticta	nitidula	Brown firefinch
Lagonosticta	rara	Black-bellied firefinch
Lagonosticta	rhodopareia	Jameson's firefinch
Lagonosticta	rubricata	Dark firefinch
Lagonosticta	rufopicta	Bar-breasted firefinch
Lagonosticta	senegala	Firefinch
Lagonosticta	vinacea nigricollis	Black-faced firefinch
Lagonosticta	vinacea vinacea	Vinaceous firefinch
Lagonosticta	virata	Kulikoro firefinch
Lepidopygia	nana	Bibfinch
Lonchura	atricapilla	Black-headed nun
Lonchura	bicolor	Blue-billed mannikin
Lonchura	caniceps	Grey-headed munia
Lonchura	cantans	Silverbill, African
Lonchura	castaneothorax	Chestnut-breasted mannikin
Lonchura	cucullata	Bronze-winged mannikin
Lonchura	flaviprymna	Yellow-rumped finch
Lonchura	forbesi	Forbes' munia
Lonchura	fringilloides	Magepie mannikin
Lonchura	fuscans	Dusky munia
Lonchura	fuscata	Brown ricebird (sparrow)

Genus	species	Common name
Lonchura	grandis	Great-billed munia
Lonchura	griseicapilla	Grey-headed silverbill
Lonchura	hunsteini	Hunstein's munia
Lonchura	kelaarti	Hill munia
Lonchura	leucogastra	White-bellied munia
Lonchura	leucogastroides	Java munia (mannikin)
Lonchura	leucosticta	White-spotted munia
Lonchura	maja	White-hooded nun
Lonchura	malabarica	Silverbill, Indian
Lonchura	malacca	Tri-colored nun
Lonchura	melaena	Thick-billed munia
Lonchura	molucca	Mollucan munia
Lonchura	montana	Snow mountain munia
Lonchura	monticola	Alpine munia
Lonchura	nevermanni	White-crowned munia
Lonchura	oryzivora	Java (rice) sparrow
Lonchura	pallida	Pale-headed munia
Lonchura	pectoralis	Pictorella finch
Lonchura	punctulata	Spice finch
Lonchura	quinticolor	Five colored munia
Lonchura	spectabilis	New Britain munia
Lonchura	striata	White-backed munia
Lonchura	striata	Society (Bengalese) finch
Lonchura	stygia	Black munia (mannikin)
Lonchura	teerinki	Grand valley munia
Lonchura	tristissima	Streak-headed munia
Lonchura	vana	Arfak munia (mannikin)
Mandingoa	nitidula	Green (Schlegel's) twinspot
Neochmia	phaeton	Crimson (Blood) finch
Neochmia	ruficauda	Star finch
Nesocharis	ansorgei	White-collared oliveback
Nesocharis	capistrata	Grey-headed olive-back
Nesocharis	shelleyi	Shelley's olive-back
Nigrita	bicolor	Chestnut-breasted negro-finch
Nigrita	canicapilla	Gray-headed negro-finch
Nigrita	fusconota	White-breasted negro-finch
Nigrita	luteifrons	Pale-fronted negro-finch
Oreostruthus	fuliginosus	Red-sided mountain finch
Ortygospiza	atricollis	Quail-finch
Ortygospiza	gabonensis	Black-chinned quail-finch
Ortygospiza	locustella	Locust-finch
Parmoptila	rubrifrons	Red-fronted ant-pecker
Parmoptila	woodhousei	Ant-pecker
Poephila	acuticauda	Shaftail (Long-tailed) grassfinch
Poephila	bichenovii	Owl (Bicheno) finch
Poephila	cincta	Parson finch
Poephila	guttata	Zebra finch
Poephila	personata	Masked grassfinch
Pyrenestes	minor	Lesser seed-cracker
Pyrenestes	ostrinus	Black-bellied seed-cracker
Pyrenestes	sanguineus	Crimson seed-cracker
Pytilia	afra	Orange-winged pytilia
Pytilia	hypogrammica	Yellow-winged pytilia
Pytilia	lineata	Red-billed aurora finch
Pytilia	melba	Melba finch
Pytilia	phoenicoptera	Aurora finch
Spermophaga	haematina	Red-breasted blue-bill
Spermophaga	poliogenys	Grant's blue-bill
Spermophaga	ruficapilla	Red-headed blue-bill
Uraeginthus	angolensis	Blue-breasted waxbill
Uraeginthus	bengalus	Cordon-bleu
Uraeginthus	cyanocephala	Blue-capped waxbill
Uraeginthus	granatina	Violet-eared waxbill
Uraeginthus	ianthinogaster	Purple Grenadier

Fringillidae:

Genus	species	Common name
Acanthis	cannabina	Linnet
Acanthis	flammea	Redpoll
Acanthus	flavirostris	Twite

Genus	species	Common name
Carduelis	carduelis	Goldfinch
Carduelis	chloris	Greenfinch
Carduelis	cucullatus	Hooded siskin
Carduelis	magellanicus	Black-headed siskin
Carduelis	sinica	Chinese green finch
Carduelis	spinoides	Himalayan greeenfinch
Carduelis	spinus	Siskin
Carduelis	tibetanus	Tibetan siskin
Carpodacus	erythrina	Common rosefinch
Carpodacus	mexicanus	House finch
Carpodacus	purpureus	Purple finch
Carpodacus	rhodopeplus	Pink-browed rosefinch
Coccothraustes	coccothraustes	Hawfinch
Coccothraustes	icteroides	Black and Yellow grossbeak
Coccothraustes	migratoria	Chinese hawfinch
Coccothraustes	vespertina	Evening grossbeak
Fringilla	coelebs	Chaffinch
Fringilla	montifringilla	Brambling
Fringilla	teydea	Blue chaffinch
Loxia	curvirostra	Common crossbill
Pinicola	enucleator	Pine grossbeak
Pyrrhula	erythrocephala	Red-headed bullfinch
Pyrrhula	pyrrhuyla	Bullfinch
Rhodopechys	githaginea	Trumpeter bullfinch
Serinus	alario	Alario finch
Serinus	atrogularis	Yellow-rumped serin
Serinus	canarius	Canary
Serinus	capistrata	Black-faced canary
Serinus	citrinella	Citril finch
Serinus	flaviventris	St. Helena seed-eater
Serinus	leucopygius	Grey singing finch
Serinus	pusillus	Red-fronted serin
Serinus	scotops	Natal linnet
Serinus	serinus	Serin
Serinus	sulphuratus	Sulphury seed-eater

Ploceidae:

Genus	species	Common name
Dinemellia	dinemelli	Dinemelli's weaver
Euplectes	afra	Napolean weaver
Euplectes	albonatus	White-winged whydah
Euplectes	ardens	Red-collared whydah
Euplectes	axilliaris	Red-shouldered whydah
Euplectes	capensis	Yellow-rumped bishop
Euplectes	diademata	Fire-fronted bishop
Euplectes	hordeacea	Crimson-crowned bishop
Euplectes	jacksoni	Jackson's whyday
Euplectes	macrourus	Yellow-shouldered whydah
Euplectes	orix	Orix bishop
Euplectes	progne	Long-tailed whydah
Foudia	madagascariensis	Madagascar weaver
Hypochera	chalybeata	Senegal combassou
Passer	cinnamoneus	Cinnamon sparrow
Passer	domesticus	House sparrow
Passer	griseus	Grey-headed sparrow
Passer	hispaniolensis	Spanish sparrow
Passer	jagoensis	Benguela sparrow
Passer	luteus	Golden sparrow
Passer	melanurus	Cape sparrow
Passer	montanus	Tree sparrow
Petronia	dentata	Bush petronia
Petronia	petronia	Rock sparrow
Ploecus	cucullatus	Rufous-necked weaver
Ploceus	luteola	Little masked weaver
Ploceus	melanocephalus	Black-headed weaver
Ploceus	nigerrimus	Vieillot's black weaver
Ploceus	philippinus	Baya weaver
Ploceus	reichenowi	Reichenow's weaver
Ploceus	velatus	Southern masked weaver
Ploceus	vitellinus	Half-masked weaver
Quelea	quelea	Red-billed weaver
Sporopipes	squamifrons	Scaly-crowned weaver
Steganura	paradisea	Paradise whydah
Vidua	macroura	Pintailed whydah
Vidua	regia	Queen whydah

19   Mendelian Genetics

Introduction

There are many aviculturists who can, because of many years of observation, predict the possible offspring resulting from the breeding of common
mutations. However, many aviculturists are confused by avian genetics. A
possible reason for this confusion is fact that many aviculturists don't have
an understanding of basic genetics. It is the hypothesis here that if aviculturists better understood basic genetics, they would have a much easier time
understanding avian genetics.

Cellular reproduction

The cell theory says that all living things are composed of cells and all
cells come from preexisting cells. Therefore, the reproduction of cells is
critical to survival of the organism. If an organism is to grow and repair itself,
there must be a mechanism for the replacement of cells. The replacement of
cells is called cell division.

The most critical element in cell division is the passing on of the hereditary material from one cell to another. Hereditary material is contained on
structures called chromosomes. The number of chromosomes in each cell is
the same throughout the body of an individual. All individuals, in the same
species, have the same numbers of chromosomes. There is, however, a
variation in the number of chromosomes found in the different species of
birds.

Mitosis

There are two types of cell division. The first is called mitosis. In mitosis
the original cell will undergo a division which will result in the production
of two "daughter cells," exactly the same as the original cell. Mitosis is
important in producing cells for the growth of the organism, from the
fertilized ovum (zygote) to the adult.

Mitosis is important in the replacement of old cells when they die. Mitosis
is also important in producing cells for repair, when injury has destroyed

cells. If the the damaged cells are not capable of undergoing mitosis, then the damage is permanent. An example of this permanent damage can be seen in a heart attack. The cardiac muscle cells of the heart are not capable of mitosis. So, if there is destruction to areas of the heart muscle, these damages are permanent.

Meiosis

The other type of cell division is called meiosis. In meiosis, as in mitosis, two "daughter cells" are produced from the original cell. There is, however, a significant difference. Meiosis results in "daughter cells" having only half as many chromosomes as the original cell. These chromosomes are in pairs. One chromosome from each pair will pass into each "daughter cell."

Meiosis is used exclusively for the production of the gametes. The gametes are the sperm cells of male birds and the ova (eggs) of female birds. For example, if the original cell had 80 chromosomes, then after meiosis the resulting "daughter cells" (sperm or egg) would each have 40 chromosomes. In contrast, after mitosis each "daughter cell" would have the full complement of 80 chromosomes (Figure 19.1).

Figure 19.1 Chromosome changes in meiosis and mitosis.

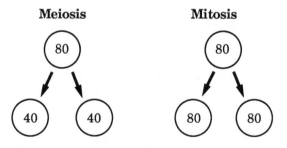

This reduction of the chromosome number in meiosis is important in reproduction. Chromosome reduction is important in regard to the number of chromosomes which will result from fertilization. For example, if the sperm cells and ova were produced by mitosis, then each would have 80 chromosomes. When fertilization occurs, the joining of the sperm and ova would result in a fertilized cell (zygote) with 160 chromosomes. The next generation would have 320 chromosomes, and so on. Obviously, this cannot continue.

However, if the sperm and ova are produced by meiosis, they will have only 40 chromosomes. Therefore, when fertilization occurs, the resulting zygote will have only 80 chromosomes. This will be repeated, generation after generation. Thus, the chromosome number of a specific species will remain the same from one generation to the next.

The significance of meiosis in genetics is that half of the chromosomes go to one "daughter cell" and half to the other. Therefore, there is a probability of different genetic potentials in each cell. This will result in many different genetic combinations. In genetics, we keep track of these different chromosomes as they go to the different gamete cells, thereby producing different genetic potentials.

Chromosomes

Located in the nucleus of each cell are long strand-like structures called chromosomes. Each chromosome is composed of small functional units called genes. The role of the gene is to code for a specific proteins. These proteins will determine the biochemical or physical characteristic of the individual cells and hence of the organism. The chromosome itself is made of a type of organic material called DNA (deoxyribonucleic acid). (Figure 19.2)

Figure 19.2   Two sets of chromosomes, showing the paired genes.

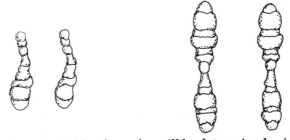

For example, cockatiel feather color will be determined primarily by the amount of melanin in each feather. A pair of genes, on two specific chromosomes, will code for the production of the melanin pigment. Genes, on chromosomes from both parents, will couple in the fertilized egg. These paired genes will interact to determine how much melanin is produced, and also where it will be distributed. This is heredity.

Chromosomes almost always exist in pairs. Because these chromosomes exist in recognizable pairs, an experienced biological technician can pair them up quickly. Figure 19.2 shows that when the pair of chromosomes are placed together, there is a definite pattern to the distribution of the genes. The location of a specific gene, on one of the chromosome pair, is in exactly the same location as the gene on the other paired chromosome.

These two genes will interact with each other to code for one of the physical characteristics of the organism. There are as many pairs of these genes as there are different physical and chemical characteristics of the organism.

These genes are usually classified as being dominant or recessive. The dominant gene characteristic is usually expressed, while the recessive gene characteristic is not. This recessive gene characteristic is "hidden", but the recessive gene is still present on the chromosome. Organisms with recessive genes that are not expressed are called carriers.

In meiosis, these paired chromosomes, and their genes, will be separated from each other in the two new "daughter" cells. In order to keep track of these genes, we assign letters to them. To solve genetics problems, we write the dominant gene with a capital letter. The recessive gene is indicated by a lower case letter. For example, in the case of a dominant red color, we use a capital "R" as the symbol for the dominant characteristic. Then a small letter "r" could be used as a symbol for the recessive characteristic.

Mendellian genetics

Gregor Mendel was an Austrian monk, who in the 1850s, made some astute observations about the different characteristics of ordinary garden peas. The first thing he noticed was that there was some predictability to the types of offspring they produced.

He also noticed some strange phenomena. Pea plants bearing red flowers, crossed with pea plants bearing white flowers, did not produce pea plants bearing pink flowers. There was no blending. Another observation was that red-flowering plants crossed with white-flowering plants most often produced all red-flowering offspring. However, in some cases there were some white-flowered offspring.

Mendel noticed that other characteristics tended to appear in two contrasting forms as well. The forms he noticed most were yellow seeds versus green seeds and smooth seeds versus wrinkled seeds. Observing many crosses of these traits, Mendel decided to call those characteristics which showed up in the first generation (red, yellow, round), dominant characters. Those which did not show up until the second generation, or later, (white, green, wrinkled), were called recessive characters.

From his observations, he postulated that there are two hereditary factors (genes) for each character. He further postulated that these hereditary factors (genes) segregate and pass into the separate gametes. The gametes here are the pollen grain and the female ovum of the pea plants. Although he could not see chromosomes or genes at that time, his hypothesis is consistent with what we know today about the segregation of chromosomes in meiosis.

Mendel published his work and hypothesis in 1866, but this cornerstone of present day genetics was ignored by the scientific community of his day. However, his hypothesis is still valid today, although we have discovered many variations of it. Let's apply Mendel's hypothesis to the crossbreeding of pea plants.

Mendel crossed one plant which produced red flowers with one plant which produced white flowers, both of which breed true. A plant which breeds true is one which always produces offspring of the same color, etc. When he crossed these two (red and white) plants which bred true, the offspring were always red.

If however, he crossed two of the resulting red-flowering offspring, he found that some white-flowering plants would result. The typical offspring ratio was three red-flowering plant for each white-flowering plant, when two red-flowering, first generation plants were crossed.

The crosses would look like this:

Cross	Parents	Offspring
1st	red x red	all red
2nd	red x white	3 red & 1 white

To understand the above Mendelian cross, we must take a look at the genes which determine flower color. The letters representing the two genes are called the genotype ("type of genes"). The interpretation of these crosses is as follows. The gene called (R) codes for a red flower, whereas, the gene (r) codes for a white flower. The red gene (R) is dominant to the white gene (r). Since the genes are typically found in pairs, the following gene combinations (genotypes) are possible:

Genotypes	Physical characteristic
(RR)	red flower
(Rr)	red flower
(rr)	white flower

If the flower is white, we immediately know that the genotype is (rr), since (rr) always produces white flowers. However, if the flower is red, there are two possible genotypes, (RR) or (Rr), which will produce red flowers. Looking at the red flowers won't tell you whether the red-flowering plant is (RR) or (Rr). The only way to find out the genotype of a red-flowering pea plant is to cross (mate) it with other pea plants and observe the offspring. This type of a cross is called a test cross and will be discussed later.

Plants reproduce in a specific sequence. First, the gametes (pollen grains and ova) are produced and then unite in a process called fertilization. In plants, this is usually accomplished by either wind or insects carrying the pollen grains to the ova of the flowers.

To understand genetics, we must follow the chromosomes and their genes, as they move first to the gametes and then as they unite in fertilization. The first step then is the formation of the gametes. As we said earlier, this comes about in a process called meiosis.

In meiosis, one chromosome from each pair goes to each of the two "daughter" cells. Since our concern here is with one characteristic (flower color) we need only to follow one pair of chromosomes. Actually, we need to follow only one pair of genes on that one pair of chromosomes. As explained earlier, these genes have been labeled with the letters (R) and (r).

Now let's review the Mendelian cross mentioned earlier. We take a red-flowering plant that always breeds true. If the red-flowering plant always breeds true, then it must have two dominant genes (RR). We will cross this plant with a white-flowering plant, which also breeds true. All white plants have two recessive genes (rr). So we will be crossing two plants with the genotypes of (RR) and (Rr).

The first step then is meiosis:

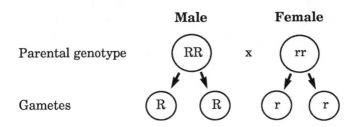

Notice that in the male, all the pollen grains have the same gene because the parent had only R genes. Also, notice that the female ova all have the same gene (r).

The second step is fertilization:

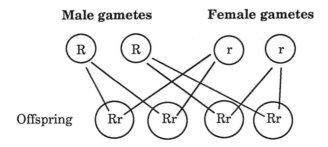

An easier way to determine the results of fertilization is to use what is called the Punnett square. To use this square, you simply write the genes of the male gamete on one axis and the genes of the female gamete on the other axis. Then fill in the boxes as shown in the example below:

	R	R
r	Rr	Rr
r	Rr	Rr

To fill in the Punnett square you simply write the (R) and (R) in the two boxes directly below them. Then write (r) and (r) in the boxes directly to their right.

The results from this Punnett square show that all the offspring from this cross have the genotype (Rr). All of these offspring therefore will be red-flowering. Having one dominant and one recessive gene is called a "split" in the avicultural world. What would happen now if we were to cross two of the (Rr) red-flowering plants? Again, we first form the gametes and then use the Punnett square for fertilization.

The first step is gamete formation (meiosis):

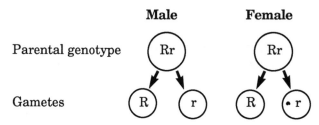

We will again use the Punnett square to see what will result from fertilization of these gametes. Notice that we now have some different genetic potentials.

	R	r
R	RR	Rr
r	Rr	rr

The results indicate three different genotype, which would result in two different flower colors. The theoretical ratio is three reds for each white.

Genotype	Physical characteristic
1 (RR)	1 red flower (will breed true)
2 (Rr)	2 red flower (which are "splits")
1 (rr)	1 white flower (will breed true)

These results show that, when you cross two plants, who have one dominant and one recessive gene, the expected offspring ratio will be three offspring exhibiting the dominant characteristic and one offspring exhibiting the recessive characteristic.

While this three to one ratio is fine for predicting the type of offspring in the long term (many offspring), it can be unpredictable in the short term. For example, in flipping a coin you would guess that there is a 50/50 chance for a head or a tail. If you flipped a coin, let's say a 1,000 times, the number of heads and tails would be just about the same.

However, if you flipped the coin only two times, it is quite possible that it will come up heads both times. This would imply, incorrectly, that there is a 100% probability of the flipped coin coming up heads. In other words, probability, while useful for predictions in the long term, can be unreliable in the short term.

Let's examine, more closely, the problem of determining whether the red flowering plant has a genotype of (RR) or (Rr). The surest way to determine which plants are "split" (Rr) is to perform what is called a test cross. In a test cross, the unknown plant is cross pollinated with a recessive plant, in this case the white flowering plant (rr). The result might look like this:

If the unknown was (RR):
(RR) x (rr)

If the unknown was (Rr):
(Rr x (rr)

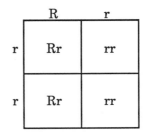

There would be only one genotype:
(Rr)   red flowers

There would be two genotypes:
(Rr)   red flowers
(rr)   white flowers

So, if the unknown was a "split" (Rr) then theoretically
half of the offspring would be red and half white.

These results tell us a lot about the genotype of the unknown parent. A parent who has two dominant genes (RR) cannot produce any white offspring. A parent who is a "split" (Rr) will produce offspring with both red and white flowers, usually in a 50/50 ratio. The most significant point here is that a (RR) parent cannot produce offspring with white flowers. Therefore, if any white flowering plants show up in the offspring, the unknown parent must be a "split" (Rr).

Lets say that white-flowering plants were twice as valuable to a nursery as red-flowering plants. Then it would be in the best economic interest of the nurseryman to select out those plants which would produce white flowers. Obviously, a white to white breeding would produce all white flowering plants.

What if there were very few white plants available, or the white to white cross produced smaller plants? The nurseryman would then have to produce white-flowering plants from red-flowering plants. The only red-flowering plants that would do this would be those whose genotypes are (Rr). Those with (RR) would produce offspring, all of which produce red flowers.

Using the test cross demonstrated above, the nurseryman can isolate those red-flowering plants which are (Rr) and cross them. As we saw earlier, this cross will produce plants in a ratio of three red-flowering plants for each white-flowering plant. Theoretically, the nurseryman can expect 25% of the plants to be white. He could increase this to 50% by crossing a "split" (Rr) red-flowering plant with a white-flowering plant. (refer back to the test cross on the previous page).

The crosses we have been looking at are called monohybrid crosses. Monohybrid crosses are those in which we look at only one characteristic, such as flower color, at a time. If you understand what we have done in these monohybrid crosses, you have the knowledge to understand basic genetics. Although they may seem more complex, all other genetic problems are just variations on this same concept.

Let's use what we have learned to solve a problem. The facts are: peas with smooth coats (S) are dominant to peas with wrinkled coats (s). We chose here to use the letters "S or s" to represent the genes. Any letter which makes sense to you can be used as a symbol for the gene. Usually the first letter of the dominant characteristic is used. What would be the theoretical offspring ratio if a plant with smooth seed, which always bred true (SS), was crossed with a plant with smooth seeds which was "split" (Ss)?

Genotypes of patent plants: (SS) x (Ss)

Cross:

	S	S
S	SS	SS
s	Ss	Ss

There are two genotypes produced from this cross, (SS) and (Ss), both of which produce the dominant characteristic, smooth coats. However, half of the offspring would be "splits" (Ss). This cross demonstrates that there is very little problem producing adequate numbers of the dominant offspring. This is fine if the dominant characteristic is the most desirable trait.

However, the recessive characteristic is the most desirable trait in most avicultural birds. Therefore, a knowledge of genetics is important to maximize the probability of producing more of these recessive characteristics in the offspring.

An example of a monohybrid cross in a bird would be the pied mutation found in cockatiels. The pied color pattern of these birds is a simple recessive characteristic. We will use (P) as the symbol for the dominant gene, which results in the normal gray color. We will use (p) as a symbol for the recessive gene, which will result in a pied bird. First we will cross a normal gray male bird, with no mutated genes (PP), with a female bird who is pied (pp):

The first step is gamete formation (meiosis):

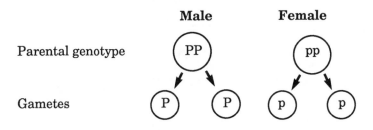

	Male	**Female**
Parental genotype	PP	pp
Gametes	P P	p p

Now to see the offspring, we fertilize using the Punnett square:

	P	P
p	Pp	Pp
p	Pp	Pp

All the offspring would have the same genotype (Pp), resulting in offspring all normal gray in appearance, but split for the pied characteristic.

What would we get if we now cross two of these "split offspring?"

The first step is gamete formation (meiosis):

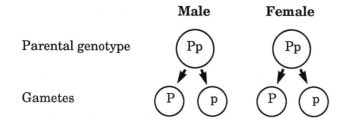

	Male	**Female**
Parental genotype	Pp	Pp
Gametes	P p	P p

Now to see the offspring, we fertilize using the Punnett square:

	P	p
P	PP	Pp
p	Pp	pp

The results indicate three different genotypes, producing birds with two different feather colors.

$$1 \text{ (PP)} = 1 \text{ gray}$$

$$2 \text{ (Pp)} = 2 \text{ grays, split to pied}$$

$$1 \text{ (pp)} = 1 \text{ pied}$$

Theoretically, this cross produces only 25% of the offspring which are pied, but 50% of the offspring are "splits." Only 25% would be completely dominant gray birds. This is not a sex-linked trait, therefore the sex of the offspring has nothing to do with whether they are gray or pied. We will discuss sex-linked traits later in this chapter.

The genetics discussed so far involves what is called "complete dominance." This is the case where the "split" (Rr) is controlled by the dominant gene and the recessive gene has no effect. In some organisms, there is what is called "incomplete dominance", where the dominant gene does not control the recessive gene. In other words, both play a role in determining the characteristic. Here is an example of "incomplete dominance" in a plant which produces red and white flowers:

$$\text{(RR)} = \text{red flowering plant}$$

$$\text{(Rr)} = \text{pink flowering plant}$$

$$\text{(rr)} = \text{white flowering plant}$$

In incomplete dominance, the interrelationship of the (R) gene and (r) gene in a "split" (Rr), results in an offspring which does not look like either of the parents. Some might call it a blending of the two colors. The basic human hair textures of curly, wavy and straight are examples of "incomplete dominance." It should be pointed out, that in almost all genetic characteristics studied, "complete dominance" is the rule. There are very few examples of "incomplete dominance" in avicultural genetics, which are known at this time.

It is obvious that organisms are made up of more than one characteristic. We have looked at just one characteristic, such as flower color or the texture of the pea coat. If one were to look at two characteristics together, such as the two just mentioned, this would be called a dihybrid cross. Since most avicultural genetics do not involve dihybrid crosses, we won't look at them here. Any basic biology textbook will explain the dihybrid cross.

Sex-linked traits

There is one variation on the basic monohybrid cross that bears our attention, since it shows up often in avian genetics. We are talking about sex-linked characteristics. In our discussion so far, we have talked about the interaction of two genes to determine a characteristic.

We have said that there are two genes which interact to determine a characteristic. There are two genes because the chromosomes are in pairs. Each chromosome has one of the two complementary genes for each of the genetically determined characteristics. We will now modify this statement to say that most chromosomes have two complementary gene for each characteristic, but not all do.

There is a pair of chromosomes called the sex-chromosomes, so called because they determine the sex of the offspring. These chromosomes have names using the letters "X" and "Y". In birds, the male is a male because he has two "X" chromosomes in each of his cells (XX). The female is a female because of the presence of one "X" and one "Y" in each of her cells (XY).

Unlike the other chromosomes of the cell, the sex chromosomes are not exactly alike (Figure 19.3). Notice that for the first two-thirds of the chromosome, the "X" and "Y" are identical. However, the lower one-third of the "Y" chromosome is permanently missing.

Figure 19.3   Comparison of the X and Y Chromosome.

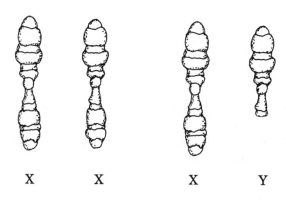

X   X   X   Y

This difference in sex chromosome size has significant implications for heredity. Any gene located on the lower one-third of the "X" chromosome won't have a complementary gene on the "Y" chromosome. So, there will be only one gene, on this lower one-third, to determine a characteristic. Thus, recessive characteristics can be expressed as easily as dominant characteristics, if the gene is located on this lower one-third of the chromosome.

Normally it takes two recessive genes (rr) to produce a recessive characteristic, such as white flower color to be exhibited. However, if the genes for flower color are located on the lower one-third of the "X" chromosome, there is only one gene position. Therefore, only one recessive gene (r) would be required to produce a white-flowering plant.

There are many sex-linked traits in avian genetics. Therefore, it becomes essential to understand this variation. The determination of offsping involving sex-linked characteristics is essentially the same as in a simple monohybrid cross. We first determine the genes passed on to the gametes (meiosis). Then we use a Punnett square to determine the genotypes of the offspring. The main difference, in a sex-linked problem, is that we must keep track of the sex chromosomes ("X" or "Y"), as well as the gene symbol ("R" or "r", or whatever). In sex-linked traits, the sex of the bird is an important factor to consider.

Before we begin looking at sex-linkage, there is one important difference between human genetics and avian genetics to mention. As mentioned earlier, in birds, (XX) produces the males and (XY) produces the females. In humans, it's just the opposite, (XX) produces females and (XY) produces males. Sex-linked traits, in humans, show up more readily in males (baldness). In birds, recessive sex-linked characteristics show up more readily, and thus more often, in female birds.

The most abundant cockatiel mutation is the one resulting in the white/lutino/albino cockatiel. These birds are known by all three names, two of which are incorrect. These birds are definitely not albinos. They are not yellow and so they are not lutinos. White is probably the best descriptive term, but since most aviculturists refer to them as lutinos, we will do so here for the sake of uniformity.

The lutino trait is a sex-linked recessive trait in cockatiels. The normal bird is gray. Again, the gene for the gray feather color is on the lower one-third of the "X" chromosome. This is why we call it sex-linked.

When working with a sex-linked trait, it is necessary to indicate the sex chromosome, as well as the gene symbol. For example, the following would be the genotypes for the various possibilities for the lutino mutation. The dominant gene "L" results in the normal gray bird. The recessive gene "l" results in the lutino bird. If the lutino were not a sex linked characteristic, we would write the genotypes like this:

(LL)   =   gray

(Ll)   =   gray, split to lutino

(ll)   =   lutino

However, the lutino characteristic is sex linked, so we must include the sex chromosome in the genotype:

$X_L X_L$ =   gray male

$X_L X_l$ =   gray male, split to lutino

$X_l X_l$ =   lutino male

$X_L Y$ =   gray female

$X_l Y$ =   lutino female

Note that for a sex linked characteristic, there is no such thing as a split female. Only the male has two X chromosomes and therefore can be "split."

We shall cross a normal gray male ($X_L X_L$) with a lutino hen ($X_l Y$):

The first step is gamete formation (meiosis):
(remember to keep track of the sex chromosome)

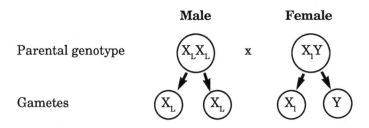

	Male		**Female**
Parental genotype	$X_L X_L$ x		$X_l Y$
Gametes	X_L X_L		X_l Y

Now to see the offspring, we fertilize using the Punnett square:

	X_L	X_L
X_1	$X_L X_1$	$X_L X_1$
Y	$X_L Y$	$X_L Y$

The results show two different genotypes. As expected, there is a 50/50 sex ratio. All the males are gray, but are split to lutino. All the females are gray. So, from this cross of a gray bird and a lutino bird, none of the offspring will be lutino.

Note that the procedure used, in the above cross, was exactly the same as the procedure used in the monohybrid crosses that we did earlier. The only difference is that the sex chromosomes were included in the figures.

The above cross goes against our intuition. If one of the birds is lutino, we would expect at least some of the offspring to be lutino. Here is another cross, with unexpected results. Two gray birds will produce a lutino. In this cross, a male split to lutino (but gray in color) will be mated to a gray female:

The first step is gamete formation (meiosis):
(remember to keep track of the sex chromosome)

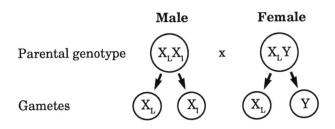

Now to see the offspring, we fertilize using the Punnett square:

	X_L	X_l
X_L	$X_L X_L$	$X_L X_l$
Y	$X_L Y$	$X_l Y$

The results of this cross show that all the males will be gray, but half will be split to lutino. One-half of the females will be gray and one-half will be lutino. We have a cross which will produce 25% lutino, all of them females.

All sex linked characteristics are calculated in the same way as demonstrated in the crosses above. The only difference is that a different letter would be used for a different color or other physical characteristic.

For example, the red or black head color in the Gouldian finch (*Chloebia gouldiae*) is a sex linked trait. The significant difference in the Gouldian finch is that the red-headed mutation is dominant. This is unusual, since most mutations are recessive.

Let's cross a red-headed male, split to black, with a red-headed female:

The first step is gamete formation (meiosis):
(remember to keep track of the sex chromosome)

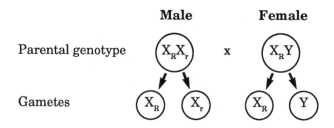

	Male		**Female**
Parental genotype	$X_R X_r$	x	$X_R Y$
Gametes	X_R X_r		X_R Y

Now to see the offspring, we fertilize using the Punnett square:

	X_R	X_r
X_R	$X_R X_R$	$X_R X_r$
Y	$X_R Y$	$X_r Y$

These results show four different genotypes. One fourth of the birds will be red-headed males with only dominant genes. One-fourth of the birds will be red-headed males, split to black. One-fourth of the birds will be red-headed females and one-fourth of the birds will be black-headed females.

None of the offspring will be black-headed males. Will the substitution of a black-headed male, for the "split" male, result in black-headed male offspring? Lets see:

The first step is gamete formation (meiosis):
(remember to keep track of the sex chromosome)

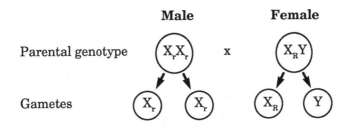

Now to see the offspring, we fertilize using the Punnett square:

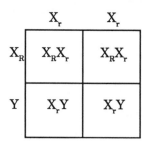

These results show that, while all the females are black-headed, we still cannot produce a black-headed male. What parents are needed to produce a black-headed male? Obviously two black-headed parents would breed true. Here is the only other crossing which will produce a black-headed male. We will cross a red-headed male, split to black, with a black-headed female:

The first step is gamete formation (meiosis):
(remember to keep track of the sex chromosome)

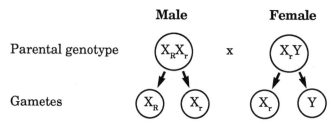

Now to see the offspring, we fertilize using the Punnett square:

	X_R	X_r
X_r	$X_R X_r$	$X_r X_r$
Y	$X_R Y$	$X_r Y$

These results show that we have, in fact, produced a male black-headed bird. One half of the males will be black-headed and one half will be red-headed, split to black. One half of the females will be black-heads and one half will be red-heads. So, the cross of a red-headed male, split to black, with a black-headed female results in, theoretically, half of the offspring with the black-head, half of whom are males.

In the next two chapters we will discuss the characteristics of both finch and parrot type birds, in terms of their genetic potential. Those characteristics which are dominant, recessive or sex-linked will be covered.

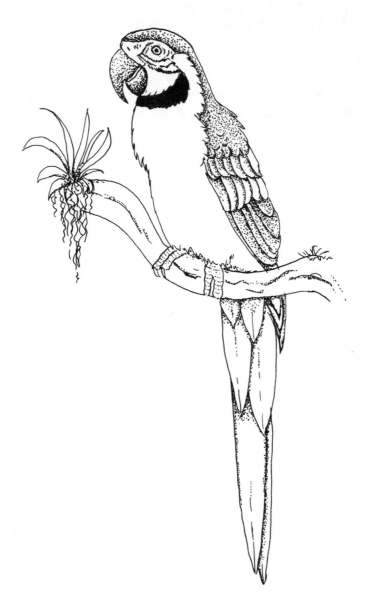

Figure 20.1   Blue and gold macaw.

20   Psittacine Genetics

Mutations

A physical or chemical characteristic that is different from the norm is called a mutation. This difference is brought about by changes in the gene structure. Mutations are events which result from mostly unknown causes and are random in their appearance.

There are many mutations established in aviaries throughout the world, as well as in the wild. The greatest variety of mutations are found in aviary birds. This happens because once a desirable mutation shows up, aviculturists will selectively bred those birds. The greater the number of birds bred, the greater the chance of a mutation occurring.

The avian leader in mutations is the Budgerigar. No other species of birds has the number of color mutations that occur in budgies. Next, in numbers of mutations are the cockatiels and Indian ringnecks. Lovebirds also have exhibited many mutations. In recent years, mutations have been appearing in the grass parakeets of the genus Neophema, probably because they are being bred in increasing numbers in aviaries.

Psittacine Mutations:

Cockatiel (*Nymphicus hollandicus*):

There are many cockatiel mutations, most of which have shown up in captivity. Most of these mutations affect the amount, placement, and color of the melanin (black) pigment. Some mutations also involve the yellow pigments. These mutations fall into two genetic categories:

Simple recessive	Sex linked
Pied	Cinnamon (Isabelle)
Fallow	Lutino (White)
Silver	Pearly (Laced or Opaline)
Charcoal	

Figure 20.2 Normal gray cockatiel (*Nymphicus hollandicus*).

The lutino mutation, a sex-linked trait, results in a bird which lacks melanin in all areas where melanin is normally found. The pied mutation, a simple recessive, results in a bird which lacks melanin in some of these areas where the melanin is normally found. What if a bird was bred to have both the lutino and pied mutations? Since these two mutations are on two separate gene pairs, the bird's feathers are getting two different genetic signals. What would this bird look like?

One gene pair says no melanin and the other pair says only produce melanin in certain areas. Since the lutino mutation codes for "no melanin at all," there will be no melanin produced. It does not matter that the pied gene codes for "making melanin only in specific areas." There is no melanin to express this code. Therefore, the bird would be a lutino, who would pass on to its offspring the genes for the pied mutation, but not exhibit it.

The fallow and cinnamon cockatiels are birds whose melanin pigment appears brown, not the black which is typical of the normal gray cockatiel. In the pearly, the contour feathers on the back lose the melanin in the center of the feathers. This results in feathers which are scalloped with melanin and have white to yellow coloration in the center.

The charcoal mutation does not involve a change in the melanin pigment. It involves the loss of the ability to produce the yellow pigment. Therefore, there is no yellow head or orange cheek patch. All areas which would normally be yellow or orange are white.

Cockatiel crosses:

Simple recessive offspring ratios (theoretical):
(Sex of the bird is not a factor.)

Simple recessive traits are: Pied, fallow, silver and charcoal.

Split to Pied x Normal Gray	=	50% Normal Grays 50% Split to pied
Split to Pied x Split to Pied	=	25% Normal Grays 50% Split to Pied 25% Pied
Split to Pied x Pied	=	50% Split to Pied 50% Pied
Pied x Pied	=	100% Pied

The following is a formula to be used to determine the offspring of crosses involving simple recessive mutations. To use this formula, simply write one of the four simple recessive mutations (pied, fallow, silver or charcoal) in all of the blanks in Formula 19.1 (the same name must go in all blanks):

Formula 19.1   Simple recessive mutation offspring ratios (theoretical).
(pied, fallow, silver & charcoal)

Split to _____   x   Normal Gray   =   50% Normal Grays
                                                     50% Split to _____

Split to _____   x   Split to _____   =   25% Normal Grays
                                                             50% Splits
                                                             25% _____

Split to_____   x   _____   =   50% Split to _____
                                                        50% _____

_____   x   _____   =   100% _____

The same kind of "fill in the blank" formula can be used to calculate the theoretical offspring in the breeding of the sex-linked mutations . To use Formula 19.2 simply write the sex-linked mutation (lutino, cinnamon, or pearly) in all of the blanks.

The most effective way to use these formulas is to make a photo-copy of them and then fill in the blanks.

Formula 19.2   Sex-linked offspring ratios (theoretical)
(lutino, cinnamon & pearly)

Remember that the sex of the bird is an important factor in the calculation of offspring ratios of sex-linked traits.

Gray male x Gray female   =   100% Gray

Gray male x _____ female   =   50% Split males
                                                            50% Gray females

Split male x _____ female =   25% _____ males
                                                            25% Split males
                                                            25% _____ females
                                                            25% Gray females

Split male x Gray female   =   25% Gray males
                                                            25% Split males
                                                            25% Gray females
                                                            25% _____ females

_____ male x Gray female   =   50% Split males
                                                            50% _____ females

_____ male x _____ female = 100% _____

Sex-linked mutations occur on different chromosomes than the simple recessive mutations. This makes it possible to combine these different chromosome mutations to produce an entirely different looking bird. For example, there are cinnamon pieds and cinnamon pearly cockatiels. In this case, the gene for the brown melanin is exhibited along with the gene for pied or pearly. Remember that if the lutino gene is expressed, none of the other melanin mutations will be exhibited.

Since these mutations have been in aviculture for many years, quite a few breeders have combined two or more of these mutations in the same bird. Let's look at a dihybrid (two characteristic) crosses which will combine two of these mutations. We will make a cross with the sex-linked trait, pearly (gene symbol E or e) and a simple recessive trait, pied (gene symbol P or p):

Parents:
  Gray male, split to pearly and split to pied ($X_E X_e Pp$).
  Pearly female, split to pied ($X_e YPp$)
Offspring (theoretical):

	$X_E P$	$X_e P$	$X_E p$	$X_e p$
$X_e P$	$X_E X_e PP$	$X_e X_e PP$	$X_E X_e Pp$	$X_e X_e Pp$
$X_e p$	$X_E X_e Pp$	$X_e X_e Pp$	$X_E X_e pp$	$X_e X_e pp$
YP	$X_E YPP$	$X_e YPP$	$X_E YPp$	$X_e YPp$
Yp	$X_E YPp$	$X_e YPp$	$X_E Ypp$	$X_e Ypp$

Females:	Males:
1 pearly pied	1 pearly pied
1 pearly	1 pearly
2 pearly - split to pied	2 pearly, split to pied
1 pied	1 pied, split to pearly
2 gray - split to pied	1 gray, split to pearly
1 gray	2 gray, split to pearly and pied

This cross breeding produces a 12.5% chance of getting a pearly pied bird, with a 50% chance of this pearly pied bird being either male or female. By substituting cinnamon for pearly in the above cross, we see that the odds for producing a cinnamon pied will also be 12.5%. Substituting the lutino mutation for the pearly would prevent the pied from being exhibited.

What about combining two sex-linked mutations? The sex-linked genes are carried on the X chromosomes. Since the two mutations are contributed by different parents, they will be on different X chromosomes. There is a process called crossing-over in which both recessive mutated genes could end up on the same X chromosome, but this is rare. Most likely the mutated genes will be on different chromosomes. The cross presented below will assume that the two sex-linked gene mutations are on different X chromosomes.

Parents:

Male gray, split to cinnamon and split to pearly ($X_{Fp}X_{fP}$).

Offspring (theoretical):

If female is gray ($X_{FP}Y$):
    1 male - split to cinnamon
    1 male - split to pearly
    1 female cinnamon
    1 female pearly

	X_{Fp}	X_{fP}
X_{FP}	$X_{FP}X_{Fp}$	$X_{FP}X_{fP}$
Y	$X_{Fp}Y$	$X_{fP}Y$

If female is pearly (X_{Fp}):
    1 male - pearly
    1 male - split to pearly
        and cinnamon
    1 female pearly
    1 female cinnamon

	X_{Fp}	X_{fP}
X_{Fp}	$X_{Fp}X_{Fp}$	$X_{fP}X_{Fp}$
Y	$X_{Fp}Y$	$X_{fP}Y$

If female is cinnamon (X_{fP}):
    1 male cinnamon
    1 male split to pearly
        and cinnamon
    1 female pearly
    1 female cinnamon

	X_{Fp}	X_{fP}
X_{fP}	$X_{Fp}X_{fP}$	$X_{fP}X_{fP}$
Y	$X_{Fp}Y$	$X_{fP}Y$

The dihybrid crosses shown above were performed to show some of the possibilites when two characteristics are considered in a cross. The dihybrid crosses above are somewhat misleading since each produced only two different types of gametes. Therefore, the Punnett square was quite simple. In a typical dihybrid cross, such as the one on the previous page, there are usually four different types of gametes produced instead of two. Therefore, there would be 16 squares in the grid instead of the four squares seen above.

Budgerigar (*Melosittacus undulatus*)

Generally, the greater the number of birds bred, the greater the chance of a mutation occurring. No bird supports this statement better than the budgerigar. Budgies have been bred in high numbers for many years and exhibit the greatest number of mutations.

Also, the greater the number of mutations for different colors, the greater the chance of having more than one color mutation in the same bird. This is true of the budgie.

The standard budgie in the wild is a light green bird, probably resulting from a combination of yellow and blue colors. The first recorded mutation was a yellow bird, resulting from a loss of the ability to produce the blue. Next, were the sky blue mutations, resulting from the loss of the ability to produce yellow color.

There are so many color variations of the budgie that it is beyond the scope of this book to explain them all. There are many simple recessive and sex-linked characteristics. Also there are some examples of incomplete dominance. Below are a list of the genes as we understand them:

Simple recessive	Sex-linked recessive
Yellow	Opaline
Sky blue	Cinnamon wing
Clearwing	Lutino
Fallow	Albino
White	Lacewing
Pied (harlequin)	

Some other psittacine mutations which have been established in aviculture are listed below:

Peachface lovebirds (*Agapornis roseicollis*):

Simple recessive	Simple Dominant	Sex-linked recessive
parYellow	Pied	Lutino
parBlue	Olive	

Indian Ringneck parakeets (*Psittacula krameri manillensis*):

Simple recessive	Simple dominant	Sex-linked recessive
Blue	Gray	Lutino
par Blue		Cinnamon
		Fallow

Princess of Wales (*Polytelis alexandrae*):

Simple recessive	Sex-linked recessive
Blue	Lutino

Turquoisine (*Neophema pulchella*):

Simple recessive	Sex-linked recessive
Yellow	Pied

Scarlet-chested Parakeet (*Neophema splendida*):

Simple recessive
Blue

Bourkes Parakeet (*Neophema bourkii*):

Simple recessive	Sex-linked
Yellow	Rosy
Cinnamon	

Elegant Parakeet (*Neophema elegans*):

Simple recessive
Lutino

While this is not a comprehensive list, it does include many of the psittacine mutations which have been estabished in aviaries in various areas of the world.

Figure 21.1 The zebra finch.

21   Finch Genetics

Mutations

In the previous chapter on psittacine genetics, we defined a mutation as a change in the gene structure which results in a new physical or chemical characteristic. We also discussed the fact that the budgie has the largest number of known color mutations, primarily because it's bred in such high numbers.

The same can be said for the zebra finches. In terms of the numbers bred, the zebra finchs, along with canaries, are the leaders in the finch world. Because so many more are bred, there is an increased chance of mutations showing up in the species. There are more known color mutations in zebra finches than in any other species of finch-type birds, with the exception of the canary.

Canary (*Serinus canarius*)

The canary is one of the oldest species of birds kept in captivity. Any bird which is bred frequently will exhibit this increased number of mutations. The canary is no exception. To explain the genetics of canaries requires an entire book, not just a chapter in a book. Also, to understand the genetics of the canary one must be very familiar with the various canary mutations. For these two reason there will be no attempt here to cover the genetics of the canary.

Zebra finch (*Poephilia guttata*)

Simple recessive	Simple dominant	Sex-linked recessive
White	Silver	Fawn
Pied		Chestnut-flanked
Penguin		

Zebra finch crosses:

Simple recessive offspring ratios (theoretical):
    (white, pied & penguin)

Sex of the bird is not a factor.

Gray x Split to white	=	50% Grays
		50% Split to white
Split to white x Split to white	=	25% Grays
		50% Split to white
		25% white
white x white	=	100% white

The following is a formula to be used to determine the offspring of crosses involving simple recessive mutations. To use this formula, simply write one of the three simple recessive mutations (white, pied, or penguin) in all of the blanks in Formula 20.1 below (the same name must go in all blanks):

Formula 20.1   Simple recessive offspring ratios (theoretical):
             (white, pied, & penguin)

Gray x Split to _____	=	50% Grays
		50% Split to _____
Split to _____ x Split to _____	=	25% Grays
		50% Splits
		25% _____
_____ x _____	=	100% _____

Simple dominance offspring ratios (theoretical):
    (silver)

Gray x Split to Silver	=	50% Grays
		50% Silver

Split to Silver x Split to Silver	=	25% Grays
		50% Silver
		25% Silver split to gray

Silver x Silver	=	100% Silver

Formula 20.2   Sex-linked offspring ratios (theoretical):
                (fawn & chestnut-flanked)

Remember that the sex of the bird is an important factor.

Gray male x Gray female   =   100% Gray

Gray male x _____ female   50% Split males
                                  50% Gray females

Split male x _____ female = 25% _____ males
                                  25% Split males
                                  25% _____ females
                                  25% Gray females

Split male x Gray female   =   25% Gray males
                                   25% Split males
                                   25% Gray females
                                   25% _____ females

_____ male x Gray female = 50% Split males
                                 50% _____ females

_____ male x _____ female = 100% _____

To use Formula 20.2, simply write one of the two sex-linked mutations (fawn or chestnut-flanked) in all of the blanks. (Write the same name in all of the blanks). **The most effective way to use Formulas 20.1 & 20.2 is to make a photocopy of them and then fill in the blanks.**

As we saw in budgie genetics, breeding zebra finches that have more than one mutated gene often results in birds with a completely different color pattern. For example, crossing a silver bird with a bird exhibiting the fawn color pattern results in a zebra finch called a cream.

Gouldian finch (*Chloebia gouldiae*)

There are a few new mutations in the Gouldian finch, but there are only two which have been established for many years. They are the red-head and orange-head mutations. These mutations are genetically interesting for a couple of reasons. One is that the red-head mutation is a dominant gene. This is unusual since most mutations are recessive. The other interesting fact is, that the orange-head mutation requires the red-head mutation before it can be expressed.

Let's take a closer look at these mutations, all three of which are found in the wild. Because of their different head colors, they were initially each given a different scientific name:

Poephilia gouldiae	=	black-head Gouldian finch
Poephilia mirabilis	=	red-head Gouldian finch
Poephilia armitiana	=	orange-head Gouldian finch

They are all the same species, and freely interbreed if given the opportunity. Therefore, they have all been given the same scientific name *Chloebia gouldiae*. The black-head Gouldian finches outnumber the red-head Gouldian finches by 3 to 1 ratio in the wild. Although the orange-heads are found in the wild, they are rare. They are estimated to represent less than 0.05% of the Gouldian population in the wild.

The presence of red or black-head color is determined by genes located on the sex chromosomes. In the black-head, the gene codes for the production of melanin pigments, resulting in the black-head. In the red-head, the gene is sex-linked dominant. This gene stimulates the conversion of beta carotene to a compound called lutein. The lutein is then converted to a red pigment called canthaxanthin that is responsible for the red head.

The presence of the orange (yellow) head is determined by another pair of genes on the autosomes (non-sex chromosomes). Orange-head is a recessive characteristic, which is not sex-linked. However, the expression of this mutation is dependent on the red-head mutation, which is sex-linked. In the orange-head, the bird lacks the ability to convert lutein to canthaxanthin. Instead, the end product is lutein epoxide, which produces the orange or yellow head color.

So, to produce an orange-head, the bird must first be genetically a red-head bird. In other words, it must be able to convert beta carotene to lutein. If the orange-head recessive genes are present the bird will convert the lutein to lutein epoxide instead of canthaxanthin producing an orange-head. Even if the autosomal pair of genes is recessive, black-head birds will not exhibit the orange-head, because there is no lutein to convert. However, the black-head with autosomal recessive genes for orange-head will have a telltale yellow tipped beak.

Summary of the biochemistry of head color:

melanin pigment production		=	black-head
beta carotene → lutein → canthaxanthin		=	red-head
beta carotene → lutein → lutein epoxide		=	orange-head

Summary of the genetics of head color:

Sex-linked gene	Autosomal gene	Head color	Tip of beak
recessive	dominant	black	red
recessive	recessive	black	yellow
dominant	dominant	red	red
dominant	recessive	orange	yellow

We will determine the offspring from a cross of two Gouldian finches with different head colors. To do this, we will use the same method for determining a sex-linked cross, as we used in the last two chapters. However, in the case of Gouldian head color, we must also keep track of the pair of autosomal genes which also affect head color.

We will use the following letters for gene symbols:

Sex-linked male:

$X_R X_R$ = red head
$X_R X_r$ = red head
$X_r X_r$ = black head

Sex-linked female:

$X_R Y$ = red head
$X_r Y$ = black head

Autosomal:

NN = normal
Nn = normal (split)
nn = orange-head

As an example, we will cross a black-head male, split for orange in the autosomal gene position ($X_r X_r$ Nn), with a red-head female who is also split in the autosomal gene position ($X_R Y$ Nn).

The first step is gamete formation (meiosis):

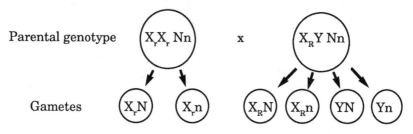

Notice that in this dihybrid cross we produce six different gametes rather than the four different gametes possible in the monohybrid crosses we have been doing. Many dihybrid crosses have eight different gametes. So, we put the two gametes of the male on one axis and the four gametes of the female on the other axis. The resulting Punnett square will have eight squares instead of the four that we have been using. Otherwise, the method is the same. There is no difference in setting-up and using the Punnett square:

	X_RN	X_Rn	YN	Yn
X_rN	X_RX_rNN	X_RX_rNn	X_rYNN	X_rYNn
X_rn	X_RX_rNn	X_RX_rnn	X_rYNn	X_rYnn

Summary of results:

1 X_RX_rNN	=	red-head male, split to black
2 X_RX_rNn	=	red-head males, split to black and to orange
1 X_RX_rnn	=	orange-head male, split to black
1 X_rYNN	=	black-head female
2 X_rYNn	=	black-head females, split to orange
1 X_rYnn	=	black-head female, yellow tip of beak

In this cross, all the females will be black-heads. Theoretically, 75 % of the males will be red-heads and 25% will be orange-heads. A dihybrid cross such as this is not difficult as it seems. We used the same principles as in the monohybrid crosses that we have been performing. The difference is, now we have to keep track of another set of genes. This is the only difference.

There are other Gouldian color mutations. Some of these mutations involve the chest color, which normally is purple. The primary mutation is one in which the ability to produce color in the chest feathers is lost. This results in a bird with a white chest. White-breasted is a simple recessive characteristic:

Genotypes:
(PP)	=	purple breast
(Pp)	=	purple breast
(pp)	=	white breast

White-breasted crosses:

Purple x Split to white	=	50% Purple
		50% Purple Split to white

Split to white x split to white	=	25% Purple
		50% Purple split to white
		25% White

White x Split to white	=	50% Purple
		50% White

White x White	=	100% White

Other Gouldian mutations have appeared in aviaries, but to date, none of them have been firmly established in aviculture. The mutations which have appeared are:

Lilac-breasted	Lutino
Cobalt-breasted	Blue-backed
Blue-breasted	Dilute-backed

Shafttail (*Poephila acuticauda*):

Simple recessive	**Sex-linked recessive**
Fawn (Isabel)	White (Ino)
Brown (dark fawn)	

There are other finch mutations. However, few of them have been well enough established in aviculture to provide a pool of offspring large enough for the mutation to be perpetuated and so are not included here.

Prologue

The Breeding Imperative

Keeping birds in captivity is a very emotional issue. There are those who believe that no wildlife should be in captivity. At the other extreme are those who believe animals have no rights or value and can be done with as we please. Most of us, I suspect, are somewhere in between.

However, there is more to this issue than emotion. The main concern is survival of the species. Many birds are becoming extinct. Habitat destruction is reducing the home range of so many birds that their only chance for survival as a species is captive breeding.

There are some who would blame the aviculturists and pet trade for the decreasing numbers of birds in the wild. Unfortunately, there have been cases where the trapping of wild birds has had a negative impact on some bird populations. However, by far, the dominant factor in the decline of worldwide bird populations is habitat destruction.

Habitat destruction is occurring for one significant reason: the rapid increase of the human population. Many people in Third World countries are simply trying to survive. The land is needed for farming and for resources. As the worldwide population continues to grow, the demands on forested land increases.

As the voracious consumption of raw materials grows, so does the demand on the land. We live in a "throwaway" society in which very few resources are recycled. Also, most of us are too often unaware of the habitat devastation our lifestyles can cause. For example, many forests are destroyed for cattle grazing land so that inexpensive beef can be shipped to fast food restaurants around the world. Compounding the problem, commercial interests often have more concern for profits than habitat protection.

The recreational needs of man also increase the pressure on the land. As the human population continues to grow, more people want to use recreational habitats (often forests). The increased use results in more destruction of these lands, thereby further reducing forest size. This results in even less recreational land, for a greater number of people. This is an alarming trend, the impact on the wildlife in these areas can be devastating.

"We are facing the 'enlightenment fallacy,' " states Michael Robinson of the National Zoological Park, Washington, D. C. "The fallacy is that if you educate the people of the Third World, the problem will disappear. It won't. The problems are not due to ignorance and stupidity. The problems of the Third World derive from the poverty of the poor and the greed of the rich."

The green forest belt (tropical rain forests) around the Earth's equator represents only 7% of the earth's land surface. Astoundingly, this 7% of the land surface contains 50% of all species of plants and animals. It is the tropical rain forests which are the most threatened by the forces of deforestation. The animals supported by these forests have nowhere else to go. They will perish.....

The tropical rain forests are being destroyed at the rate of 5.9 million hectares (2,471 acres) per year, an area larger than the country of Costa Rica. This represents 0.7% of the total rain forest being destroyed per year. If this rate of destruction continues, unchecked, all tropical rain forests will be clear-cut or seriously damaged by the year 2135.

If this destruction continues there will only be small areas remaining for the wildlife. Edward O. Wilson, Harvard University biologist, makes the following assessment: "When the islands (remaining forests) are in the range of 1 to 25 square kilometers - in other words the size of many small parks and reserves - the rate of extinction of bird species during the first 100 years is 10% to 50%. Extinction rates rise steeply when the area drops below 1 square kilometer. The tropical world is clearly headed towards an extreme reduction and fragmentation of tropical forests, which will be accompanied by a massive extinction of species"

Faced with these possibilities, we have some difficult decisions to make. Do we want to let many species of birds "die with dignity" as a species? This is suggested by some. Or do we want to take an active part in decreasing habitat destruction? More relevant to the aviculturist, do we take a more active role in the breeding of endangered species?

Captive breeding will preserve some species which otherwise would be lost forever. Also, captive breeding will decrease the number of birds trapped in the wild to supply the pet trade. Aviculturists need to become more selective breeders. We also need to become more knowledgeable and efficient at breeding threatened species.

Some aviculturists, both privately and in zoos, have successfully bred species previously not well established in aviculture. An example of this is the keeping of Australian finches. In the 1950's, Australia halted the export of all wildlife. Faced with the prospect of the low availability of Australian birds, aviculturists became quite active in learning how to manage and breed these birds. Now there are many self-sustaining captive populations of Australian finches in the world.

Unfortunately, we cannot say the same thing about the African finches. They continue to be imported in such numbers that the cost of most of these finches is relatively low. There is little pressure to bred them since we can always replace lost birds for a low cost. There are few, if any, self-sustaining populations of African finches in captivity.

It is inevitable that the importation of large numbers of these birds will eventually stop, and it should. If we don't begin to learn more about these birds and make a strong effort to breed them, they will no longer be available in our collections. Worse yet, with the continued pressure on their environment, there may not be any more of these birds in the wild either!

Can this task be left to zoos? There are still many zoos with a stronger commitment to displaying animals in small cages than to breeding endangered or threatened species. Even if all zoos were to make a commitment to this effort, it would not be enough. Noting that all the zoos of the world would fit within the confines of the District of Colombia, William Conway of the New York Zoological Society, states the number of animals they contain "is roughly 1% of the quantity of domestic cats in American households." The number of animals kept in zoos is approximately 540,000 individuals, representing 4,000 species.

The zoos can be the technological and spiritual leaders in the preservation of our disappearing wildlife. However, the saving of large numbers of avian species can be done only if private aviculturists make a conscious decision to be an active part of this effort. "If you're not part of the solution, you're part of the problem" was a rallying cry of the ecological movement of the 70s. It's just as true today. Please, get involved, in any way you can, in the preservation of our wildlife.

Bibliography

A Selected Avicultural Bibliography

Ornithology

1. Burtt, Edward H . *The Behavioral Significance Of Color*. New York: Garland STPM Press, 1979.

2. Burton, Robert. *Bird Behavior*. New York: Alfred A. Knopf, 1985.

3. Campbell, Bruce. *The Dictonary of Birds*. London: Peerage Books, 1974.

4. Cruickshank, Allen D., and Helen G. Cruickshank. *1001 Questions Answered About Birds*. New York: Dover Publications Inc., 1958.

5. Darling, Louis, and Lois Darling. *Bird*. Boston: Houghton Mifflin Company, 1962.

6. Freethy, Ron. *How Birds Work: A Guide To Bird Biology*. Poole & Dorset, England, 1982.

7. Gooders, John. Birds: *An Illustrated Survey Of The Bird Families Of The World*. Melbourne: Lansdowne Press, 1975.

8. Gotch, A.F. *Birds-Their Latin Names Explained*. Poole: Blanford Press, 1981.

9. Grzimek, Bernard. *Grzimek's Animal Life Encyclopedia*. Vol. 7, Birds I. New York: Van Nostrand Reinhold Co., 1972.

10. Grzimek, Bernard. *Grzimek's Animal Life Encyclopedia*. Vol. 8, Birds II. New York: Van Nostrand Reinhold Co., 1972.

11. Grzimek, Bernard. *Grzimek's Animal Life Encyclopedia*. ol. 9, Birds III. New York: Van Nostrand Reinhold Co., 1972.

12. Harter, Walter. *Birds In Fact & Legend*. New York: Sterling Publishing Co., 1979.

13. Lucas, Alfred M. and Peter R.Stettenheim. *Avian Anatomy, Integument. Parts I & II*. Washington D.C.: U.S. Government Printing Office, 1972.

14. Manning, Aubrey. *An Introduction to Animal Behavior*. Menlo Park: Addison-Wesley Publishing Company, 1967.

15. McCaulely, William J. *Vertebrate Physiology*. Philadelphia: W.B. Saunders Company, 1971.

16. Perrins, Dr. Christopher. *Birds*. San Francisco: W.H.Freeman, 1980.

17. Perrins, C. and C.J.O. Harrison. Ed. *Birds - Their Life . Their Ways Their World.* Pleasantville, N.Y. Readers Digest Assn. Inc., 1980.

18. Pettingill, Olin Sewall, Jr. *A Laboratory and Field Manual of Ornithology.* 3rd Ed. Minneapolis: Burgess Publishing Co., 1980.

19. Pettingill, O. S. Jr. *Ornithology: in Laboratory and Field.* 4th Ed Minneapolis: Burgess Publ. Co., 1970.

20. Prosser, C. Ladd and Frank A. Brown, Jr. *Comparative Animal Physiology.* 2nd Ed. Philadelphia: W.B. Saunders Co., 1962.

21. Saunders, Aretas A., *An Introduction to Bird Life for Bird Watchers.* New York: Dover Publications, 1971.

22. Scientific American. *Birds.* San Francisco: W.H.Freeman, 1980.

23. Skrutch, Alexander F. *Parent Birds and Their Young.* Austin: Univ. of Texas Press, 1979.

24. Snow, David W. *The Web of Adaptation - Bird Studies in the American Tropics.* Ithaca: Cornell Univ. Press, 1976.

25. Stokes, Donald W. *A Guide to Bird Behavior.* Vol. 1. Boston: Little Brown and Co., 1979.

26. Storer, John H. *The Flight of Birds.* Bloomfield, Michigan: Cranbrook Press, 1948.

27. Sturkie, P.D., ed. *Avian Physiology.* 3rd Ed., New York: Springer-Verlag, 1976.

28. Van Tyne, Josselyn, and Andrew Berger. 2nd Ed., *Fundamentals of Ornithology.* New York: Dover Publications, 1976.

29. Wallace, George J. and Harold D. Mahan. *An Introduction to Ornithology.* New York: Macmillan Publ. Co., 1975.

30 Walters, Michael. *The Complete Birds of the World - Illustrated Edition.* Neptune, N.J.: TFH, 1980.

31. Welty, Joel Carl. *The Life of Birds.* 3rd Ed., New York: Saunder College Publishing, 1982.

Aviculture General

1. Australian Society of Aviculture. *Australian Aviculture.* Victoria: W.D. Vaughan, PTY. LTD, 1970.

2. Avon, D. and Tilford, T. *Aviary Birds in Color.* New York: Pitman Publishing, 1974.

3. Christie, Irene. *Birds: A Guide To A Mixed Collection.* New York: Howell Book House, 1985.

4. Clear, Val. *Common Cagebirds in America.* New York: Bobbs-Merrill Co., Inc., 1966.

5. Clear, Val. *Making Money With Birds.* Neptune, N.J.: TFH Publishing, 1981.

6. Harman, Ian. *Bird-Keeping in Australia.* Sydney: Angus and Robertson Publishing, 1962.

7. Low, Rosemary. *Mynah Birds.* Edinburg: John Bartholomew & Sons. 1976.

8. Meaden, F. *A Manual of European Bird Keeping.* Poole and Dorset, England: Blanford Press, 1979.

9. Morcombe, M. *Birds of Australia.* New York: Charles Scribners & Son, 1971.

10. Morcombe, M. *The Great Australian Birdfinder.* Sydney: Lansdowne Press, 1986.

11. Readers Digest: *Complete Book of Australian Birds.* Sydney: Readers Digest Services, PTY LTD, 1976.

12. Rogers, C. H. *Encyclopedia of Cage and Aviary Birds.* New York: MacMillan Publishing Co., 1975.

13. Rutgers, A. and Norris, K.A. *Encyclopaedia of Aviculture. Vol I. Cranes, Gamebirds, Waterfowl, Birds of Prey and Doves.* Poole and Dorset, England: Blandford Press, 1970.

14. Rutgers, A. and Norris, K.A. *Encyclopaedia of Aviculture. Vol. II. Parrots, Budgies, Cuckoos, Nightjars, Hummingbirds and Owls.* Poole and Dorset, England: Blandford Press, 1972.

15. Rutgers, A. and Norris, K.A. *Encyclopaedia of Aviculture. Vol. III. Passeriformes of Africa, Australia and America, Including Canaries, Zebra and Bengalese Finches.* Poole and Dorset, England: Blandford Press, 1977.

16. Skutch, Alexander F. *Birds of Tropical America.* Austin: Univ. of Texas Press, 1983.

17. Slater, Petrer, Pat Slater & Raoul Slater. *The Slater Field Guide to Australian Birds.* Dee Why West, NSW, Australia.: Rigby Publishers, 1986.

18. Sutherland, Patricia. *The Pet Bird Handbook.* New York: Arco Publishing Co., 1981.

Parrots

1. Allen, Dr. Gerald R. and Connie J. Allen. *All About Cockatiels.* Neptune, N.J. TFH Publications, 1977.

2. Arndt, Thomas. *Encyclopedia of Conures.* Newton, N.J.: TFH Publications, 1982.

3. Bates, Henry J. and Robert L. Busenbark. *Parrots and Related Birds.* Neptune, N.J.: TFH Publications, 1969.

4. Bedford, The Duke of. *Parrots and Parrot-Like Birds.* Neptune, N.J.: TFH Publications, 1969.

5. Bielfeld, Horst. *Handbook of Lovebirds.* Neptune, N.J.: TFH Publications, 1982.

6. Bosch, Klaus and Ursula Wedde. *Encyclopedia of Amazon Parrots.* Neptune, N.J.: TFH Publications, 1984.

7. Diefenbach, Karl. *The World of Cockatoos.* Neptune, N.J.: TFH Publications, 1985.

8. Decoteau, A.E. *The Handbook of Amazon Parrots.* Neptune, N.J.: TFH Publications, 1983.

9. Decoteau, A.E. *Handbook of Macaws.* Neptune, N.J.: TFH Publications, 1982.

10. Forshaw, Joseph M. *Parrots of the World.* 2nd Ed., Melbourne: Lansdowne Press, 1978.

11. Forshaw, Joseph M. *Australian Parrots.* 2nd Ed., Melbourne: Lansdowne Press, 1981.

12. Freud, Arthur. *All About Parrots.* New York: Howell Book House, 1980.

13. Groen, Dr. H.D. *Australian Parakeets.* 5th Ed., Holland: Drukkerijdijkstraniuemeyerbv.

14. Hall, Jo. *Cockatiels ...Care and Breeding.* Austin, Texas: Sweet Publishing Co., 1976.

15. Harmon, Ian. *Australian Parrots in Bush and Aviary.* London: David & Charles, 1981.

16. Harris, Robbie. *Breeding Conures*. Neptune, N.J.: TFH Publications, 1983.

17. Hart, Earnest H. *Budgerigar Handbook*. Neptune, N.J.: TFH Publications, 1978.

18. Hoppe, Dieter. *The World of Macaws*. Neptune, N.J.: TFH Publ. 1986.

19. Hutchins, B.R. & R.H. Lovell. *Australian Parrots: A Field and Aviary Study*. Melbourne: The Avicultural Society of Australia, 1985.

20. Immelmann, Dr. Klaus. *Australian Parakeets*. Belgium: Association Ornithologique de Belgique, 1968.

21. Kates, S. *Encyclopedia of Cockatoos*. Neptune, N.J.: TFH Publications, 1980.

22. Lendon, Alan H. *Australian Parrots in Field and Aviary*. London: Angus and Robertson Publishers, 1979.

23. Low, Rosemary. *Endangered Parrots*. Dorset: Blandford Press, 1984.

24. Low, Rosemary. *Lories and Lorikeets*. Neptune, N.J.: TFH Publications, 1977.

25. Low, Rosemary. *Parrots: Their Care and Breeding*. Revised and Enlarged Edition. New York: Blandford Press, 1986.

26. Moon, Mrs. E.L. *Experiences With My Cockatiels*. Chicago: Audubon Publishing Co., 1962.

27. Mulawka, Edward J. *African Grey Parrots*. Neptune, N.J.: TFH Publications. 1983.

28. Mulawka, Edward J. *Taming and Training Parrots*. Neptune, N.J.: TFH Publications, 1981.

29. Mulawka, Edward J. *Yellow-Fronted Amazon Parrots*. Neptune, N.J.: TFH Publications, 1982.

30. Murphy, Kevin. *Training Your Parrot*. Neptune, N.J.: TFH Publ., 1983.

31. Nothaft, Ann. *Breeding Cockatoos*. Neptune, N.J.: TFH Publications, 1979.

32. Paradise, Paul R. *African Grey Parrots*. Neptune, N.J.: TFH Publications, 1979.

33. Radtke, George A. *Encyclopedia of Budgerigars*. Neptune, N.J.: TFH Publications, 1981.

34. Rogers, Cyril H. *Parrot Guide.* Neptune, N.J.: TFH Publ., 1981.

35. Rutgers, A. *The Handbook of Foreign Birds.* Vol. 2, London: Blandford Press, 1965.

36. Smith, George A. *Encyclopedia of Cockatiels.* Neptune, N.J.: TFH Publications, 1978.

37. Smith, George A. *Lovebirds and Related Parrots.* Neptune, N.J.: TFH Publications, 1979.

38. Smith, Ralph. *Breeding the Colorful Little Grass Parakeet.* Neptune, N.J.: TFH Publications, 1979.

39. Soderberg, P.M. *All About Lovebirds.* Neptune, N.J.: TFH Publications, 1977.

40. Starika, W.A. & E.L. Richardson (ed). *The T.F.H. Book of Parrots.* Neptune, N.J.: TFH Publications, 1982.

41. Stoodley, John & Pat. *Parrot Production.* Portsmouth, England: Bezels Publications, 1983.

42. Stoodley, John & Pat. *Pionus Parrots.* Portsmouth, England: Bezels Publications, 1984.

43. Vriends, Matthew M. *Encyclopedia of Lovebirds.* Neptune, N.J.: TFH Publications, 1978.

44. Vriends, Matthew M. *Parakeets of the World.* Neptune, N.J.: TFH Publications, 1979.

45. Vriends, Dr. Matthew M. *Popular Parrots.* New York: Howell Book House Inc., 1983.

Finches

1. Bates, Henry and Robert Busenbark. *Finches and Soft Billed Birds.* Neptune, N.J.: TFH Publications, 1970.

2. Black, Robert G. *Problems with Finches.* Lakemont, Georgia: Copple House Printing, 1980.

3. Black, Robert G. *Society Finches as Foster Parents.* Crystal River, Florida: Achbach Corporation, 1977.

4. Dodwell, D.E. *Encyclopedia of Canaries.* Neptune, N.J.: TFH Publications, 1976.

5. Evans, Stewart and Mike Fidler. *The Gouldian Finch*. London: Blandford Press, 1986.

6. Goodwin, Derek. *Estrildid Finches of the World*. Ithica, N.Y.: Cornell University Press, 1982.

7. Immelman, Klas. *Australian Finches in Bush and Aviary*. Australia: Angus and Robertson Publishers, 1974.

8. Mobbs, A.J. *Gouldian Finches: Their Care and Breeding*. Liss, Hants, GU337PR, England: Nimrod Book Services, 1985.

9. Iles, G.W. *Breeding Australian Finches*. Bristol: Isles d'Avon LTD.

10. Naether, Carl. *Soft-Billed Birds*. Chicago: Audubon Publishing Company, 1955.

11. Noreen, George W. *Finches...In Color*. Neptune, N.J.: TFH Publishers, 1969.

12. Queensland Finch Society. *Finch Breeders Handbook*. Queensland Australia: Queensland Finch Society, 1982.

13. Restall, Robin L. *Finches and Other Seed-eating Birds*. London: Faberand Faber, 1975.

14. Roberts, Mervin F. *Gouldian Finches*. Neptune, N.J.: TFH Publications, 1984.

15. Rutgers, A. *The Handbook of Foreign Birds*. London: Blandford Press, 1964.

16. Scheider, Earl, ed. *Enjoy Your Finches*. New York: The Pet Library LTD.

17. Soderberg, P.M. *Waxbills, Weavers and Whydahs*. Chicago: Audubon Publishing Co., 1963.

18. Vriends, Matthew M. *Handbook of Canaries*. Neptune, N.J: TFH Publications, 1980.

19. Ziegler, Gert. *The Gouldian Finch*. Australia: The Australian Finch Society.

Diseases

1. Arnall, L and I.F. Keymer. *Bird Diseases: An Introduction to the Study of Birds in Health and Disease*. Neptune, N.J.: TFH Publications, 1975.

2. Baer, J.G. *Animal Parasites*. New York: McGraw-Hill Book Co., 1971.

3. Burr, Elisha W. *Diseases of Parrots*. Neptune, N.J.: TFH Publ., 1982.

4. Cooper, J.E. (Ed.) *First Aid and Care of Wild Birds*. London: David & Charles, 1979.

5. Coutts, G.S. *Poultry Diseases Under Modern Management*. Surrey, England: Saiga Publication Co., 1981.

6. Gallerstein, Dr. Gary A. *Bird Owners Home Health and Care Handbook*. New York: Howell Book House, 1984.

7. Gerstenfeld, Sheldon L., V.M.D. *The Bird Care Book*. Menlo Park: Addison-Wesley Publications Co., 1981.

8. Harrison, Greg J., DVM and Linda R. Harrison. *Clinical Avian Medicine and Surgery*. Philadelphia: W.B. Saunders. 1986.

9. Petrak, Margaret L. *Diseases of Cage and Aviary Birds*. Philadelphia: Lea and Febiger, 1969; 2nd Ed., 1982.

10. Raethel, Heinz-Sigurd. *Bird Diseases*. Neptune, N.J.: TFH Publ. 1981

11. Roach, Peter. *The Complete Book of Pet Care*. New York, N.Y.: Howell Book House, Inc., 1983.

12. Siegmund, Otto H. (Ed.). *The Merck Veterinary Manual*. 6th. edition Rathway, N.J.: Merck & Co., 1986.

13. Steiner, Charles V., D.V.M. and Richard B Davis, D.V.M. *Caged Bird Medicine - Selected Topics*. Ames, Iowa: Iowa State University Press, 1981.

14. Stunkard, J.A., Russell, R.J. and Johnson, D.K. *A Guide to Diagnosis, Treatment and Husbandry of Caged Birds*. U.S. Veterinary Medicine Publ. Co., 1982.

15. Stroud, Robert. *Stroud's Digest on the Diseases of Birds*. Neptune, N.J.: TFH Publications, 1964.

16. Veterinary Advisers to "Caged Birds." *Bird Ailments and Accidents*. London: Dorset House, 1959.

17. Viguie, J., and M. Viguie. *Diseases of Canaries, Budgerigars, Parakeets, and Other Cage Birds*. Verzeille, France: Avicophrms, 1977.

Breeding

1. Anderson Brown, A.F. *The Incubator Book*. Surrey, England: Spur Publishing Company, 1979.

2. Stromberg, Janet. *A Guide to Better Hatching.* Fort Dodge, Iowa: Stromberg Publ. Co., 1975.

3. Stromberg, Loyl. *Sexing All Fowl, Baby Chicks, Game Birds and Cage Birds.* Pine River, Minn.: Stromberg Publishing Co., 1977.

Nutrition and Diet

1. Berthelet, J.T. *All About Mealworms.* La Jolla, CA.: Olympic Mealworm Company, 1981.

2. Black, Robert G. *Nutrition in Finches.* Franklin, N.C.: Copple House Printing and Binding, 1981.

3. Clarke, Charlotte B. *Edible and Useful Plants of California.* Berkeley: Univ. of California Press, 1977.

4. Department of Agriculture. *Handbook of the Nutritional Contents of Food* (U.S.D.A. Handbook #8). New York: Dover Publishing, 1975.

5. James, Wilma R. *Know Your Poisonous Plants.* Happy Camp, CA: Naturograph Publ. Co., 1973.

6. Lint, K.C. and A.M. Lint. *Diets for Birds in Captivity.* Poole and Dorset, England: Blandford Books, Inc., 1981.

7. Martin, A.C., Zin, H.S. & Nelson, A.L. *American Wildlife and Plants: A Guide To Wildlife Food Habits.* New York: Dover Publ., 1961.

8. Pennington, Jean A.T. and Helen N. Church. *Bowes and Church's Food Values of Portions Commonly Used.* Philadelphia: J.P. Lippinctt Co. 1980.

9. Tucker, J.M. & Kimball, M.H. *Poisonous Plants In The Garden.* Berkeley: Div. of Agriculture, Univ. of Calif. Leaflet 2561, 1976.

10. U.C.S.D. Medical Center. *Common Poisonous Plants.* San Diego Regional Poison Center, 1975.

11. Whitney, E. and Hamilton, M. *Understanding Nutrition.* Los Angeles: West Publishing Company, 1977.

Aviary Construction

1. Larosa, Don. *How to Build Everything You Need For Your Birds.* Simi, CA: La Rosa Publishers, 1973.

2. Naether, C. and Vriends, M.M. *Building an Aviary.* Neptune, N.J.: TFH Publications, 1978.

Glossary

Albumen White of the egg. Source of protein for developing chick.

Altricial bird Birds (e.g. finches) born without feathers, eyes closed, very dependent on parent.

Alveoli Area of lung where oxygen and carbon dioxide are exchanged.

Amino acid Basic building block of protein. There are over 20 types.

Animal pole The embryo portion of the yolk complex.

Atrophy A decrease in cell size, thus organ gets smaller (e.g. muscle).

Barb The structures which project outward from the feather shaft forming the main part of the feather vane.

Barbicel The parts of the feather that hook, holding the barbs together.

Barbule Small projections from the barb. Barbicels project from them.

Bile salts Compounds necessary for the digestion of fats.

Bilirubin The compound resulting from the breakdown of old hemoglobin. Accumulation in skin is called jaundice.

Blood feather (see pin feather)

Caeca Small pouches in the lower part of the intestines.

Calamus (Quill) Portion of feather found primarily under skin.

Calcite crystals A mostly calcium material which forms egg shell.

Carnivore Animal who feeds primarily on meat.

Carotenoids Pigments responsible for yellow, red, and orange colors.

Cerebellum Area of the brain associated with controlling movement.

Cerebrum Area of the brain associated with intellectual activities.

Chalaza Albumen cord causing the rotation of yolk and embryo.

Chromosome Units in nucleus containing genetic material, the genes.

Cloaca Area in the lower abdomen of the bird through which sperm, eggs, urine, and feces all pass.

Clutch The number of eggs laid by a bird for one incubation sitting.

Complete protein One which contains all of the essential amino acids.

Copulation The act of male depositing sperm cells in vent of female.

Coverts Small feathers covering the quills of the flight feathers.

Crop Storage area for food immediately after eating or being fed.

Determinate layer Bird who lays a certain number of eggs per clutch, even if they are removed.

Diarrhea Excess water in feces caused by disease or other conditions.

Diastolic pressure Blood pressure when the heart is relaxed.

Dimorphic Sex of the bird can be determined by external features.

Disaccharide Carbohydrate consisting of two monosaccharides. Sucrose, maltose, and lactose are examples.

Droppings Waste products of birds consisting of both urine and feces.

Edema An accumulation of water in the tissues.

"Egg tooth" Small bony projection on beak used by chick in pipping.

Ejaculation The forceful expulsion of the semen.

Embryo The chick in its early stages of development.

Esophagus First part of the digestive tract. Passageway to stomaches.

Essential amino acids Amino acids which must be obtained in the diet because the organism cannot produce them.

Fallopian tube (see oviduct)

Fecal sac Sac containing feces of the chicks in the nest.

Feces Waste products from the digestive system. One part of droppings.

Feral Wild or untamed.

Fledging Young leaving the nest.

Fledgling A bird that has or is ready to fledge.

Follicle stimulating hormone (FSH) One of the main hormones controlling reproduction.

Gaping When a bird opens its mouth wide, usually to be fed.

Gene Unit on the chromosome which codes for a genetic characteristic.

Genotype Combination of genes that determine a characteristic.

Genus A taxonomic category. Part of the scientific name.

Gizzard Muscular stomach used to mechanically digest food (e.g. seed).

Goiter Enlarged thyroid gland.

Gonads The sex organs. Ovaries in females and testes in males.

Habituation Behavior in which bird adapts to a situation.

Hemoglobin The oxygen carrying pigment of the red blood cell.

Hemostasis Blood clotting.

Herbivore An animal who eats primarily vegetable matter.

Heredity The passage of characteristics via genes from parent to young.

Homothermic The maintenance of a constant body temperature.

Hypertrophy Increase in cell size. The organ gets larger (e.g. muscle).

Hypothalamus Area of the brain associated with functions, such as body temperature, hunger, control of hormones, etc.

Immunity The development of antibodies against various diseases.

Imprinting Behavior of precocial chicks to follow parents or objects.

Incomplete dominance Rare genetic variation where both dominant and recessive genes have similar influence. Causes "blending."

Indeterminate layer Bird who continues to lay eggs, even if the eggs are removed (e.g. chicken).

Infundibulum First part of oviduct, Egg is released (ovulated) into it.

Innate behavior Behavior that does not have to be learned.

Insemination The placement of semen into the vent of the hen.

Intestines Area in digestive system where most digestion and absorption takes place.

Isometric muscle contraction Contraction in which the muscle doesn't shorten. Important in posture and balance.

Isotonic muscle contraction Contraction in which the muscle shortens and causes movement.

Istmus Area of the oviduct where the egg shell membranes are formed.

Jaundice Yellow cast of skin or eyes due to presence of bilirubin.

Keel Broad portion of sternum used for attachment of flight muscles.

Keratin Protein found in feathers, nails and covers beak.

Lactose Carbohydrate. A disaccharide found in mammal's milk.

Leukocytes White blood cells.

Lutenizing hormone (LH) One of the main hormones controlling reproduction.

Lipids Fatty materials such as fats (triglycerides) and steroids.

Lumen The inside of any tube-like structure.

Magnum Area of the oviduct where albumen is deposited.

Maltose Carbohydrate. A disaccharide found in germinating seeds.

Medullary bone Long bones in female storing high amounts of calcium prior to egg laying. Formation stimulated by female sex hormones.

Meiosis Cell division resulting in cells having half the chromosomes of the normal cell. Used to produce the ovum and sperm cells.

Melanin Dark pigment found in eyes and feathers of birds.

Mendel Austrian monk who is the father of the study of heredity.

Metabolic rate Rate at which all biochemical reactions are occurring.

Microorganism Small organsims such as viruses, bacteria, or fungus.

Mitosis Cell division in which the resulting cells have the same chromosome number as original cell. Used for growth and repair.

Molting The orderly process of replacing old feathers.

Monohybrid cross Genetic cross involving only one characteristic.

Mutation A change in physical or chemical characteristics of an organism due to changes in the gene, often with a negative effect.

Nephron The functional unit of the kidney.

Nictitating membrane Birds' third transparent eyelid. Protects eye.

Non-essential amino acid Amino acids which need not be obtained in the diet because the organism can produce them.

Nutrient Any substance the bird needs for maximum health, but cannot produce or get enough of in its diet.

Omnivore A bird that eats just about everything that is edible.

Opportunistic feeder. A bird who changes food sources as different foods become available.

Organic materials Any materials which contain carbon.

Ova The eggs (ovum is singular) before fertilization.

Ovary Reproductive organ that produces ova, estrogen, & progesterone.

Oviduct (Fallopian tube) Passageway for the sperm cells to reach the ova, area where egg forms, passageway for eggs to pass outward.

Ovulation The release of ova by the ovary.

Pelvic girdle Primary area for the support of the wing.

Phalanges Small finger bones. Highly modified in birds.

Pin feather Newly erupted feather. Often have pulp filled with blood.

Pineal gland Endocrine gland close to brain. Most functions unknown.

Pipping The process in which chick breaks thru the egg shell to hatch.

Pituitary gland Gland located in the near the center of brain. Very important in controlling other glands.

"Plumping" Enlargement of the developing egg due to an increase in the uptake of water and minerals.

Pneumatized bone Bones which have air spaces and are therefore lighter in weight.

Precocial birds Birds (e.g. quail) that hatch fully feathered, eyes open, and not nearly as dependent on parents as altricial birds.

Preening Behavior in which birds clean their feathers and also hook the baricels to strengthen the feather.

Proventriculus Glandular stomach. Enzymatic digestion begins here.

Releasing stimuli Stimuli which have the effect of triggering a specific behavior (e.g. cry of a chick).

Saturated fatty acid Type of fat found in animal tissues. Semi-solid.

Scientific name The specific name given an organism. Consists of the genus and species name. Is recognized throughout the world.

Semen Fluid ejaculated by the male containing sperm cells.

Seminiferous tubules. Area in the testes where sperm are stored.

Sex chromosomes Chromosomes are named "X" and "Y." A female bird has an "X" and a "Y" and a male has two "X" chromosomes.

Sex hormones Hormones which control breeding. Estrogen and progesterone of females and testosterone of males.

Sex-linked traits Genetic trait affected by the presence of "X" or "Y" chromosomes. Sex of the parent makes a genetic difference.

Shell gland (see uterus)

Species Most specific taxonomic category, usually defining organisms that reproduce with one other. Part of the scientific name.

Spermatozoa Sperm cells.

Starch Carbohydrate. Polysaccharide formed by plants. Glucose chain.

Sucrose Carbohydrate. A disaccharide known as table sugar.

Supplement Nutrients given to the bird beyond its normal food.

Symbiosis Organisms living together.

Syrinx The song producing organ of birds. Unique to birds.

Systolic pressure Blood pressure when heart is pumping.

Taxonomy The study of classification.

Territory A specific area defended by a bird against the intrusion of other birds, especially birds of the same species.

Testes The reproductive organs of males (singular: testis).

Testosterone The sex hormone of males.

Thalamus An area of the brain involved with homeostasis.

Wet bulb thermometer A thermometer which is designed to register temperature in humid conditions.

Thermoregulation The regulation of body temperature.

Thrombocytes Blood clotting cells.

Thymus gland Gland important in developing immunity in young.

Thyroxine Hormone produced by the thyroid gland. A main regulator of metabolism.

Trachea Passageway from the mouth into the lungs.

Triglycerides Fats. Used for energy storage.

Tympanum The external membrane of the ear. Important in hearing.

Unsaturated fatty acids Type of fat found in plants. Usually liquid.

Ureter Passageway from the kidney to the cloaca.

Uric acid Waste product to remove nitrogenous waste from bird's body.

Uterus (shell gland) Area in oviduct where egg plumps and egg shell is formed.

Vagina Last portion of the oviduct.

Vane The major part of the feather on either side of the shaft.

Vas deferans Passageway for the sperm cells to exit the testes.

Vegetative pole The yolk portion of the egg (see animal pole).

Vent The opening to the outside. It represents the end of the reproductive, excretory, and digestive tracts.

Yolk sac The sack surrounding the yolk. It is used to pull the yolk into the abdominal cavity just prior to hatching.

Zygote Cell resulting when the sperm enters ovum. First cell of all life.

Index

9/94²